THE MAHATMA AND THE POET
LETTERS AND DEBATES
BETWEEN
GANDHI AND TAGORE
1915–1941

Compiled and Edited
with an Introduction by
SABYASACHI BHATTACHARYA

NATIONAL BOOK TRUST, INDIA

ISBN 81-237-2202-8

First Edition 1997 (*Saka* 1919)

Rs 40.00

Published by the Director, National Book Trust, India
A-5 Green Park, New Delhi-110016

THE MAHATMA AND THE POET
LETTERS AND DEBATES
BETWEEN
GANDHI AND TAGORE
1915–1941

CONTENTS

Preface   xiii

Abbreviations   xv

Introduction   1

PART I : 1915–1922

Notes on Documents

1. Tagore on the Phoenix School boys (Tagore to Gandhi,
   undated, January 1915)   44

2. Gandhi on Hindi as the national Language
   (Gandhi to Tagore, 21 January 1918)   44

3. Tagore on the use of Hindi (Tagore to Gandhi, 24
   January 1918)   45

4. Gandhi on C.F. Andrews (Gandhi to Tagore, 5 November 1918)   46

5. Gandhi's letter of thanks (Gandhi to Tagore, 5 November 1918)   47

6. Gandhi's letter asking for a message (Gandhi to Tagore,
   5 April 1919)   47

7. Tagore's letter on the eve of the Jallianwalla Bagh
   massacre (Tagore to Gandhi, 12 April 1919, published
   16 April 1919)   49

8. Gandhi's invitation to Tagore (Gandhi to Tagore, 18
   October 1919)   51

9. Gandhi on Andrews' service to the people of Punjab
   (Gandhi to Tagore, 28 October 1919)   52

10. Gandhi renews the invitation (Gandhi to Tagore, 14
    January 1920)   53

11. Gandhi on arrangements for Tagore's reception
    (Gandhi to Tagore, 11 March 1920)   53

12. Tagore's reflections on Non-cooperation and Cooperation (essay by Tagore in *The Modern Review*, May 1921, in the form of letters to C.F. Andrews)   54

13. Gandhi's reactions to Tagore's views (note by Gandhi entitled 'English Learning' in *Young India*, 1 June 1921)   63

14. The Poet's Anxiety (under this title, essay by Gandhi in *Young India*, 1 June 1921)   65

15. The Call of Truth (under this title, essay by Tagore in *The Modern Review*)   68

16. The Great Sentinel (under this title, essay by Gandhi in *Young India*, 13 October 1921)   87

PART II : 1923–1928

Notes on Documents

1. Tagore's telegram after Gandhi's release from prison (5 February 1924)   97

2. Tagore sends Andrews to Gandhi (Tagore to Gandhi, 20 February 1924)   97

3. Gandhi plans a visit to Santiniketan (Gandhi to Tagore, 18 May 1925)   97

4. Tagore on his personal relationship with Gandhi (Tagore to Gandhi, 27 December 1925)   98

5. Gandhi's letter of acknowledgement (Gandhi to Tagore, 3 January 1926)   98

6. The Cult of the *Charkha* (under this title, essay by Tagore in *The Modern Review*, September 1925)   99

7. Striving for *Swaraj* (under this title, essay by Tagore in *The Modern Review*)   113

8. The Poet and the *Charkha* (under this title, essay by Gandhi, *Young India*, 5 November 1925)   122

9. The Poet and the Wheel (under this title, essay by Gandhi in *Young India*, 11 March 1926)   127

PART III : 1929–1933

Notes on Documents

1. Birthday Greeting telegram from Tagore (2 October 1931) ... 133

2. Gandhi to Tagore on the resumption of Civil Disobedience (Gandhi to Tagore, 3 January 1932) ... 133

3. Tagore's thoughts of Gandhi in jail on the eve of fast **(Tagore to Gandhi, 19 September 1932)** ... 133

4. Gandhi seeks Tagore's blessings before starting a fast (Gandhi to Tagore, 20 September 1932) ... 134

5. Tagore's relief at abandonment of fast (Tagore to Gandhi, 30 September 1932) ... 135

6. Gandhi's letter of thanks (Gandhi to Tagore, 9 October 1932) ... 135

7. Gandhi on the fast (Gandhi to Tagore, 10 November 1932) ... 136

8. Tagore on the impact of the fast (Tagore to Gandhi, 15 November 1932) ... 137

9. Gandhi on Tagore's comforting letter (Gandhi to Tagore, 24 November 1932) ... 138

10. Tagore on Hindu sects and the prayer hall at Santiniketan (Tagore to Gandhi, March 1933) ... 138

11. Gandhi's thoughts contemplating yet another fast (Gandhi to Tagore, 2 May 1933) ... 140

12. Tagore on Gandhi's fasts (Tagore to Gandhi, 9 May 1933) ... 141

13. Tagore on the moral aspects of the fast (Tagore to Gandhi, 11 May 1933) ... 142

14. The message of the Fast (under this title, essay by Tagore, *Harijan*, 10 June 1933) ... 143

15. Gandhi to Tagore on the Yeravada Pact (Gandhi to Tagore, 27 July 1933) ... 146

16. Tagore's misgivings about Poona Pact (Tagore to Gandhi, 28 July 1933) ... 147

17. Gandhi's acknowledgement of Tagore's letter (Gandhi to Tagore, 7 August 1933)   148

18. Tagore on inclusion of Bengal in Poona Pact (Tagore to Gandhi, 8 August 1933)   149

PART IV : 1934-1941

Notes on Documents

1. Gandhi on repression in Bengal (Gandhi to Tagore, 21 January 1934)   155

2. Tagore on the "lawlessness" of the Government (Tagore to Gandhi, 31 January 1934)   155

3. Tagore on "divine chastisement" of Bihar (Tagore to Gandhi, 28 January 1934)   156

4. Gandhi's telegram to Tagore (2 February 1934)   156

5. Tagore's statement in defence of Gandhi (6 February 1934)   157

6. The Bihar Earthquake (Tagore's statement to the Press, including *Harijan*, 16 February 1934)   158

7. Superstition vs. Faith (under that title, essay by Gandhi in *Harijan*, 16 February 1934)   159

8. Tagore's appeal to Gandhi (Tagore to Gandhi, 12 September 1935)   161

9. Gandhi undertakes to help Tagore (Gandhi to Tagore, 13 October 1935)   162

10. Gandhi arranges required funds for Santiniketan (Gandhi to Tagore, 27 March 1936) enclosing Donors' letter to Tagore (27 March 1936)   163

11. Tagore nominates Gandhi as a Life-Trustee of Visva-Bharati (Tagore to Gandhi, 10 February 1937)   164

12. Gandhi asks Tagore to recall Life-Trusteeship (Gandhi to Tagore, 19 February 1937)   164

13. Tagore's reply (undated, posted on 26 February 1937)   165

14. Gandhi on Tagore's "begging expedition" (Gandhi to Tagore, 2 March 1937)   166

15. Tagore thanks Gandhi for his message of "affectionate anxiety" (Tagore to Gandhi, 19 September 1937)   167

16. Gandhi writes a letter with his left hand (Gandhi to Tagore, 23 September 1937)   168

17. Tagore's birthday greetings to Gandhi (telegram, 2 October 1937)   168

18. Tagore's letter requesting "balm to the wound" inflicted on Bengal (Tagore to Gandhi, 29 March 1939)   168

19. The Congress (under this title, essay by Tagore in *The Modern Review*, July 1939, in the form of a letter to Amiya Chakraborty, originally in Bengali in *Pravasee*)   169

20. A telegraphic invitation from Tagore (Tagore to Gandhi, 20 January 1940)   177

21. Prompt acceptance by telegram (Gandhi to Tagore, 23 January 1940)   177

22. "My life's best treasure": Tagore on Visva-Bharati (Tagore to Gandhi, 2 February 1940)   177

23. Their "common endeavour": Gandhi on Visva-Bharati (Gandhi to Tagore, 19 February 1940)   178

24. Gandhi's telegram about the health of Andrews (26 February 1940)   179

25. Tagore to Gandhi (telegram, 27 February 1940)   179

26. Proposal for a joint appeal (Gandhi to Tagore, 5 May 1940)   179

27. Gandhi's last letter to Tagore (1 October 1940)   180

28. Tagore's last letter to Gandhi (undated, during Tagore's last illness, September-October 1940)   181

29. Gandhi and Tagore exchange telegraphic greetings (on Tagore's 81st birthday, 13 April 1941)   181

APPENDIX

Notes on Documents

1. Tagore's letter to the Viceroy renouncing his Knighthood (Tagore to Viceroy, 30 May 1919)   187

2. The conditions of Swaraj (under this title, essay by Gandhi, *Young India*, 23 February 1921)   188

3. The Poet's Visit (under this title, report by Mahadev Desai on Tagore's visit to Satyagraha Ashram in Ahmedabad, *Young India*, 23 January 1930)   190

4. Tagore on Gandhi's absence at the Round Table Conference (Tagore's letter to the Editor, *The Spectator* of London, 15 November 1930)   194

5. Tagore's telegram of good wishes for the "penance" (Tagore to Gandhi, 22 May 1933)   198

6. Telegram about Gandhi's condition (Amiya to Tagore, 23 May 1933)   198

7. "Your prayer great help in this ordeal": (Gandhi, message to Tagore through Amiya Chakraborty, 23 March 1933)   199

8. Tagore's telegram on the conclusion of a fast by Gandhi (27 May 1933)   199

9. Tagore's press statement on Bengal and the Poona Pact (24 July 1933)   199

10. Gandhi on inability to visit Calcutta (telegram from Gandhi to Tagore, 13 July 1934)   200

11. Gandhi on breaking fast at Wardha (telegram from Gandhi to Tagore, 14 August 1934)   201

12. Gandhi seeks Tagore's consent to Andrews' visit to Poona (telegram from Gandhi to Tagore, 10 September 1934)   201

13. Tagore thanked for compliance with Gandhi's request (telegram from Gandhi to Tagore, 11 September 1934)   202

14. Moral Warfare (under this title, an essay by Tagore in, *The Modern Review*, September 1934)   202

15. Mahadev Desai seeks Tagore's views on conversion of Harijans to Sikhism (M. Desai to Tagore, 30 December 1936)   203

16. Tagore's clarification (Tagore to M. Desai, 4 January 1936 (sic.)   204

17. Gandhi's assurance to Tagore about Andaman prisoners (Telegram, 16 August 1937) — 205

18. About donations to Visva-Bharati (Gandhi to Tagore, 8 November 1937) — 207

19. Tagore thanks Gandhi for aid to Visva-Bharati (Tagore to Gandhi, 7 November 1937) — 207

20. Tagore's message to the Press about Gandhi's health (21 January 1938) — 208

21. Tagore's Welcome Address to Gandhi (during Gandhi's visit to Santiniketan, 17 February 1940) — 208

22. The Santiniketan Pilgrimage (under this title, report by Mahadev Desai on Gandhi's visit, *Young India*, 9 March 1940) — 209

23. Rathindranath Tagore's letter to Gandhi about a memorial for Andrews (Rabindranath's son writes to Gandhi, n.d., April 1940) — 214

24. Tagore on a suitable memorial to Andrews (Tagore to Gandhi, 13 May 1940) — 214

25. Gandhi's telegram thanks Tagore for a song (undated, approx. May 1940) — 215

26. Gandhi's enquiry about Tagore's health (telegram, Gandhi to Tagore, 16 July 1941) — 216

27. Gandhi's telegram to Rathindranath Tagore (1 May 1941) — 216

28. Obituary of Tagore by Mahatma Gandhi (7 August 1941, published in *Bombay Chronicle*, 8 August 1931) — 216

PREFACE

This collection of letters exchanged by Mahatma Gandhi and Rabindranath Tagore, along with some essays by them, began as a modest project without any funding in 1992. While I was at Visva-Bharati, the university founded by Tagore, I came across the Gandhi-Tagore correspondence in the university's archives and I was struck by the significance of these letters in terms of the differing perceptions they had of major national issues, as well as the intimate light the letters throw upon the relationship between these two friends and adversaries in debate. A collection of these letters was intended to be part of the National Book Trust's publications in the 125th Gandhi Jayanti year, 1994-95. However, as I began editing the letters I realised that the dialogue between Tagore and Gandhi needed to be contextualised by including in this collection some of the published writings in which they addressed the issues they raised in their private correspondence. Some of the sources from which material for this volume could be gathered were dispersed and not easily accessible. Thus the project demanded more time than I could devote to it until I could demit the Vice-Chancellor's office to return to my research interests. This accounts for the unconscionable delay in completing the task I had undertaken five years ago.

In the 'Introduction' to this book I have tried to sketch the historical backdrop against which we see the beginning and growth of that intellectual exchange between Gandhi and Tagore which is the focal theme of the book. I have also attempted an overview of the major issues which united or divided the two, issues which they frankly discussed in their private letters, not meant for publication, and also in a more guarded fashion in their published writings. What may be considered an unusual feature of this collection is the interweaving of the public discourse and their private communications. The documentation is designed to dovetail these two kinds of writings in the chronological framework of the four different phases into which I have periodised the narrative. Editorial notes at the beginning of each of the four parts of the collection elucidate details regarding the letters and writings which belong to each phase.

I have tried not to burden the text with footnotes which may be of no interest to most readers and redundant to the specialists of Gandhian or Tagore literature. Editorial notes, in italics, at the top of the documents indicate the source; unless stated otherwise, the letters are from the Tagore Archives in Rabindra Bhavan, Visva-Bharati. The Appendix contains letters from Tagore or Gandhi to other correspondents, statements to the Press, etc. which do not form a part of the Gandhi-Tagore correspondence but are, nevertheless, essentially relevant to that exchange. The correspondence has been reproduced in the original form, to the extent possible, with only minor editorial changes to bring consistency in the text. I may add that in transliterating non-English words diacritical marks have not been used due to technical constraints. Finally, translations from Bengali into English have been acknowledged wherever possible; in the last two decades of Tagore's life translation was done by diverse hands, not always easy to establish. Translations done by myself and not by the author or approved by the author have been indicated.

Acknowledgement and grateful thanks are due to the present Vice-Chancellor D.K. Sinha, as well as the Granthan Vibhanga and the Rabindra Bhavan Archives of Visva-Bharati; Mr Arvind Kumar, formerly Director, National Book Trust, New Delhi; Navajivan Trust, Ahmedabad; and the Gandhi Smarak Nidhi, New Delhi.

I give this book to my wife, Malabika, who helped me to put it together during our days in Santiniketan.

SABYASACHI BHATTACHARYA

ABBREVIATIONS

C.W.M.G. : *Collected Works of Mahatma Gandhi* (Navjivan Trust, Ahmedabad, and Publications Division, Government of India).

M.R. : *The Modern Review* (Calcutta) Ed. Ramananda Chatterjee.

N.A.I. : National Archives of India, New Delhi.

R.R. : *Rabindra-Rachanavalee* (Collected Works of Rabindranath Tagore, Publications Department, Visva-Bharati, Calcutta).

V.B. : Visva-Bharati Archives, Rabindra Bhavan, Shantiniketan, West Bengal.

Y.I. : *Young India.*

Dear Gurudev,

This is early morning 3 o'clock of Tuesday. I enter the fiery gate at noon. If you can bless the effort, I want it. You have been to me a true friend because you have been a candid friend often speaking your thoughts aloud. I had looked forward to a firm opinion from you one way or the other. But you have refused to criticise. Though it can now only be during my fast, I will yet prize your criticism, if your heart condemns my action. I am not too proud to make an open confession of my blunder, whatever the cost of the confession, if I find myself in error. If your heart approves of the action I want your blessings. It will sustain me. I hope I have made myself clear.

my love

mkgandhi.

Y.E.V.P. 20/9/32.

Rabindra Sadan, Santiniketan

Mahatma Gandhi's letter to Tagore, written before he began his fast on 20 September 1932

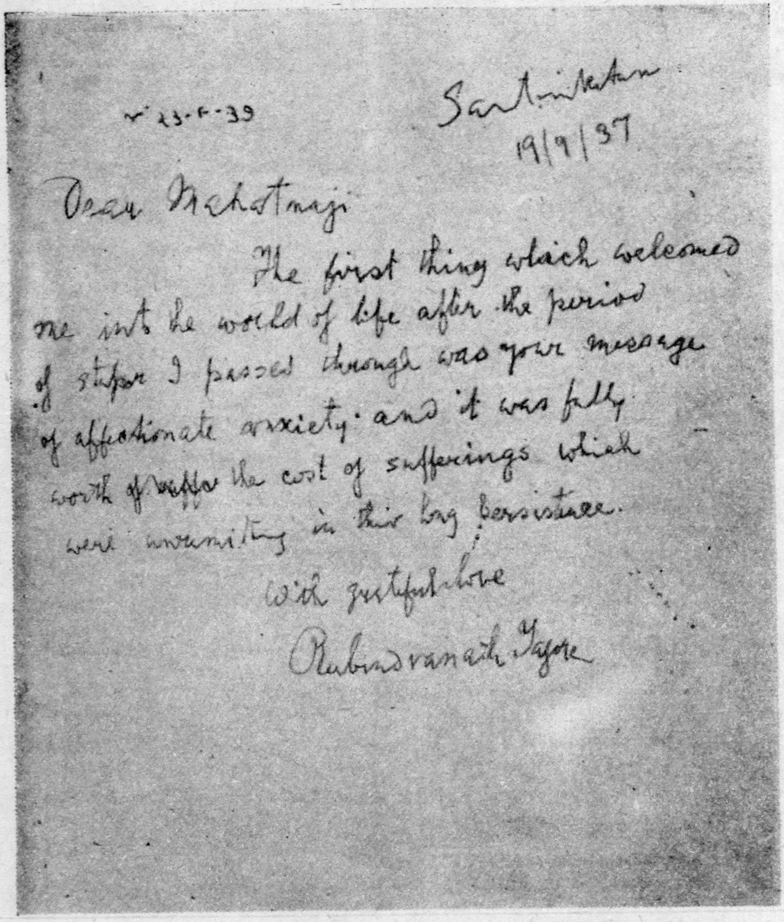

Santiniketan
19/9/37

Dear Mahatmaji

The first thing which welcomed me into the world of life after the period of stupor I passed through was your message of affectionate anxiety and it was fully worth of the cost of sufferings which were unremitting in their long persistence.

With grateful love

Rabindranath Tagore

Rabindra Sadan, Santiniketan

Tagore's letter to Mahatma Gandhi after his illness in 1937

INTRODUCTION

This book puts together letters exchanged by Mahatma Gandhi and Rabindranath Tagore along with some essays which they wrote debating major national issues. These letters, preserved in the archives at Visva-Bharati, the University founded by Tagore, are of great historical interest. Of more than historical interest is the debate between Gandhi and Tagore over certain issues and questions which continue to be relevant to this day and age. This intellectual exchange began in 1914–15 when Mahatma Gandhi along with the students of his Phoenix School in South Africa visited Tagore's Santiniketan. Gandhi recalled later: "It was here that the members of my South African family found warm hospitality in 1914, pending my arrival from England, and I too found shelter here for nearly a month"[1].

At that time, Tagore's school at Santiniketan was not yet 15 years old. Tagore was 53 years of age and he had received the Nobel Prize just a year earlier. Gandhi was younger by eight years and yet to attain a national stature in India, though his great work in South Africa was widely known. There were many striking contrasts between these two personalities. Yet, they found some common chord and there began a friendship which lasted till Tagore's death in 1941. As early as February 1915 we find Tagore referring to Gandhi as 'Mahatma' and Gandhi readily

---

[1] *Harijan,* 9 March 1940, speech by Mahatma Gandhi at Santiniketan, in February 1940, as recorded by Mahadev Desai. The boys of Phoenix School stayed at Santiniketan from 4 November 1914 to 3 April 1915. Gandhi arrived from England on 9 January 1915; D.G. Tendulkar, *Mahatma,* Vol.I (Delhi, 1951), p.157. He met Tagore at Santiniketan during his second visit on 6 March 1915; to this day to commemorate his visit, the *Gandhi Punyaha Din* is observed at Santiniketan on 10 March each year. Tagore's first letter to Gandhi was probably written in January 1915 about the time Gandhi reached India; the copy of this letter in Visva-Bharati Archives bears no date.

adopted the form of addressing Tagore as 'Gurudev'.[2]

But theirs was not a friendship based on just mutual admiration. They had differences on fundamental philosophical questions, which led to disputation about many political, social and economic matters. Both were unsparing in their debate and, indeed, it cannot be said that either of them was very successful in persuading the other towards a path of convergence of views. Each accepted cordially the other's right to differ. These differences on public issues never affected, as far as one can judge from the letters, their personal relationship.

In editing this volume, I had to choose between two possible ways of organising the letters and essays. One could place the material before the reader simply following the chronological order. Alternatively, one could group the material around the major issues discussed by Tagore and Gandhi, e.g., the efficacy of boycott of educational institutions, the possibilities and limits of handicraft industries and the *charkha*, the discourse of science as opposed to that of religiosity, etc. The course adopted in this collection of writings is to present the writings within a chronological framework, but also to highlight the issues being debated in the period to which they belong. The chronological framework in the following pages is one suggested by the private and public communications included here. It broadly corresponds to the rhythms of development of the discourse of nationalist politics and culture.

What were the circumstances in which the intellectual exchange between Gandhi and Tagore commenced and developed? Rabindranath Tagore's experience as an active participant in the *swadeshi* movement following the partition of Bengal (1905)

---

2. Tagore to C.F. Andrews, 18 February 1915, *Letters to a Friend*, ed. C.F. Andrews (London, 1928). Tagore first addresses Gandhi as 'Mahatma' in a letter on 12 April 1919, and Gandhi addresses Tagore as '*Gurudev*' in a letter of 12 January 1918 (Visva-Bharati Archives, Rabindra Bhavan).

Hereafter, in citation of documents the following abbreviations are used: V.B. Archives (Visva-Bharati Archives, Rabindra Bhavan); *CWMG* (*Collected Works of Mahatma Gandhi*, Publications Division, Government of India, New Delhi); *R.R.* (*Rabindra-Rachanavalee*, or Collected Works of Rabindranath Tagore, published by Visva-Bharati Publications Department, Calcutta, 29 volumes); *Y.I.* (*Young India*); *M.R.* (*Modern Review*).

Due to technical constraints, diacritical marks have not been used in the transliteration of non-English words.

may have sensitised the poet to the limitations of the pre-Gandhian Congress and its politics. He saw, perhaps before many of his countrymen, that Gandhi promised to give an altogether new turn to the Indian struggle for freedom. Mohandas Karamchand Gandhi of South African fame might have sent his Phoenix School students to Tagore's Santiniketan because he saw that something was under way in that remote corner of Bengal, which shared some traits with his own endeavour and philosophy.

They were not total strangers to each other. It is on record that in 1901 at the Calcutta Session of the Indian National Congress, M.K. Gandhi moved a resolution "as a petitioner on behalf of the hundred thousand British Indians in South Africa."[3] On that occasion, he met Rabindranath's elder brother Jyotirindranath and, shortly after that, a translation of one of Gandhi's articles on the Indian settlers in South Africa was published in the journal *Bharati*, with which the Tagores were associated.[4]

There is no evidence of personal encounter at this time between Rabindranath and Gandhi. However, there is an affinity of spirit evident in what Tagore wrote of the Indian struggle as early as 1908: "God save us from the disastrous notion that *dharma* is not for the powerless. Let us not depart from the path of Truth (*satya*), that which is Right.... It is regrettable that the terror and upheavals of Europe are the only models before us. But the Christian saints who, by the strength of their faith, withstood the oppression of the Roman Emperor triumphed in their death over the Emperor.... *dharma* can help us surpass oppression...."[5] In this statement and in others, Tagore's philosophical approach appears to approximate that of Gandhi's.

It was Gandhi's work in South Africa which made him known to Tagore, and in this matter Tagore's friend C.F. Andrews and one of his colleagues at Santiniketan, W.W. Pearson, played an important role. At the end of 1913, Andrews and Pearson

---

3. B. Pattabhi Sitaramayya, *The History of the Indian National Congress 1885–1935* (Madras, 1935), p.78.

4. Prasanta Kumar Pal, *Ravi-Jeevanee*, Vol.VI, (Calcutta, 1993), p.4.

5. Rabindranath Tagore, *Pravasee*, 16 April 1908 (my translation); see Prasanta Kumar Pal, *op. cit., p.4*; C. Sehanovis, *Rabindranath o biplabee samaj* (Calcutta, 1985), pp.24–25.

resolved to visit Gandhi and to advance his cause in South Africa. On the eve of their journey to Durban from Calcutta, they saw Tagore to seek his blessings and two days before their departure a meeting was held at the Town Hall of Calcutta on 5 December 1913 to consider the position of Indians in South Africa. Tagore was one of the organisers, and the letter requesting the Sheriff's permission to hold the meeting bore his signature.[6] Andrews, a prolific correspondent, regularly kept Tagore informed of Gandhi's activities in South Africa.

Few letters of this early period have survived. Nor do we have any account of Gandhi's first visit to Santiniketan except for Gandhi's own words quoted earlier and a letter Tagore wrote to him thanking him for sending the Phoenix School boys to Santiniketan—for "allowing your boys to become our boys as well."[7] But it is evident that from 1914 a close friendship burgeoned rapidly.

Despite formal address till 1919 ("Dear Mr. Gandhi") Tagore refers to Gandhi as the 'Mahatma' as early as February 1915. His friend C.F. Andrews used this nomenclature for Gandhi in a letter to Tagore even earlier, in January 1914: "I had no difficulty in seeing from the first Mr. Gandhi's position and accepting it; for in principle, it is essentially yours and Mahatmaji's—a true independence, a reliance upon spiritual force, a fearless courage in the face of temporal power, and withal a deep and burning charity for all men."[8]

1915–1922

The years between 1914 and 1922 were crowded with events in national life. In 1914–15, Gandhi was about to re-enter public life in India. The Lucknow Session of the Indian National Congress in 1916 and the so-called Lucknow Pact revived hopes of unity between the moderate and extremist wings and between the Congress and the Muslim League. The declaration by the British Government in August 1917 regarding the future policy of

---

[6] *Amrita Bazar Patrika*, 25 November 1913 cited in Pal, *op cit.*, VI, p.456.

[7] Tagore to Gandhi, n.d. (January 1915?), V.B. Archives; letters between Gandhi and Tagore cited hereafter are from the V.B. Archives, unless stated otherwise, and are reproduced in this book verbatim.

[8] C.F. Andrews to Tagore, 4 January 1914 (Durban), cited in Pal, *op. cit.*, vol.VI, p.456.

promoting self-governance and a "responsible government of India" raised expectations, which were soon dashed to the ground by the Montagu-Chelmsford Reforms. A sense of disappointment was transformed into outrage by the enactment of the Rowlatt Act of 1919, which undermined basic civil liberties.

Gandhi, with the achievements of 1917–18—the Champaran *satyagraha*, the Ahmedabad mill-workers' strike, and the Khaira struggle—behind him, appeared on the national scene as the man of the hour. The *satyagraha* against the Rowlatt Act in March and April 1919 evolved unprecedented participation of ordinary citizens, far removed from the till now edifying resolutions and unedifying squabbles of the Congress. On 12 April 1919, Tagore, then at Santiniketan, wrote to Gandhi: "Our authorities have shown us their claws, whose sure effect is to drive some of us into the secret path of resentment and others into utter demoralisation. In this crisis you, as a great leader of men, have stood among us to proclaim your faith in the ideal, which you know to be that of India.... 'Conquer anger by the power of non-anger, and evil by the power of good'."[9] On the next day, 13 April, took place the Jallianwalla Bagh massacre. As the facts of the atrocities in Punjab began to spread, the entire country was anguished.

On 30 May 1919, Tagore wrote in his own hand that justly famous letter to the Viceroy renouncing his knighthood: "The enormity of the measures taken by the Government in the Punjab for quelling some local disturbances has, with a rude shock, revealed to our minds the helplessness of our position as British subjects in India.... [T]he very least I can do for my country is to take all consequences upon myself in giving voice to the protest of the millions of my countrymen, surprised into a dumb anguished terror. The time has come, when badges of honour make our shame glaring in their incongruous context of humiliation...."[10]

From 1919 to 1922, the Khilafat and Non-cooperation movements catapulted Mahatma Gandhi to the leadership of a mass movement, which included a programme of "boycott of government schools" and of "inducing the people" to give up foreign cloth and take to *swadeshi* products. Tagore began to feel

---

9. Tagore to Gandhi, 12 April 1919.
10. Tagore to H.E. the Viceroy, 30 May 1919; the original draft written by Tagore is in the Visva-Bharati Archives, Rabindra Bhavan (see Appendix).

uncomfortably at variance with some of the actions, agenda and practices which these programmes led to.

At the same time, Gandhi and Tagore continued to enjoy each other's confidence and support on some basic issues. Gandhi sought Tagore's opinion on the use of Hindi as a national language. Tagore was of the view that Hindi was "the only possible national language" at the inter-provincial level, but a period of preparation was necessary to "pave the way towards its general use by constant practice as a voluntary acceptance of a national obligation."[11] In 1921, the new Constitution of the Congress adopted at the Nagpur Session, accepted Hindustani as the language of proceedings "as far as possible", also allowing the use of English and the language of the province.[12] We also find Gandhi writing to Tagore requesting a message on the eve of the massive *hartal* he had called on 6 April 1919; likewise he invited Tagore's message at the National Week Conference in Bombay.[13] In the message, read out by Tagore's emissary C.F. Andrews, Tagore condemned in eloquent words "the great crime" that was done in the name of law in Punjab, "the cowardliness of the powerful", and the "dastardliness of cruel injustice confident of its impunity."[14]

In March 1920, Gandhi wrote to Tagore inviting him to visit Ahmedabad and his *ashram* on the occasion of the Gujarat Literary Conference in April 1920.[15] After Tagore's visit, his companion C.F. Andrews stayed on in Sabarmati. Gandhi wrote to Tagore, a restless traveller all his life: "If... you could at all rest anywhere in India, I would ask you and Mr. Andrews to remain in India," because "I would like all the pure forces to be physically in the country during the process of her new birth."[16]

Despite this cordial relationship, Tagore began to express doubts about some aspects of the political movement Gandhi led.

[11] Tagore to Gandhi, 24 January 1918.
[12] D. Chakrabarty (ed.), *Congress in Evolution: A collection of Congress Resolutions* (Calcutta, 1935), p.221.
[13] Gandhi to Tagore, 5 April 1919 (the letter has not been traced in V.B. Archives, but it is referred to by Tagore in his letter to Gandhi of 12 April 1919).
[14] The message, printed in *Young India*, has not been preserved in the V.B. Archives.
[15] Gandhi to Tagore, 11 March 1920.
[16] Gandhi to Tagore, 30 April 1918.

A series of articles written by both of them appeared in *Modern Review* and *Young India* debating the questions raised by Tagore. The debate took place when the Non-cooperation movement was at its height, and nationalist public opinion, very naturally, was hostile to Tagore's critique. Gandhi was arrested on 10 March 1922 and thereafter Tagore desisted from writing on the subject.

In the meantime, there was a revulsion of feeling as regards Gandhi's leadership: his decision to call off the movement in February 1922 after the Chauri Chaura incident, puzzled and disappointed his followers and comrades. Tagore did not lend his support to the veiled attacks on Gandhi at that hour.

Tagore's critique appeared in 1921 in the form of some letters to his friend, C.F. Andrews, published in *Modern Review* (May 1921) and this was answered by Gandhi in two articles in *Young India* (June 1921); there followed a long rejoinder from Tagore (first published in *Prabasi* in Bengali and later in *Modern Review* under the title "Call of Truth"). Gandhi responded with a well-known essay entitled 'The Great Sentinel' (*Young India*, 13 October 1921), preceded by shorter essays published in *Young India*, entitled 'English Learning' and 'The Poet's Anxiety' (June 1921).

It is unnecessary to present their arguments in this 'Introduction', since these have been reproduced in their entirety in the following pages. The argument was at two levels, so to speak. At one level, fundamental philosophical issues were raised; we shall return to them towards the end of this essay. At another level, the debate focused on some immediate questions relating to the programme and practice of Non-cooperation in 1920-21.

The issues were: first, Tagore abhorred an instrumentalist view of *satyagraha*. He felt that the politicians were using Mahatma's *satyagraha* as a stratagem in politics, as another "ingenious move in their political gamble. With their minds corroded by untruth, they cannot understand what an important thing it is that the Mahatma's supreme love should have drawn forth the country's love."[17] They had converted Gandhi's message into a mindless *mantra* and thus they strengthened bigotry and inertia. Secondly, Tagore was unhappy with the call to boycott govern-

---

[17] Tagore's 'Call of Truth' reproduced in this book, was published in Bengali under the title *'Satyer ahvan'* in *Kalantar*, a collection of socio-political essays, *R.R.*, Vol.XXIV (Calcutta, 1947).

ment schools, when there was no alternative educational system to impart better education. The existing British-sponsored education was undoubtedly abominably poor — and Tagore was its severest critic — but the question remained: "Our students are bringing their offering of sacrifice to what? Not to a fuller education, but to non-education."[18] Such a programme could not be sustained for long. Thirdly, Tagore was sceptical of the *charkha* and the burning of foreign cloth as the panacea for India's problems. And, finally, he was apprehensive that an isolationist obscurantism might develop if India, obsessed with the 'sins' and shortcomings of Western civilisation, failed to take a broader view of humanity as a whole.

Mahatma Gandhi's answer to the problems thus posed were very precise. He agrees that those who slavishly mimic his message do beget more bigotry; but he believed that his followers were not among them. "I regard the Poet as a sentinel warning us against the approaching enemies called Bigotry, Lethargy, Intolerance...." But he could not agree that the Non-cooperation movement had fallen prey to those enemies.

As regards boycott of government schools and colleges, Gandhi maintained that boycott was fully justified, for the training imparted there "rendered us helpless and godless. It is no argument against the soundness of the proposition laid down by me that the vast majority of the students went back after the first flush of enthusiasm. Their recantation is proof rather of the extent of our degradation than of the wrongness of the step."[19] Gandhi rejected Tagore's view on the *charkha* and put forward his rationale for *khadi*. "It was our love of foreign cloth that ousted the wheel from its position of dignity. Therefore I consider it a sin to wear foreign cloth. I must confess that I do not draw a sharp or any distinction between economics and ethics."[20]

On the *charkha* and the related question of acceptance or rejection of "the machine and the materialism of the West", the battle was not yet fully joined in 1921; it developed in the next phase, around 1925.

---

[18] Tagore, 'Letter to a Friend', *Modern Review*, May 1921 (the friend is C.F. Andrews).

[19] Gandhi, 'The Poet's Anxiety', *Young India*, 1 June 1921.

[20] Gandhi, 'The Great Sentinel', *Young India*, 13 October 1921.

1923–1928

In the period between the arrest of Mahatma Gandhi in March 1922 and his release in February 1924, the Tagore-Gandhi debate was, so to speak, suspended since Tagore did not pursue his line of criticism when Gandhi was incarcerated. Immediately on Gandhi's release, Tagore sent him a cable: "We rejoice". He sent C.F. Andrews to meet Gandhi at Sassoon Hospital in Pune where he was recuperating. Gandhi visited Santiniketan in 1925.[21] About this time, Tagore took up the threads of the earlier debate in a series of articles in *Modern Review* while Gandhi responded through essays in *Young India*.

It may be recalled that this was the year when Gandhi retreated from the world of active politics for the time being and remained in self-chosen exile from that world till 1927. He had declared that a "constructive programme" of rural upliftment and economic regeneration through the propagation of the *charkha* and removal of untouchability were his first objectives. National politics was in a morass: the elan of the Non-cooperation movement turned into disillusionment in the years following its withdrawal and hence, led to a kind of disarray and directionlessness.

The tussle in the Indian National Congress between the Swarajists led by Motilal Nehru and C.R. Das, and the "No-changers" led by Vallabhbhai Patel and Rajendra Prasad from 1923; the death of C.R. Das in June 1925; the resurgence of communalism in its most violent form despite Gandhi's efforts (his fast in September 1924); a further split within the Swarajists' ranks — all this added up to present a gloomy prospect for the forces in national life that Gandhi had once led. Although Gandhi was "in retirement", Tagore, once again, addressed his questions to Gandhi.

These questions basically were concerned with Gandhi's "constructive programme", especially the economic programme focusing upon the *charkha* and casteism. Leaving aside, for the present, the wider-ranging philosophical issues, the immediate pragmatic problem pointed out by Tagore in the essay 'Cult of the *Charkha*' (1925) was the economic efficacy of the *charkha* programme. He had written in 1921: "The question of using or refusing cloth of a particular manufacture belongs mainly to

---

21   Tagore to Gandhi, 5 February 1924 (cable), and letter, 20 February 1924.

economic science", but a tendency was abroad to use the "magical formula that foreign cloth is impure" and thus "economics is bundled out and a fictitious moral dictum dragged in its place."[22] The objection here is not to the substantive point about foreign cloth but to the terms of discourse, the use of moral language in place of the economic. To this, Gandhi's reply was that he had not drawn any distinction between economics and ethics.[23]

Tagore pursues the question of economic rationality further. The causes of poverty, he says, are "complexly ramified" and we have the British "sweeping away" wealth across the seas, something that did not happen in the preceding Mughal and Pathan regimes.[24] The ruination of handicrafts was "only one of the external symptoms" of the process of impoverishment. A programme that concentrated only on this to the exclusion of all else gave undue prominence to it. Tagore recommended that the leaders of the nation should think more broadly (e.g., in terms of a rural cooperative movement) and comprehensively address the totality of the problem.

Further, Tagore makes another point which is of interest in the light of later developments. How long would it be possible "to hide ourselves away from commerce with the outside world?" As we shall see later, from a philosophical standpoint, Tagore had other doubts as well about the *charkha* programme.

Mahatma Gandhi's response to the economic question was that Tagore had denounced what he imagined to be the excesses of the *charkha* cult from sheer ignorance. "All he knows about the movement is what he has picked up from table-talk."[25] Secondly, poets are given to exaggeration and what is said under "poetic licence" is not to be taken literally. The exaggeration consisted of imagining that Gandhi wanted every one to spin all the time, whereas all he wanted was at least half an hour a day from those who had other means of livelihood and as much spinning as possible from the unemployed or underemployed. Those who had taken to European textiles should try to clothe themselves without depending on importation. He was prepared to push the

---

[22] Tagore, 'The Call of Truth'.
[23] Gandhi, 'The Great Sentinel'.

[24] Tagore, 'The Cult of the *Charkha*'.
[25] Gandhi, 'The Poet and the *Charkha*', *Young India*, 5 November 1925.

self-sufficiency argument "to the logical limit" and say that Bengal need not import from Bombay.

Finally, Gandhi was not recommending *charkha* alone, but a chain of activities promoting rural cooperation; the only difference in this regard from Tagore was that Gandhi preferred to put the *charkha* at the focus of these cooperative activities. Gandhi also noted that Tagore put his signature on programmes propagating the *charkha* and visited and addressed Khadi Ashram, and thus, Gandhi presumed the poet did not oppose the *charkha* per se.[26] Tagore seems to have retained a qualified scepticism, and nationalist public opinion at that time was vociferous against him.

In this period, the other issue on which Tagore implicitly, though not explicitly, differed from Gandhi was the latter's defence of the *varna* order. Tagore's essay, 'Shudra Dharma' does not form a part of the Gandhi-Tagore debate and has been excluded from this collection of their writings. We may, however, note the substance of it because it provides the background to some later writings reprinted here, occasioned by a debate in 1934 on Gandhi's statement about casteism.

In 1928, Gandhi reiterated his position in *Young India* that the *varnashrama*—defined as "pre-determination of the choice of man's profession" according to his ancestors' occupation—was the best means of preventing encroachment on others' spheres and competitiveness in pursuit of wealth.[27] "Our failure to follow the law of *varna* is responsible both for our spiritual and economic ruin.... *Varna* is the best form of insurance for happiness and for religious pursuit.... I derive it from the *Bhagvad Gita*." He also said: a *shudra* who acquires the qualities of a *brahmin* "may not be called a *brahmin* in this birth. And it is a good thing for him not to arrogate a *varna* to which he is not born." At the same time, Gandhi maintained that untouchability and the evils of the caste system were "excrescences" upon Hinduism and "*varna* had nothing do with caste"; he conceded that parts of *Manusmriti* were "open to grave objections" in that these were unjust to women and the so-called lower castes.

Tagore was completely in accord with Gandhi in the latter's

---

[26] Gandhi, 'The Poet and the Wheel', *Young India*, 11 March 1926.
[27] 'The Caste System' (record of the conversation with Gandhi), *Young India*, 3 January 1928.

struggle against casteism and untouchability; however, the defense of *varnashrama* by Gandhi might have caused Tagore an acute moral discomfort. In a very elliptical fashion, Tagore addressed the question in an essay entitled 'The *Shudra* Habit'.[28] One set of argument here concerns the practical effects of *varna*, the other set the moral effect. As regards the first: "how far by this means (*varna*) our national efficiency has or has not been achieved", he asked. His answer was that it did not make for efficiency in allocating people to occupation according to birth, instead of individual capacity; further, the pursuit of hereditary occupations, generation after generation, involves mindless repetition and degrades the quality of mind that is needed to make innovations even within the limited sphere of an occupation.

As for the moral effects, Tagore found nothing defensible in the *varna* order assigning some to 'lowly' occupations and others to 'superior' ones by birth. It enshrined at best "fixed external observances" being kept up without reference to their significance or utility, at the cost of restricting human freedom. It imprisoned the mind in rituals, blindly repeated among *brahmins*, without elevating the mental and moral qualities the ideal originally prescribed. The true *kshatriya* was "nowhere to be found" in India.

Tagore goes on to say in a rhetorical vein: "the *dharma* of the *shudra* is the only one that is as a matter of fact extant today in this land of India, a state of things complacently accepted by the orthodox believers in the perpetuation of the *dharma* of caste.... Where else, indeed, in all the world can be found the like of those whose very *dharma* has reduced them to hereditary slaves?" The *shudra* habit was so ingrained in the culture of the nation, Tagore said, that Indians were the best servants of the British empire. Whether it is the "liveried brethren in government service" in India, or the Indian policeman in China, or the Indian soldier in other parts of the world, injunctions of *dharma* ensure that India

---

[28] Tagore,'The *Shudra* Habit', *Modern Review*, May 1927; the Bengali original entitled '*Shudra Dharma*' appears in *Kalantar* (Calcutta, 1937; 7th ed. 1993), p.286, *R.R.*, Vol.XXIV. It is well-known that Dr. B.R. Ambedkar's main point in criticism of Gandhi in *What Congress and Gandhi have done to the Untouchables*, was Gandhi's defence of *varnashrama*; Tagore does not voice such criticism, his tenor in this essay being obliquely ironical.

fulfills her functions as *"Shudra India"*. "She will say: Better to die in one's *dharma*.... Everywhere is she the bearer of menial burdens.... Those whom she rushes to attack at the behest of her British master are not her enemies. And, as soon as her fighting is done, she is hustled back into her servant quarters." This essay, rather poorly translated in *Modern Review* in 1927, is one of the best examples of Tagore's ironical polemics in Bengali.

1929–1933

There commences a large spate of letters between Tagore and Gandhi in the early 1930's. In 1928–29, the Congress emerged from the doldrums and Gandhi re-entered political activities at the national level. Although the attempt to frame a constitution for India (Nehru Report, August 1928) failed due to communalist obduracy, the Simon Commission (1928) provided a common object of opposition to all sections of political opinion. In the previous few years the recrudescence of Hindu and Muslim communalism was a marked feature of Indian social and political life and eradication of communalism became a common cause for Tagore and Gandhi.

In 1928–29 the Bardoli *satyagraha* on the one hand and, on the other, the communist-led industrial strikes in Bombay and other cities, became landmarks in mass politics. The organisation of the Hindustan Socialist Republican Association of Chandra Shekhar Azad and revolutionary terrorist activities in Bengal offered an alternative to the path treaded by the Congress, and this political alternative attracted the younger generation.

A new agenda of action was virtually forced upon the Congress. The adoption of *Purna Swaraj* as the Congress objective at the Lahore session (1929), the adoption of the tricolour flag of freedom, the declaration of 26 January 1930 as the Independence Day, and finally the launching of the Civil Disobedience Movement with Gandhi's march to Dandi (12 March 1930)—all these developments marked a new phase in the nationalist movement. Many of the letters in the following pages relate to these events.

On many occasions, Gandhi sought Tagore's advice and intellectual support before launching on a major course of action. Thus, for instance, he wrote to Tagore a few hours before the resumption of Civil Disobedience in January 1932: "I try to steal

a wink of sleep and I think of you. I want you to give your best
to the sacrificial fire that is being lighted."[29] (From a forwarding
note by Mahadev Desai, it seems that Gandhi was arrested at 4
a.m. before he could sign this letter.) Again, on the day he started
his famous fast at Yeravada on the issue of depressed castes and
separate electorates, he scribbled (3 a.m., 20 September 1932) a
few lines to Tagore: "If you can bless the effort, I want it. You
have been a true friend because you have been a candid friend,
often speaking your thoughts aloud."[30] It so happened that
Tagore's cable to him was already on the way with the message
that" our sorrowing hearts will follow your sublime penance with
reverence and love."[31]

Similarly, just before he began his fast in protest against
orthodox Hindus' attitude on the entry of the so-called lower
castes at the Guruvayyur Temple, Kerala, Gandhi wrote to
Tagore in November 1932: "I want your whole-hearted cooperation if you feel as I do."[32] Tagore was supportive and, while
expressing concern that "the sacrifice of your life for our sins"
would be an unthinkable calamity, doubted whether Gandhi
should take such an extreme step; in Tagore's opinion, except for
some isolated groups, the majority were already "overwhelmingly on the side of reforms" of the kind Gandhi desired.[33] Tagore
proved to be wrong in this optimistic assessment of the general
trend, and Gandhi was, of course, right.

There is the same protective love in Tagore's protest against
Gandhi's resolve to fast in May 1933; but Tagore added that he
could not possibly "fully realise the call, which has come only to
yourself" and that he would "try to believe that you are right in
your resolve" and that Tagore's misgivings might be "the outcome of a timidity of ignorance."[34]

Thus, at moments of crisis Gandhi and Tagore seemed to
draw together seeking a kind of companionship of the mind,
although they differed on many issues. One of these issues was

---

[29]   Gandhi to Tagore, 3 January 1932.
[30]   Gandhi to Tagore, 20 September 1932.
[31]   Tagore to Gandhi, 19 September 1932.
[32]   Gandhi to Tagore, 10 November 1932.
[33]   Tagore to Gandhi, 15 November 1932.
[34]   Tagore to Gandhi, 9 May 1933, in reply to Gandhi's request for blessings on 2
       May 1933.

the efficacy of fasting. Tagore found it painful to contemplate the suffering Gandhi brought upon himself by fasting. Tagore also feared the possibility of lesser men fasting for any cause, noble or otherwise; it opened up "an easy and futile path... into a dark abyss of self-mortification."[35] Although Gandhi said that this extreme form of sacrifice was for him alone as an individual, Tagore realized that others would follow his example. He seems to have anticipated that protest fasting was soon to be trivialised and thus lose its moral content. "As far as I can understand, the fast that you have started [May 1933] carries in it the expiation for the sins of your countrymen. But I ask to be excused when I say that the expiation can truly and heroically be done only by daily endeavours for the sake of these unfortunate beings, who do not know what they do." Mahatma Gandhi's reply: "Your prayer [is a] great help in this ordeal. God's will be done."[36]

On two major questions of the day, communalism and casteism, Gandhi and Tagore were completely in accord. From 1926 onwards, Tagore's writings against communalism became sharper than ever. This might have been partly due to the fact that in 1926 he personally witnessed the Calcutta riots which, in fact, began with an incident in the locality where his Calcutta residence was situated.

These riots were preceded and followed by similar events in Lahore, Panipat, Hyderabad, Bombay, Rawalpindi, Allahabad, Dacca (Dhaka) and Delhi. The national conference of the Hindu Mahasabha in Delhi in May 1926; dangerous ambiguities in the government's policy on the question of music in the vicinity of mosques; the opposition within the Congress to the 'Bengal Hindu-Muslim Pact' which C.R. Das had piloted with difficulty—all this made 1926 a watershed in communal relations. About this time, Tagore wrote a poem well-known in Bengali, 'Dharmamoha': "They altar awash with blood/Smash, smash that into nothingness/Strike your thunderbolt on the prison-walls around faith/And bring the light of knowledge to this benighted land."[37]

---

[35] Tagore to Gandhi 11 May 1933.
[36] Gandhi to Tagore (cable), 23 May 1933.
[37] The historical background to these writings has been discussed in Sabyasachi Bhattacharya, 'The Archaeology of a Poem', *The Telegraph* (Calcutta), 12 March 1993.

In the later twenties Tagore's battle against communalism continued. He went so far as to say that "straightforward atheism" was "preferable to this terrible thing, delusion of religiosity... the satanic bestiality which wears the garb of religion."[38] This was scarcely the kind of language Gandhi would have employed, but they were both striving for a common cause. Tagore began to send some of his writings and translations for publication in Gandhi's *Harijan*; the first English translation of two famous poems were published in that journal in 1933, 'The Great Equality' and 'The Cleanser'.[39] The *Harijan* also carried some of Tagore's letters. Between Tagore's visit to Gandhi's Ashram in Ahmedabad on 18 January 1930 (an account of it by Mahadev Desai in *Harijan*, is reprinted here in the Appendix) and by the end of 1933, there is virtually no issue dividing the two.

1934–1941

Unlike the 1920's, the political waves raised by Gandhi did not cast up many issues in the 1930's to cause a difference of opinion with Tagore. In 1934, the formal withdrawal of the Civil Disobedience Movement passes unnoticed in their correspondence. What caused a debate may appear to be trivial, but it was not so to Tagore.

This was when Gandhi was reported in the Press to have made a statement to the effect that the calamitous Bihar earthquake of 1934 was 'divine chastisement' for the sin committed against the so-called untouchable castes. Tagore was shocked to see the element of irrationality in the statement, while he was totally in agreement with Gandhi on the evil of untouchability. He drafted a statement and sent it to Gandhi requesting him to release it to the Press, if Gandhi had indeed said what was reported.

Tagore expressed "painful surprise" that Gandhi should have lent his authority to "this kind of unscientific view of things," which many in India readily accept.[40] He apologised for stating the truism "that physical catastrophes have their inevita-

---

[38] *ibid.*; This was a statement in a sermon at Santiniketan, recorded by Kshitimohan Sen in 1926 (my translation); this essay was, curiously enough, excluded from the collected works of Tagore later (almost certainly without his authority).

[39] *Harijan*, 25 March 1933, 5 May 1933.

[40] Tagore to Gandhi, 28 January 1934.

ble and exclusive origin in a certain combination of physical facts." Generally, Tagore said, we should not "associate ethical principles with cosmic phenomena." Man's iniquities—including the exploitation that happens in the factories or oppression that takes place in prisons—may crack the moral foundations of society, but laws of nature are something apart. "We who are immensely grateful to Mahatmaji for inducing by his wonder-working inspiration a freedom from fear and feebleness in the minds of his countrymen feel profoundly hurt, when any words from his mouth may emphasize the elements of unreason in these very minds, the unreason which is the fundamental source of all the blind powers that drive us against freedom and self-respect."[41]

Gandhi published this statement in the *Harijan* with his own rejoinder. "Gurudev and I early discovered certain differences of outlook between us", he began. He went on to say that despite Tagore's statement on this occasion, Gandhi adhered to his position. "To me the earthquake was no caprice of God nor a result of a venting of mere blind forces.... I cannot prove the connection of the sin of untouchability with the Bihar visitation even though the connection is instinctively felt by me. If my belief turns out ill-founded, it will still have done good to me and those who believe with me."[42] Tagore did not pursue the debate further: they stood at two polar opposites and a debate, after Gandhi's gentle reply to Tagore's unwontedly sharp words, was not perhaps possible.

The provincial Congress Committee of Bengal often sought Tagore's intervention and occasionally he acceded to such requests. Thus there was an exchange of letters with Gandhi in July-August 1933 on resentments in Bengal concerning the Poona Pact of 1932, and again in January 1934 on police atrocities in Midnapore in Bengal. Likewise there was an exchange of letters occasioned by the tussles and tensions regarding the election of Subhas Chandra Bose to the position of President of the Indian National Congress and his resignation in 1939. Both the young leaders,

---

[41] Tagore's statement, *Harijan*, 16 February 1934. This debate reminds one of the famous disputation between Voltaire and J.J. Rousseau on the earthquake of Lisbon in 1755.

[42] Gandhi, 'Superstition versus Faith', *Harijan*, 16 February 1934.

Bose and Jawaharlal Nehru, visited Tagore at Santiniketan frequently and Nehru formed some permanent ties, with his daughter Indira's admission to Visva-Bharati as a student. Tagore might have had an empathy with Nehru in whom he noted a readiness "to lead an assault against abuse of power by wealth, or blind faith, or imperialistic policy". As for Bose, Tagore recognized the fact that "the leadership of Bengal has now fallen on Subhas Chandra", although he professed to be unable to see through "the dust that has been raised" by "party feelings."[43] Tagore did not directly intervene in matters internal to the Congress, but after the fact became known that Subhas Chandra Bose was being eased out of the Congress, he wrote a very brief letter in March 1939 consisting of one sentence to Gandhi: "Some rude hands have deeply hurt Bengal with an ungracious persistence, please apply without delay balm to the wound with your kind hands."[44] In December 1939, he requested Gandhi to "invite his [Subhas Bose's] cordial cooperation in supreme interest of national unity."[45]

Gandhi tried to set at rest these anxieties. He asked Andrews to explain matters to Tagore: "I feel that Subhas is behaving like a spoilt child of the family.... And then his politics show sharp differences. They seem to be unbridgeable. I am quite clear that the matter is too complicated for Gurudev to handle. Let him trust that no one in the Committee has anything personal against Subhas."[46] By April, 1940 Tagore is said to have been disillusioned with the continued squabbles between sections of Bengal leadership; in particular a scuffle in public between Gandhian Congressmen and followers of Subhas in Calcutta, is reported to be the cause of severe comments by Tagore on the immaturity of the leaders and a certain tendency in Bengal to "wail and complain", a decline from the glorious role that was

---

43   Tagore to Amiya Chakraborty, published as an essay entitled 'The Congress' in *Modern Review*, July 1939 and in Bengali in *Pravasee*, Ashadh, 1346 B.S. (Bengal era).

44   Tagore to Gandhi, 29 March 1939.

45   Tagore to Gandhi, 20 December 1939.

46   Gandhi to C.F. Andrews, 15 January 1940. It is doubtful if the message conveyed by Andrews changed Tagore's mind; what seems to have led him to re think on the question was the undisciplined behaviour of Subhasists in full public view on some occasions in Calcutta.

Bengal's at one time.[47]

While maintaining a certain distance from what was commonly perceived as manifestations of Bose-Nehru antagonism in 1939–40, Tagore addressed the problem at a general level. First, "in spite of the uniting centre, which the Congress represents, the provinces are showing lamentable signs of separatist tendencies."[48] It was this which, he thought, merited more attention. Like a carriage that seemed all in one piece while it was propped up in the stable, the Congress had appeared to be whole at one time; when it was driven on to the streets it began to come apart. The fissures in the unity of the nation began to show when it came "on the highway of a common political freedom". As for feelings in some sections in Bengal regarding her role in the Congress, Tagore wrote that a readiness to see conspiracy was "a sign of weakness" and to be suspicious of everyone around is to lack "political sanity."[49]

In February 1937, we find Tagore requesting Gandhi to be a life trustee of the Visva-Bharati; in 1934, Gandhi had become at Tagore's request 'Adviser' to the Village Industries Association in Santiniketan.[50] What was more, Gandhi had on several occasions mobilised funds for Visva-Bharati. In 1935, Tagore confided in him that a crisis faced Visva-Bharati. Being outside of the university system erected by the British Government, it obtained no aid in any form; Tagore kept it going with the royalty income from his writings. (The Nobel Prize money had gone mainly into Tagore's rural cooperative bank, with dubious results.) "Over 30 years I have practically given my all to this mission of my life.... And now, when I am 75 I feel the burden of my responsibility growing too heavy for me...."[51] Gandhi immediately assured his friend of support and within six months a substantial sum, contributed by Gandhi's friends and admirers in business circles, was remitted by him to Tagore.[52] An interesting aftermath of this

---

[47] See contemporary observers' impressions and news-reports in Prabhat Mukhopadhyay, *Rabindra-Jeevanee* (Calcutta, 1994), Vol.IV, pp.231–32.

[48] Tagore to Amiya Chakraborty, letter published in *Pravasee*, 1346 B.S. and Eng. trans. in *Modern Review*, July 1939.

[49] *ibid.*

[50] Tagore to Gandhi, 10 February 1937, 21 November 1934.

[51] Tagore to Gandhi, 12 September 1935.

[52] Gandhi to Tagore, 13 October 1934, 27 March 1936.

was an exchange of angry letters between the two in 1937. Gandhi thought that Tagore's further efforts to raise funds for Visva-Bharati through song and dramatic performances was damaging to the dignity of the poet and his institution. Tagore argued that these were not "begging expeditions", but an expression of that artistic self which was part of the culture and personality he tried to build in Santiniketan. "It is part of a poet's religion...."[53]

In February 1940, Gandhi visited Santiniketan. In his address of welcome Tagore expressed the hope that "eternal values of our true endeavour", beyond "the moral confusions of our distracted politics", would be revealed.[54] Neither could have known that this was to be Gandhi's last visit to Rabindranath at Santiniketan. But, it is possible that Tagore might have sensed that he would not live for many more days. He wrote to Gandhi a letter, which was handed over to Gandhi at the time of his departure from Santiniketan: "Accept this institution under your protection.... Visva-Bharati is like a vessel, which is carrying the cargo of my life's best treasure and I hope it may claim special care from my countrymen for its preservation."[55] Gandhi wrote back on the train, as he was often in the habit of doing, reassuring Tagore that he would do all he could to preserve Santiniketan, his "second home."[56] These were among the last letters exchanged between them. Tagore was old and ailing. On 13 April 1941 when

---

53. Tagore to Gandhi, 26 February 1937.

54. Tagore's Address of welcome to Gandhi, 17 February 1940, Santiniketan.

55. Tagore to Gandhi, 19 February 1940.

56. Gandhi to Tagore, 19 February 1940. It may be appropriate, before we enter into a discussion on some general issues, to note that the letters which passed between them are relatively unknown, though the public debate between the two has received some attention from commentators, particularly those of the Gandhian school. These include: B.K. and S. Ahluwalia, *Tagore and Gandhi* (New Delhi, 1981); Gurdial Mallik, *Gandhi and Tagore* (Ahmedabad, 1961); R.K. Prabhu and R. Kelkar (eds), *Truth Called Them Differently* (Ahmedabad, 1961); J.P. Chander, *Tagore and Gandhi Argue* (Lahore, 1945); *Gandhi Centenary Volume* (Visva-Bharati, Santiniketan, 1969); Sudhangshu Mohan Bannerji, 'Rolland, Tagore and Gandhi' in *Tagore Studies* (Tagore Research Institute, Calcutta, 1969); Krishna Kripalani, 'Gurudev and Gandhiji', *ibid*; of more general interest is B. Parekh, *Gandhi's Political Philosophy* (McMillan, U.K., 1989). Most of the letters from Gandhi to Tagore are in the *CWMG*, scattered in over 30 volumes; the letters from Tagore to Gandhi have not been collected in any book yet, but the Bengali house journal of Rabindra Bhavan called *Raveendra-Veeksha (Poush, 1398* Bengal era, pp.1-33) carried them with excellent notes by S.K. Bagchi.

Tagore completed his eightieth year, Gandhi cabled "Four score not enough. May you finish five. Love." Tagore cabled back: "Four score is impertinence. Five score intolerable." Rabindranath died a few months later, on 7 August 1941.

'The Spirit of Philosophy'

The intellectual quality of the dialogue between Mahatma Gandhi and Rabindranath Tagore is such that it possesses an enduring interest. In these pages, I have tried to situate their debates, in private letters and in public statements, in the historical context of India's national life and the cultural and political discourse of those times.

"Until philosophers are kings or the kings and princes of this world have the spirit and power of philosophy, and political greatness and wisdom meet in one, and those commoner natures who pursue either to the exclusion of the other are compelled to stand aside, cities will never have rest from... evils—no, nor the human race, as I believe—and then only will this our State have a possibility of life and behold the light of day."[57] Thus in Plato's *Republic* an ideal was posited, an ideal that became a central one in the civilized world for many centuries. However, the pursuit of political ends and philosophical truths remained separate paths for almost all "the commoner natures."

The most remarkable thing about the intellectual exchange between Gandhi and Tagore is the high philosophical plane to which they elevated a political debate, and the extent to which each of them—one holding the highest degree of political power in the sub-continent and the other at the pinnacle of intellectual eminence—was willing to learn from the other. Once we recognise this fact, the uniqueness of the intellectual exchange between the Mahatma and the Poet becomes self-evident.

There are some questions which underlay the immediate issues debated by Gandhi and Tagore. What is the role in politics of a poet or an intellectual disengaged from active politics? What are the limits of the individual's right to think and act on his own,

---

[57.] Book V, 473, *Plato's Republic*, ed., A.D. Lindsay (London, 1929), p.189. A.E. Taylor in his commentary on Plato surmises that "the actual Socrates, whose standing complaint against Athenian democracy in the dialogues is that he has no respect... for the 'man who knows' shared these ideas." Taylor, *Plato: The Man and his Work* (London, 1960), p.284.

when such thoughts or actions are in conflict with prescriptions and proscriptions emanating from a collective entity like the Nation or the State? Is there any value higher than the free and rational exercise of one's mind? What are the limits of nationalism, and are there values higher than nationalism?

As regards the first of these questions, there is no doubt that there was an overwhelmingly strong public opinion that the poet was encroaching on a sphere beyond his proper limits in engaging in debates with Gandhi on what were commonly perceived to be political issues. Although Gandhi never for a moment suggested it, many of his followers thought that a *mere* poet should refrain from offering unwanted advice to those who were leading the political struggle of the Indian nation.

A typical statement in a contemporary Bengali newspaper by a Gandhian appeared in 1928: "It will not be unjust to say that he [Tagore] is unfit to be a priest at the sacred sacrificial rites [*yagna*] for freedom.... Few have won accolades of the world equal to what Rabindranath has won and he deserved it. But, why should he be aggrieved if he does not get accolades which he cannot claim in other spheres. And is that sufficient reason to heap ridicule upon those who have earned through their labours the devotion of the people?"[58]

This trend of thinking was premised upon the idea that a 'pure' intellectual who had not actively engaged in the political battle had no place in the vast endeavour called the 'freedom struggle.' Gandhi on the other hand realised that this endeavour was a battle for the mind of the nation, not merely a series of political exercises and stratagems. In that larger perspective, the Poet had a role to play. It was not just a matter of Gandhi's personal regard for Tagore.

Although Gandhi does not explicitly state it in these terms, I think such a reading of his interventions in the debate would be justified. While saying that "our fields are absolutely different", Gandhi also said: "The poet lives in a magnificent world of his own creation—his world of ideas. I am a slave of somebody else's creation—the spinning wheel.... But I may say in all humility that we complement each the other's activity."[59] And again: "I do indeed ask the poet and the sage to spin the

---

58. Kshitish C. Dasgupta in *Ananda Bazar Patrika*, 20 April 1928.
59. Gandhi, 'The Poet and the *Charkha*', *Young India*, 5 November 1925.

wheel as a sacrament."[60]

Where the two differed was when Gandhi goes on to say that "when there is war, the poet lays down the lyre.... The poet will sing the true note after the war is over...."[61] Tagore was unwilling to suspend the poetic life, to depart from "the poet's religion" and suggested that to demand otherwise is to destroy the *swadharma* of all creative minds and that is self-defeating as a means, however noble the ends. Hence, we have an accord between the two on the ends, but a difference on the means. Tagore's plea to Gandhi was that at no time should the poet "lay down his lyre" or the scholar his books for the sake of *swaraj*: "its foundation [i.e. the foundation of *swaraj*] is in the mind, which, with its diverse powers and its confidence in those powers, goes on all the time creating *swaraj* for itself."[62]

An editorial in the *Ananda Bazar Patrika* may be noted to show the severity of media comments against Tagore's position on the question of the *charkha*, even in Bengal where he was beginning to be regarded as an icon. "The *charkha* movement has been revealed to the Poet's intelligence as a hoax. There are some others in the country, respected thinkers, who are critical of the *charkha*; but no one has raised such an objection. Only an extraordinary genius can say such an extraordinary thing—anyone who is not a child can see that.... The ludicrous opinions of the Poet may appeal to those who live in a dream-world, but those who are grounded in the soil of this country and know of the realities... will, no doubt, feel that the Poet's useless labours are sad and pitiful."[63]

Likewise, the editorial comments of *Bombay Chronicle*, about the same time in 1925, were directed against the Poet's rhetoric, his ironical style, his emotionalism—which, it was said, failed to convince any one who looked for reasoning.[64] Highly scurrilous poems and spoofs on Tagore's writings were published in Bengali newspapers.[65] At a more serious level khadi organisations and

60. Gandhi, 'The Great Sentinel', *Young India*, 13 October 1921.

61. *ibid.*

62. Tagore, 'The Call of Truth'.

63. Editorial, *Anada Bazar Patrika*, 19 August 1925 (my translation).

64. *Bombay* Chronicle, 9 September 1925.

65. For example, 'Visva-Varan: A New Musical Drama', *Ananda Bazar Patrika*, 24 September 1925; other examples in C. Bandyopadhyay (ed.), *Rabindra Prasanga*: *Ananda Bazar Patrika, 1922–32* (Calcutta, 1993).

Gandhians in general were forthright in their condemnation of
Tagore's critique of the message of the *charkha*.[66] Some of them
went so far as to say that Tagore's statements would have been,
had India been independent, tantamount to treason.[67]

In contrast, Gandhi's was a temperate, measured response,
"to ensure a dispassionate view being taken of the Poet's criticism." He knew that Tagore fundamentally disagreed with him,
but "frank criticism pleases me. For our friendship becomes all
the richer for our disagreements."[68]

Tagore's tranquil courage in facing the revulsion of popular
feelings against him was matched by Gandhi's generosity in
allowing the right of criticism. Tagore, however, continued to
maintain that a certain distance and autonomy was essential for
creative minds in order that they give their best to the society and
polity in a sphere beyond the immediate demands of politics of
the day.

In this regard his views are close to Benedetto Croce's, who
coined the term 'sympolitical' to describe the ideal role of artists
or philosophers or poets—a role of transmuting their political
concerns into their own discourse, in their own sphere of creativ-
ity, without being either apathetic to politics or bad propagan-
dists in politics.[69]

Swaraj and the State
In Tagore's impatience with any tendency to restrict or discipline
freedom in the world of the mind, there is something more than
a concern for the intellectuals' or the creative artists' role in

---

66. *Ananda Bazar Patrika*, 22, 23, 25 and 26 August 1925 carried a series of polemics
    issued by *Khadi Pratishthan* of Calcutta.
67. C. Bandyopadhyay (ed.), *op. cit.*, p.287.
68. Gandhi, 'The Poet and the *Charkha*', *Young India*, 5 November 1925.
69. It is not known whether Benedetto Croce's essay, 'Unpolitical Man' in *My
    Philosophy* (Tr. Carriett) was accessible to Tagore; see Prabhat Kumar
    Mukhopadhyay, *Rabindra-Jeevanee*, Vol.IV (Calcutta, 1994) on Croce; Tagore
    met Croce in Italy and his books might have been gifted to Tagore in 1928 by the
    Italian Government. Suresh Sharma in '*Swaraj* and the Quest for Freedom:
    Tagore's critique of Gandhi's Non-cooperation', *Studies in Humanities and Social
    Sciences*, II, 1995, pp. 111-122, makes an interesting point that to Tagore "the
    knowledge that the word of Truth was there and known, was sufficient
    assurance of its final triumph." In this Tagore was more of an 'intellectual'; in
    moderating this faith with attention to practice in life. Gandhi was, one may
    say, more pragmatic.

national political life. Is there something akin in temper if not in ideas to the aristocratic anarchists, Prince Kropotkin or Count Tolstoy? This question is difficult to answer.

Of this there is no doubt that there is an element of anarchistic thinking in Tagore as much as in Gandhi. In an essay on the *swadeshi* era he repeatedly cifed later, '*Swadeshi Samaj*' (1905), Tagore put forward an anit-statist position that he never resiled from. He made two basic points. First, that, unlike in Europe, the State has never been in India a central thing in the life of the nation. While European civilization assigned a central position to the State, Indian civilization from ancient times put in that place society guided by *dharma* as it was conceived by the people. Tagore's second proposition was that in modern times "the European State is founded upon the acquiescence of society as an essential part thereof—the State has evolved from the inherent tendencies therein.... In our country [in British India] the State is no part of our Society, it is external to Society."[70]

Hence, Tagore opposed tendencies of thought elevating the State above society, and that applied equally to political struggle to capture state power. Insofar as the national movement was directed primarily towards this latter objective, Tagore was sceptical of it. This is why he repeatedly stressed in his debates with Gandhi the need to extend the political battle into a battle for the mind and the inner powers (or soul-force, *atmasakti*) of the nation and thus to aim at a change beyond the mere replacement of one set of rulers by another. "Alien government in India is a chameleon. Today it comes in the guise of the Englishmen; tomorrow perhaps as some other foreigner; the next day, without abating a jot of its virulence, it may take the shape of our own countrymen. However determinedly we may try to hunt this monster of foreign dependence with outside lethal weapons, it will always elude our pursuit by changing its skin, or its colour."[71]

This statement, prophetic in more ways than one, has one implication which has a bearing on the immediate issue. To Tagore, the struggle did not consist of political strategem for capturing state power. At its basics, it is a kind of philosophical

---

70. Tagore, '*Swadeshi Samaj*' in *Atmashakti* (1st ed. 1905) in *R.R.*, Vol.III, (Calcutta, 1940); my translation.
71. Tagore, 'The Call of Truth'.

anarchism, dismissive of the state and political power; he even permitted himself the exaggeration of calling it mere *maya*.[72]

Gandhi has also been described by many commentators as an anarchist in the ultimate analysis.[73] There may be, however, a difference between the approaches of Tagore and Gandhi in that the latter, as a pragmatic political leader, could not accept Tagore's approach. While he agreed that the aim should be *swaraj* "for the soul", his programme, without an alternative, was a political one: Non-cooperation. "It had become disloyal, almost sacrilegious to say 'no' to the government. This deliberate refusal to co-operate is like the necessary weeding process that a cultivator has to resort before he sows.... The nation's non-coooperation is an invitation to the Government to cooperate with it on its own terms as is every nation's right and every government's duty."[74]

In Tagore, there is a strain of individualism founded on the belief that it is the destiny of the human mind to "create *swaraj* for itself". To subject "the free play of our intellect" to any restraint, such as collective action without conviction of the intellect, would be to deny to the mind its creative powers. There was a period of history when individual intellect was constrained by traditional wisdom in a static society: when India had been "content with surrendering our right—the right to reason and to judge for ourselves—to the blind forces of *shastric* injunctions and social conventions."[75] No "unreasoned creed" deserves obedience at any time, not even in the interest of *swaraj*, for no *swaraj* will be complete without "*swaraj* of the mind." If there are questions

---

[72] *ibid.*; Benoy Kumar Sarkar, *Political Philosophies since 1905* (Madras, 1925), p.142, noted the anarchistic tone in Tagore.

[73] Some of the pioneering analysts of the anarchistic elements in Gandhi's thoughts are Gopinath Dhawan, *The Political Philosophy of Mahatma Gandhi* (Allahabad, 1951), pp. 5, 317; Nirmal Chandra Bhattacharya, 'Is A Non-violent State possible?' in B.B. Majumdar (ed.), *Gandhian Concept of State* (Calcutta, 1957); A.H. Doctor, *Anarchist Thought in India* (Bombay, 1964), ch. III; Joan V. Bondurant, *Conquest of Violence: The Gandhian Philosophy of Conflict* (OUP, 1959), p.173, who is inclined to emphasise the retention of the State and political means and ends rather than its opposite; Nirmal Kumar Bose, *Studies in Gandhism* (Calcutta, 1940), pp. 85–86, similarly suggests that Gandhi's views on the State and the anarchistic vision are inconsistent, though as the ultimate end Gandhi posits the end of the State.

[74] Gandhi, 'The Poet's Anxiety', *Young India*, 1 June 1921.

[75] Tagore, 'The Call of Truth'.

raised about the path to freedom, that should cause no misgivings. Through the free exercise of intellect alone "the attainment of *swaraj* becomes thinkable."[76]

Now, it was obviously difficult for a political movement to accommodate this form of individualism. And Gandhi was the pragmatic leader of a delicately engineered movement facing heavy odds.

To Marjorie Sykes, an English authoress who spent a good deal of time at Gandhi's ashram and with Tagore at Santiniketan, it appeared that a "divergence of temperament between Gandhi and Tagore was reinforced by the difference in their family backgrounds and traditions. The Tagore family had a strong tradition of personal liberty, personal decision and enterprise. From boyhood, Rabindranath had rebelled against rules, against schools, against accepted social norms. Gandhi's family tradition was one of sober, social responsibility, of the administration of a State.... Tagore's unspoken concern was to guard the integrity of personal action. Gandhi turned his mind to the administrative question of how any particular programme might be carried out with equal integrity at State level and with country-wide impact."[77] Although Sykes' observation possibly exaggerates the degree of personal freedom under the regimes of Dwarakanath and Debendranath in the Tagore household—for each was a stern *pater familias*—she gets to the heart of the matter in emphasising Tagore's individualistic notion of freedom.

This regard for individual freedom also accounts for Tagore's failure to push ahead in practice, in many instances, what he believed in theory. A telling example is the fact that although Tagore abhorred casteism and himself defied its rules almost daily, from 1901 to 1915 in his students' hostels inter-dining among different castes was unknown. The students and their parents, he thought, should not be forced to accept such a practice, however desirable it was in his own opinion.[78] It was Gandhi's presence and forceful persuasion, which persuaded the Santiniketan community in 1915 to accept inter-dining, much to the delight of Tagore. Inter-dining had come to stay, but another

---

[76.] Tagore, 'The Cult of the *Charkha*'.

[77.] J.P. Patel and Marjorie Sykes, *Gandhi and the Gift of the Fight* (Rasulia, 1987), p.62.

[78.] Krishna Kripalani, *Rabindranath Tagore: A Biography* (Calcutta, 1980), p.258.

change introduced by Gandhi at Santiniketan was short-lived. Pramatha Nath Bishi, a student at Santiniketan in 1915, recounts how Tagore yielded to the protest of students' parents, when Gandhi persuaded students to take upon themselves the so-called menial tasks in the hostel and the school, tasks assigned to servants by the traditional *bhadralok*.[79] "The revolution created by Mahatma Gandhi" was cut short by the compunctions of Tagore regarding the willing and considered consent of the persons affected.

Somewhat similar was Tagore's objection to the imposition of the boycott of foreign cloth by the socially dominant (e.g. the Bengal zamindars) over the lesser folk.[80] In such matters, his critics in the field of practical politics felt Tagore's idea of freedom hampered collective action. Perhaps, this is why a participant in the politics of those times remarks that Gandhi proved to be more of a revolutionary in practice, although Tagore's ideas might have been more advanced.[81] A consciousness of this is reflected in Tagore's tribute to Gandhi on his seventieth birthday: Gandhi, whose "realm of activity lies in practical politics", was one of "the makers of history", said Tagore.[82]

Limits of Nationalism

That leads us to another aspect, the critical stance of Tagore with respect to the idea of Nationalism, derived from the European paradigm and internalised by Asian societies, sometimes in the form of ethnic and cultural chauvinism. It is well-known that Tagore, although an ardent and articulate proponent of nationalism during the *swadeshi* agitation in the first decade of the twentieth century, began to be increasingly critical of the kind of nationalism he saw at work in the process of Japan's growth into an aggressive imperialist power, the synergistic thrust in Europe towards the global conflict of 1914–18, and the emergence of nationalist terrorism in Bengal. On the latter development,

---

[79] Pramatha Nath Bishi, *Rabindranath o Santiniketan* (V.B. Publications, Calcutta, n.d.), p.93.

[80] Sumit Sarkar, *The Swadeshi Movement in Bengal 1903–08* (Calcutta, 1973), is an outstanding analysis of the subject.

[81] Pannalal Dasgupta, *Gandhi-gaveshana* (Calcutta, 1986), p.230.

[82] Tagore's message on Gandhi's 70th birthday was sent to S. Radhakrishnan in October 1939 and printed in *Visva-Bharati News*, October 1939, p.31.

Tagore's deeply searching questions in the novel *Char Adhyay* (Four Chapters) in 1934 created adverse reactions in Bengal.[83] That apart, there was a strong tendency among those in the mainstream of the nationalist movement to look askance at Tagore's 'internationalism', however lofty the idea was and however well-crafted its expression in Tagore's hands. Fairly typical was this editorial in a leading Bengali newspaper in 1929: "Those who are familiar with the *swadeshi* era know how much the new nationalism or patriotism of Bengal or of India owes to Rabindranath Tagore. Today, after only a few years, the same Rabindranath is putting all his force against nationalism! Perhaps the terrible destructiveness of the last World War of Europe and the ugly face of nations mutually at loggerheads, have hurt the poet's soul. But, however much the poet's soft and idealistic soul may be hurt... there is no denying that nationalism is a necessity for the oppressed countries like India.... In the present world the effort to bind the strong and the weak by the bond of love may be nice to imagine, but it is hopeless as a practical proposition."[84]

Ironically, while Tagore thus alienated many nationalist enthusiasts, the British Government in India looked upon him with equal suspicion. Documents in the National Archives now authenticate what was rumoured in the twenties, that Tagore was under surveillance of the British Indian police, his mail was censored, and he was regarded as a "constant opponent of the government."[85] The Director of the Intelligence Bureau of the Government of India writes in 1925: "It is, of course, well-known that in 1920–21 [sic] he resigned his Knighthood, becoming to all intents and purposes a non-cooperator"; political activities of his associates like C.F. Andrews and W.W. Pearson, the visit of teachers and scholars from Central European countries allied to the Axis Powers, the employment of former nationalists and terrorists at Santiniketan, etc. were cited by the police and

---

[83]. Chinmohan Sehanovis, *Rabindranath o biplabi samaj* (Calcutta, 1985), p.91 et seq.

[84]. Editorial, *Ananda Bazar Patrika*, 5 June 1923 (my translation). Ashis Nandy's argument on the nuances of the concept of nationalism in Tagore is very persuasive.

[85]. D. Petrie, Director, Intelligence Bureau, Government of India, 15 May 1925, Home (Political) F.181/25, National Archives of India; see S.K. Bagchi, 'The Poet and the Raj', *V.B. Quarterly*, Vol.50, April 1985, p.94.

intelligence chiefs. The Indian Home Department reported to India Office in London: "Past experience shows that in India attempts by private enterprise to organise educational institutions on what are conceived to be indigenous national lines are very susceptible to political influences, which usually tend to be of an undesirable character."[86] Loyal subjects were encouraged to withdraw their wards from the undesirable nationalist institution, Visva-Bharati. Thus, Tagore was, as it were, caught in the cross-fire between the nationalists and their enemies.

Between Tagore's ideas on the limits of nationalism and Gandhi's, there was a resonance, although they employed different idioms of discourse. Gandhi himself tried, time and again, to correct the excesses of what he called the "exclusive nationalism" of his political following. In response to Tagore's warning against the dangers of "an isolated view of the country", a parochial nationalism, Gandhi's response was clear: "Our non-cooperation is neither with the English, nor with the West. Our non-cooperation is with the system the English have established", because "Indian nationalism is not exclusive", it is "humanitarian". This Gandhi wrote in his essay 'The Great Sentinel', addressed to Tagore in 1921.[87]

In the twenties, Gandhi elaborated on this idea, particularly in a series published in *Young India*: "Patriotism for me is the same as humanity" (1921); "patriotism includes the service of humanity" (1925); "it is the narrowness, selfishness and exclusiveness, which is the bane of modern nations, which is evil" (1925); "through the realization of freedom of India, I hope to realize and carry on the mission of brotherhood of men" (1929).[88]

However, this universalistic spirit in Gandhi's and Tagore's philosophy and their effort to create a space for the concept of *swaraj*, beyond the narrow limits of the dominant paradigm of nationalism derived from the West, remained far removed from the realities of politics and the political consciousness that took

---

[86] T. Sloan, Home Department to Secretary, Public and Judicial Department, India Office, London, 22 October 1925, Home (Pol) F.181/25, National Archives of India.

[87] Tagore, 'The Call of Truth'; Gandhi, 'The Great Sentinel'.

[88] Gandhi's essays in *Young India*, 16 March 1921; 18 June 1925, 9 September 1925; 14 April 1929.

shape in India. When the concept of nationhood itself was fractured by the increasing conflict between two religious communities in India, their message of brotherhood with the world was no more than mere words from two visionaries.

As for Europe, for a while such words touched a common chord in some minds and this partly accounted for the very favourable manner in which Tagore's writings were received in Europe just before the World War, at the time of the Nobel Prize award. The reversal of the tide during the War and the devaluation of Tagore in the West in the twenties, coincided with a recrudescence of ethnocentrism.[89]

We find Stefan Zweig writing in 1929 to Romain Rolland: "A country which has produced within fifty years Rāmakrishna, Vivekananda, Gandhi and Tagore is not decadent or *passe*, as European arrogance would have us believe." Zweig went on to say that in the West "on an intellectual level we shall become more universal in our range than ever."[90] The wave of Fascism which engulfed Europe soon after Zweig wrote thus, put to an end such fond hopes.

Science and the *Yantra-Danava*

When we turn to the differences in outlook between Gandhi and Tagore in respect of their approaches to science and technology, we have to bear in mind that these were far from being static. At some points of time, there is clearly a confrontation between two contrary approaches. We have seen that in the debate on the implications of the Bihar earthquake in 1934 in Gandhi's pronouncements, there is an inherent theodicy as distinct from Tagore's rejection of any explanation in terms of divine intervention in physical phenomena. Again, in the twenties, in the debate on the *charkha* , there is a similar confrontation. Tagore contended that the gifts of modern technology or science must not be judged by criteria which are irrational or alien to science. "Where Mahatma Gandhi has declared war against the tyranny of the machine which is oppressing the whole world, we are all enrolled

---

[89]. This has been recently documented by Krishna Dutta and Andrew Robinson, *Rabindranath Tagore: The Myriad-minded Man* (New York, 1996).

[90]. Stefan Zweig to Romain Rolland, 26 November 1929, cited in Martin Kampchen, *Rabindranath Tagore and Germany: A Documentation* (Calcutta, 1991), p.64; this commendable piece of research merits wider attention.

under his banner."[91] But, Tagore objected to the "magical formula that foreign cloth is impure" for it was not part of the language of science.

As we have seen earlier, he was critical of moral dicta in a discourse that properly belongs to "economic science", or else people would be driven "from one injunction to another", without applying the test of reason, out of "the terrible habit of obeying orders". To Gandhi, on the other hand, the test of morality was supreme. This was his cardinal point, even in his earlier writings. "I have ventured utterly to condemn modern civilization because I hold that the spirit of it is evil. It is possible to show that some of its incidents are good, but I have examined the tendency in the scale of ethics...."[92] Or again, on the Bihar earthquake, in refutation of Tagore's view: "visitations like droughts, flood, earthquake and the like, though they seem to have only physical origins, are, for me, somehow connected with man's morals."[93]

However, it must be conceded that the system of ideas in Gandhi's and Tagore's writings is in each case more complex than what the simple oppositions, as above, would suggest. In the play *Mukta-dhara* (1922) Tagore presented an allegory about the prostitution of science for purposes of domination and exploitation. Exactly when he was engaged in the debate on the *charkha*, Tagore depicted in this play the revolt of a subject people to the construction of an enormous dam by alien rulers, a dam which would control the vital source of water, on which the life of the subject people depended. The play continues to be relevant to this day.

An analogous creation was the play *Rakta-karabi* (1926) which reflects Tagore's deep concern about the exploitation of technology to extract profit from the labour of men, who are reduced to tools. The tyranny of the *yantra-danava*, the monster machine, was a recurring theme in Tagore's poetry as well.

At the same time, when Tagore considered the role of science and technology, he spoke as an inheritor of the faith of post-Renaissance era of Enlightenment. He saw the application of science as the means of liberating man from poverty. "One thing is certain, that the all-embracing poverty, which has overwhelmed

---

91. Tagore, 'The Call of Truth'.
92. Gandhi to W.J. Wybergh, 10 May 1910, *CWMG*, Vol.X, pp. 246–250.
93. Gandhi, 'Superstition versus Faith', *Harijan*, 16 February 1934.

our country cannot be removed by working with our hands to the neglect of science."[94] Tagore probably conceived of a via media between the two polarities, rejection of each gift of modern science and technology on the one hand, and passive unquestioning acceptance of it on the other: "If the cultivation of science has any moral significance it is in its rescue of man from outrage by nature, not its use of man as a machine but its use of machine to harness the forces of nature in man's service."[95]

As for Mahatma Gandhi, a number of commentators have noted the evolution of his uncompromising position in *Hind Swaraj* towards a more complex and flexible stance typified by this statement in 1921: "I am not aiming at destroying railways and hospitals, though I would certainly welcome their natural destruction... they are a necessary evil.... Still less am I trying to destroy all machinery and mills."[96] One may surmise that Gandhi and Tagore were able to define and perhaps modify their positions more accurately by the debate their differences compelled them to enter.

Two Philosophies of Education

On another question where they differed, no debate developed and the matter did not receive public attention. This was the question of the philosophy of education and more particularly the Gandhian scheme of Basic Education, enunciated in 1937. In the early years of their development, Santiniketan and Sabarmati offered many striking parallels. Both Gandhi and Tagore were in a common enterprise of building educational institutions outside of the state-sponsored system in the colonial mould.[97] Both of them emphasised the primacy of the mother-tongue in teaching;

[94.] Tagore, 'The Cult of the *Charkha*'.

[95.] *ibid.*

[96.] Gandhi, 'A Word of Explanation', *Young India*, 26 January 1921; *Young India*, 8 December 1920. Although there are now many recent commentaries in India on Gandhi's views on technology, thanks to the current Western interest in it arising out of Environmentalist concern, the older expositions remain the most useful since they are faithful to Gandhi's text; e.g. D.P. Mukherjee, *Diversities* (Delhi, 1958); Visvanath Prasad Varma, *The Political Philosophy of Mahatma Gandhi* (Agra, 1959); Buddhadeva Bhattacharya, *Evolution of Political Philosophy of Gandhi* (Calcutta, 1969).

[97.] Sabyasachi Bhattacharya and Ashoke Mukhopadhyay (eds.), *The Common Pursuit: Convocation Addresses at Visva-Bharati* (Calcutta, 1995), Introduction by Sabyasachi Bhattacharya.

both tried to shape the schooling system in the mould of India's culture and way of life; and both gave salience in their scheme to students' participation in the kind of creative and productive activities, which did not find a place in the conventional schooling system.

Tagore's village school, *Shiksha Satra*, founded in 1924 in Sriniketan was visited by Gandhi in 1925.[98] Its Principal, A. Williams Aryanayakam, was invited by Gandhi in 1934 to head an experimental school on Gandhian lines at Wardha and it was Aryanayakam, who was commissioned by Gandhi in 1937 to be the Secretary to the Committee he set up to frame the Basic Education Scheme.[99]

When the scheme, also known as the Wardha Scheme, was published in *Harijan* in 1937 and discussed in the ensuing meeting of the Indian National Congress, Tagore raised some questions. His comments centred around two features of the scheme.[100] First, Tagore questioned the utilitarian centrality given to productive manual work in the Basic Education Scheme. "As the scheme stands on paper, it seems to assume that material utility, rather than development of personality is the end of education." It put excessive stress on "the market value of the pupil's labour." Incidentally, Dr. Zakir Hussain had misgivings of the same kind and the part of the scheme which suggested that teachers' salary would be funded from sale of their pupils' products was dropped eventually.[101] Secondly, Tagore was uncomfortable with the idea of earmarking for the rural poor a special type of education which destined them to a limited vocation. Was there to be a schooling offered to some, who could afford to pay for it different from those who could not? "It is true that as things are even that [in Wardha Scheme] is much more than what the masses are actually getting but it is nevertheless unfortunate that even in our ideal

[98] J.C. Kumarappa, *Rabindranath Tagore: India's School-Master* (New York, 1928); W.W. Pearson, *Santiniketan: The Bolpur School of Rabindranath Tagore* (London, 1916).

[99] Prabhat Kumar Mukhopadhyay, both a school-teacher and librarian at Santiniketan, has left a personal account of great value in *Rabindra-Jeevanee*, Vol.IV (Calcutta, 1994).

[100] The Wardha Scheme was published in *Harijan*, 11 December 1937; Tagore's comments in *Visva-Bharati News*, January 1938, pp.51–53.

[101] M. Mujeeb, *Dr. Zakir Hussain* (New Delhi, 1985), contains a detailed account of Dr. Hussain's critique.

scheme, education should be doled out in insufficient rations to the poor...."

To Mahatma Gandhi, these questions might have been irrelevant since his object was, first, to make the schools financially viable and independent of government support, and, secondly, to use productive manual work as "the prime means of intellectual training."[102] Tagore did not press his points and readily conceded: "Gandhiji's genius is essentially practical, which means his practice is immeasurably superior to his theory.... We may be sure that when the scheme is actually worked out, we shall discover in it only one more testimony to the genius of this practical sage whose deeds surpass his words."[103] How the Gandhian scheme failed to get a fair trial and the misfortunes it met in the hands of educational bureaucrats is another story which need not detain us here.

The Long View

Our effort to understand the nuances of the debates between Gandhi and Tagore and putting together discrete pieces of their writings may sharpen certain hidden polarities, which were more softly defined in their writings. Gandhi is reported to have said, when he visited Santiniketan for the last time, four years after the death of Tagore: "I started with a disposition to detect a conflict between Gurudev and myself but ended with the glorious discovery that there was none."[104]

But this view, coloured with friendly generosity, is probably as correct as his earlier perception. I have argued above that the differences between them were real and at the same time they shared a common highground above the terrain of differences. Despite their differences on many crucial questions, they were willing to learn from each other.

There is an interesting anecdote from Krishna Kripalani, who was a resident in Santiniketan for many years. When the Non-cooperation movement was at its height and Tagore's dissent on some issues was well-known, Tagore presided over a

---

[102.] *Harijan*, 18 September 1937.

[103.] Tagore in *V.B. News*, January 1938, pp. 51–53.

[104.] Krishna Kripalani, *Rabindranath Tagore: A Biography* (Calcutta, 1980), p.339; Kripalani who married into the Tagore family and served Visva-Bharati with distinction, was present on this occasion.

debate organized by his students on the relative merits of Tagore's
and Gandhi's points of view. When votes were taken the majority
were in favour of Mahatma's point of view. And Tagore, in his
presidential remarks, observed that "nothing could have made
him happier than the result of the debate, for it had vindicated the
basic principle of education. He had taught his students, not to
conform but to think freely for themselves."[105]

As we have seen, Gandhi was equally open to candid
criticism. It is possible that in some respects his outlook evolved
in response to the debates with Tagore. Consider, for instance, his
approach in *Hind Swaraj*: "I believe that the civilization India has
evolved is not to be beaten in the world. Nothing can equal the
seeds sown by our ancestors.... India remains immovable and
that is her glory.... India has nothing to learn from anybody else
and this is as it should be."[106] One can compare that with his later
pronouncements, most notably his reply to Tagore in 1921, a truly
memorable statement: "I do not want my house to be walled in
all sides and my windows to be stuffed. I want the culture of all
the lands to be blown about my house as freely as possible. But
I refuse to be blown off my feet by any."[107]

Overriding the numerous differences aired in the debates
between them in public or in private correspondence, there was
a commonality at the core of their world-outlook. Jawaharlal
Nehru, who was close to both of them, explained this paradox in
terms of their rootedness in the civilization of India. "No two
persons could probably differ so much as Gandhi and Tagore,"
wrote Nehru in a letter after Tagore's death in 1941. "The
surprising thing is that both of these men with so much in
common and drawing inspiration from the same wells of wisdom
and thought and culture, should differ from each other so
greatly!... I think of the richness of India's age-long cultural
genius, which can throw up in the same generation two such
master-types, typical of her in every way, yet representing different aspects of her many-sided personality."[108]

One may ask the question whether indeed Gandhi and

105. Kripalani, *op. cit.*, p.307.
106. Gandhi, *Hind Swaraj*, CWMG, vol.X, pp. 36–37.
107. Gandhi, 'The Great Sentinel', *Young India*, 1 June 1921.
108. Jawaharlal Nehru to Krishna Kripalani, 27 August 1941, in K. Kripalani, *op. cit.*,
     p.455.

Tagore represented the "typical". Actually a kind of intellectual solitude, for want of kindred spirits in their society and times, seemed to be the lot of each of them. Yet, Nehru was perspicacious in casting his appreciation in civilizational terms. This becomes evident when we consider the intellectual exchanges between Tagore and Gandhi.

To introduce the documentation that follows, we have tried, first, to contextualise their debate in the matrix of the contemporary historical processes and events, and, second, to explore the differences between Gandhi's philosophy and Tagore's, in relation to the issues debated. In doing so, in taking a long view of the intellectual conflict and companionship, one realises that their debate forms a part of a more wide-ranging discourse which exceeds the immediate issues of the day, and touches and blends with concerns and values which have been at the core of civilizations in other times and other places as well. That perhaps is the significance of Romain Rolland's observation in a letter he wrote to Tagore in 1923: "the noble debate" between Gandhi and Tagore, he said, as it were "embraces the whole earth, and the whole humanity joins in this august dispute."[109]

SABYASACHI BHATTACHARYA

[109.] Romain Rolland to Rabindranath Tagore, 2 March 1923 (V.B. Archives).

PART I

1915–1922

1915–1922

Notes on Documents

The source of all the documents in this part and subsequent ones is the Visva-Bharati Archives, Rabindra Bhavan, unless specified otherwise. An overview of the historical context is provided in the 'Introduction' to this volume, for each of these parts: 1915–22, 1923–28, 1929–33, 1934–41. The notes on Documents are concerned mainly with the details pertaining to documents reproduced here.

The first letter from Tagore to Gandhi (Document 1) bears no date; it was almost certainly written in January 1915, after Gandhi's arrival from England and shortly before his visit to Santiniketan. The boys of the Phoenix School mentioned in this letter stayed in Santiniketan from 4 November 1914 to 3 April 1915; their stay there was arranged through the mediation of C.F. Andrews (see M.K. Gandhi to Maganlal Gandhi, 4 Dec. 1914, *CWMG*, XII, p.558). "If our Phoenix ideals", Gandhiji exhorts Maganlal, "are kept up, Gurudev's expectations will be fulfilled." Gandhi himself had great expectations of Santiniketan, as is evident from his letters (e.g. Gandhi to Swami Shraddhanand, 27 March 1914, *CWMG*, XII, p.400). At his reception in Santiniketan, Gandhi spoke of his "close kinship with this *ashram* in Bengal" (Speech, 17 Feburary 1915, *CWMG*, XIII, p.24). Although Tagore had organised the reception, he was away during Gandhi's first visit in February 1915; the two met when Gandhi visited Santiniketan the second time in March. Thereafter, they appear to have kept in touch with each other through their mutual friend C.F. Andrews (Documents 4, 5).

In 1918, Gandhi wrote to Tagore on the question of national language (Document 2; the letter is reproduced in *CWMG*). Tagore replied within three days endorsing Gandhi's well-known position on the question (Document 3).

Again, early in April 1919, Gandhi wrote to Tagore requesting a message on the "national struggle" since he felt a need "to gather round this mighty struggle the ennobling influence of those who approve it" (Document 6). It was in reply to this letter that Tagore addresses Gandhi as the "Mahatma" and as a "great leader of men;" Tagore says in his letter, India will win freedom "when she can prove that she is morally superior to the people who rule her by right of conquest" and when she undergoes "the penance of suffering." (Document 7). This letter was written on 12 April 1919. The Jallianwala Bagh atrocity took place the next day.

As the news of the Punjab events began to spread slowly and was confirmed by various witnesses, Tagore's mind was in turmoil. On 30 May 1919, he wrote to the Viceroy giving up his Knighthood as an act of protest. (See Appendix). Gandhi was appreciative of that "burning letter from the poet" and the renunciation of Knighthood; but he confided to Srinivasa Shastri, "I personally think it is premature." (Gandhi to V.S.S. Shastri, 6 June 1919, CWMG, XV, p.345).

In 1919–20, Gandhi wrote to Tagore a number of times, mainly to organise a visit by Tagore to Gujarat. (Documents 8, 9, 10, 11). Eventually Tagore visited Ahmedabad to preside over the Gujarat Literary Conference on 2 April 1920. On 13 April 1920, at the National Week Conference in Bombay organised by Gandhi, Tagore's message on the political situation was read out by C.F. Andrews. Tagore wrote of "the dastardliness of cruel injustice confident of its impunity" in Punjab. (Bombay Chronicle, 14 April 1920).

Tagore was out of India when the Non-cooperation movement started in full swing. But he observed its progress. And he shared his anxieties about some failings of the movement, as he perceived it, with C.F. Andrews. These letters to Andrews were later edited and published by him (Letters to a friend, London, 1928). Three of Tagore's letters on the Indian political situation were carried by the Modern Review of Calcutta in May 1921. (Document 12). Gandhi responded with two articles in Young India in June 1921. (Documents 13, 14). Gandhi might have had an inkling of Tagore's line of criticism, for Gandhi writes to Andrews in March 1921 that in his opinion Tagore "had not understood the simple beauty and the duty of non-cooperation." (Gandhi to Andrews, 28 March 1921, CWMG, XIX, p.483). When the criticism became public he was indeed exercised. Gandhi rejected the idea that Tagore and M.M. Malviya, who also voiced criticism, were "envious"; but he said, "Both lack fearlessness and are proud of their opinion and ideas. You can tolerate pride if not accompanied by fear...." (Gandhi to Mahadev Desai, 1 September 1921, *CWMG*, XXI, p.46; allowance may be made for the fact that this is a translation from Gujarati and that the concept of *abhaya* has many nuances.)

In August 1921, Tagore's lecture at the Calcutta University Institute was entitled *'Satyer Ahvan'* or 'The call of truth'; this appeared in the journal *Pravasee* in Bengali and in the *Modern Review* in English. (Document 15). When Gandhi visited Calcutta in September 1921 he had long discussions in camera with Tagore; various imaginary versions of this debate between the Titans circulated in the Press, but Gandhi refused to make any statement on it. (*Amrita Bazar Patrika*, 11 September 1921) Probably neither succeeded in convincing the other. In October 1921, Gandhi's response to Tagore's critique was published, the well-known essay 'The Great Sentinel'. (Document 16). A few months later Gandhi was arrested (10 March 1922) and Tagore desisted from criticism while Gandhi was incarcerated.

EDITOR

1. Tagore on the Phoenix School Boys

(Gandhi visited Santiniketan for the first time on 17 February 1915. Boys from his Phoenix School from South Africa had arrived a few days earlier. This letter is undated, but was probaby written in January 1915.)

Dear Mr. Gandhi

That you could think of my school as the right and the likely place where your Phoenix boys could take shelter, when they are in India, has given me real pleasure—and that pleasure has been greatly enhanced when I saw those dear boys in that place. We all feel that their influence will be of great value to our boys and I hope that they, in their turn, will gain something which will make their stay in Santiniketan fruitful. I write this letter to thank you for allowing your boys to become our boys as well and thus, form a living link in the *Sadhana* of both of our lives.

Very sincerely yours,
Rabindranath Tagore

2. Gandhi on Hindi as the national language

(From a photocopy of the original in Mahadev Desai's hand, CWMG, Vol.XIV.)

Motihari,
21 January 1918

Dear Gurudev,

For my forthcoming address before the Hindi Sammelan at Indore, I am trying to collect the opinions of leaders of thought on the following questions:

(i) Is not Hindi (as *bhasha* or Urdu) the only possible national language for inter-provincial intercourse and for all other national proceedings?

(ii) Should not Hindi be the language principally used at the forthcoming Congress?

(iii) Is it not desirable and possible to give the highest teaching in our schools and colleges through the vernaculars?

And should not Hindi be made a compulsory second language in all our post-primary schools?

I feel that if we are to touch the masses and if national servants are to come in contact with the masses all over India, the questions set forth above have to be immediately solved and ought to be treated as of the utmost urgency. Will you kindly favour me with your reply, at your early convenience?

I am

yours sincerely,

M. K. Gandhi

3. Tagore on the use of Hindi

(Copy of a letter written by Tagore to Gandhi.)

Santiniketan,

24 January 1918

Dear Mr. Gandhi,

I can only answer in the affirmative the question you have sent to me from Motihari. Of course Hindi is the only possible national language for interprovincial intercourse in India. But, about its introduction at the Congress, I think we cannot enforce it for a long time to come. In the first place, it is truely a foreign language for the Madras people, and in the second, most of our politicians will find it extremely difficult to express themselves adequately in this language for no fault of their own. The difficulty will be not only for want of practice but also because political thoughts have naturally taken form in our minds in English. So, Hindi will have to remain optional in our national proceedings until a new generation of politicians fully alive to its importance, pave the way towards its general use by constant practice as a voluntary acceptance of a national obligation.

Yours very sincerely,

Rabindranath Tagore

4. Gandhi on C.F. Andrews

(Copy from original letter in Gandhi's own hand.)

Delhi,
30 April 1918

Dear Gurudev,

Much as I should like to keep Mr. Andrews with me a little longer, I feel sure that he must leave for Calcutta tonight. I know you want his soothing presence by you whilst you are keeping indifferent health. And you must have him while you need him.

We are on the threshold of a mighty change in India. I would like all the pure forces to be physically in the country during the process of her new birth. If therefore you could at all find rest anywhere in India, I would ask you and Mr. Andrews to remain in the country and kindly to lend me Mr. Andrews now and then. His guidance at times is most precious to me.

Mr. Ambalal asked me to say that he will welcome you and your company as his honoured guests in his Bungalow at Matheran. The season there ends about the middle of June. Mr. Ambalal is also prepared to secure for you accommodation at [undecipherable] if you so wish. I suggest that it would be better if you would stay at Matheran for the time being and then decide whether you will pass the rest of the hot season at Ooty.

I do hope you will soon recover from the nervous strain you are suffering from.

Yours sincerely,
M.K. Gandhi

5. Gandhi's letter of thanks

(From a microfilm of the original. Courtesy: National Archives of India; CWMG, Vol.XV.)

The Ashram,
Sabarmati,
5 November 1918

Dear Gurudev,

Charlie left the Ashram yesterday and we are the poorer for his absence. I very much miss his sunny face. You will therefore understand what I mean when I tell you how deeply grateful I feel for your having allowed him to pass a few days at the Ashram.

I hope you are keeping good health under the heavy strain which the school work in Santiniketan places upon you.

Yours sincerely,
M.K. Gandhi

6. Gandhi's letter asking for a message

(From the manuscript of Mahadev Desai's diary. Courtesy: Narayan Desai; CWMG, Vol.XV.)

Bombay,
5 April 1919

Dear Gurudev,

This is an appeal to you against our mutual friend, Charlie Andrews. I have been pleading with him for a message from you for publication in the national struggle which, though in form it is only directed against a single piece of legislation, is in reality a struggle for liberty worthy of a self-respecting nation. I have waited long and patiently. Charlie's description of your illness made me hesitate to write to you personally. Your health is a national treasure and Charlie's devotion to you is superhuman. It is divine and I know that if he could help it he would not allow a single person, whether by writing or his presence, to disturb your quiet and rest. I have respected this lofty desire of his to protect you from all harm. But I find that you are lecturing in

Benares. I have, therefore, in the light of this fact corrected Charlie's description of your health which somewhat alarmed me and I venture to ask you for a message from you—a message of hope and inspiration for those who have to go through the fire. I do it because you were good enough to send me your blessings when I embarked upon the struggle. The forces arrayed against me are, as you know, enormous. I do not dread them, for I have an unquenchable belief that they are supporting untruth and that if we have sufficient faith in truth, it will enable us to overpower the former. But all forces work through human agency. I am therefore anxious to gather round this mighty struggle the ennobling assistance of those who approve it. I will not be happy until I have received your considered opinion on this endeavour to purify the political life of the country. If you have seen anything to alter your first opinion of it, I hope you will not hesitate to make it known. I value even adverse opinions from friends, for though they may not make me change my course, they serve the purpose of so many lighthouses to give out warnings of dangers lying in the stormy paths of life. Charlie's friendship has been to me on this account an invaluable treasure, because he does not hesitate to share with me even his unconsidered notes of dissent. This I count a great privilege. May I ask you to extend at this critical moment the same privilege that Charlie has?

I hope that you are keeping well and that you thoroughly recuperated after your fatiguing journey through the Madras Presidency.

Yours sincerely,
M. K. G.

7. Tagore's letter written on the eve of the Jallianwala Bagh massacre

(The following letter to Gandhi was sent by Tagore and also communicated to the Press. Reproduced from The Indian Daily News *of 16 April 1919.)*

Santiniketan,
12 April 1919

Dear Mahatmaji,

Power in all its forms is irrational, it is like the horse that drags the carriage blind-folded. The moral element in it is only represented in the man who drives the horse. Passive resistance is a force which is not necessarily moral in itself; it can be used against truth as well as for it. The danger inherent in all force grows stronger when it is likely to gain success, for then it becomes temptation.

I know your teaching is to fight against evil by the help of the good. But such a fight is for heroes and not for men led by impulses of the moment. Evil on one side naturally begets evil on the other, injustices leading to violence and insult to vengefulness. Unfortunately such a force has already been started and either through panic or through wrath, our authorities have shown us their claws whose sure effect is to drive some of us into the secret path of resentment and others into utter demoralisation.

In this crisis you, as a great leader of men have stood among us to proclaim your faith in the ideal which you know to be that of India, the ideal which is both against the cowardliness of hidden revenge and the cowed submissiveness of the terror-stricken. You have said, as Lord Buddha has done in his time and for all time to come:

"Akkodhena jine kodhan asadhum sadhuna jine"

"Conquer anger by the power of non-anger and evil by the power of good."

This power of good must prove its truth and strength by its fearlessness, by its refusal to accept any imposition, which depends for its success upon its power to produce frightfulness and is not ashamed to use its machines of destruction to terrorise a people completely disarmed. We must know that moral conquest does not consist in success, that failure does not deprive it of its dignity and worth. Those who believe in spiritual life know that

to stand against wrong which has overwhelming material power
behind it is victory itself, it is the victory of the active faith in the
ideal in the teeth of evident defeat.

I have always felt, and said accordingly that the great gift of
freedom can never come to a people through charity. We must
win it before we can own it. And India's opportunity for winning
it will come to her when she can prove that she is morally
superior to the people who rule her by their right of conquest. She
must willingly accept her penance of suffering, the suffering
which is the crown of the great. Armed with her utter faith in
goodness, she must stand unabashed before the arrogance that
scoffs at the power of spirit.

And you have come to your motherhood in the time of her
need to remind her of her mission, to lead her in the true path of
conquest, to purge her present-day politics of its feebleness which
imagines that it has gained its purpose when it struts in the
borrowed feathers of diplomatic dishonesty.

This is why I pray most fervently that nothing that tends to
weaken our spiritual freedom may intrude into your marching
line, that martyrdom for the cause of truth may never degenerate
into fanaticism for mere verbal forms, descending into self-
deception that hides itself behind sacred names.

With these few words for an introduction allow me to offer
the following as a poet's contribution to your noble work:-

I

Let me hold my head high in this
faith that thou art our shelter,
that all fear is mean distrust of thee.
Fear of man? But what man is there
in this world, what king, O King of kings
who is thy rival, who has hold of me
for all time and in all truth?
What power, is there in this world to rob
me of my freedom? For do not the arms reach
the captive through the dungeon-walls bringing
unfettered release to the soul?
And must I cling to this body in fear of
death, as a miser to his barren treasure?
Has not this spirit of mine the eternal call

to the feast of everlasting life?
Let me know that all pain and death are
shadows of the moment; that the dark force
which sweeps between me and thy truth is but the
mist before the sunrise; that thou alone art
mine forever and greater than all pride of
strength that dares to mock my manhood with
its menace.

II

Give me the supreme courage of love, this is
my prayer, the courage to speak, to do, to
suffer at thy will, to leave all things or be
left alone.
Give me the supreme faith of love, this is
my prayer, the faith of the life in death,
of the victory in defeat, of the power hidden in
the frailness of beauty, of the dignity of pain
that accepts hurt, but disdains to return it.

Yours etc.,
Rabindranath Tagore

*(The very next day, on 13 April 1919, the Jallianwala Bagh
massacre by General Dyer and his soldiers took place.)*

8. Gandhi's invitation to Tagore

(From a photocopy of the handwritten original; CWMG, Vol.XVI)

The Ashram,
Sabarmati,
18 October 1919

Dear Gurudev,

There is to be a literary conference in Ahmedabad in
December. The dates are 13th, 14th and 15th Dec. The organisers
are most anxious that you should grace the occasion by
your presence and I hope that if you could at all manage it,
you will not disappoint Gujarat.

It was good of you to have permitted Andrews to go to South Africa. I have just received a telegram from him saying he is free to go. This relieves me considerably and I am sure that his going there will do the utmost good.

I hope that you are keeping good health.

Yours sincerely,
M. K. Gandhi

9. Gandhi on Andrews' services to the people of Punjab

(From a microfilm of the original in Gandhi's hand in N.A.I. CWMG, Vol.XVI)

As at Delhi
c/o Principal Rudra
28 October 1919

Dear Gurudev,

I have just arrived in the Punjab and I feel happy that I have been able at last to visit this unhappy land. I am today in Lahore. Tonight both Andrews and I are going to Delhi in connection with the Committee.

I write this to tell you how great have been Andrews' services to the people of this Province. He has done work which no other person could have done. And with him it is a matter of the right hand not knowing what the left hand doeth. It was good of you to have spared him for the Punjab. I am now pleading with him to go to South Africa as soon as he has *finished* the Punjab work. His own intention is not to stir out of Shantiniketan. I tell him the South African work is his speciality and he may not neglect it, when the call has come. Of course he has told me that you have left him free to do as he pleases. And I am hoping that he will go to South Africa. He won't have to be there for any length of time. Two months' stay would suffice.

I have an appeal for funds for the distress in East Bengal. Could you please let me have a pen picture? It will enable me to approach the people more effectively.

Hoping you are keeping well,

Yours sincerely,
M.K. Gandhi

10. Gandhi renews the invitation

(From a photocopy of the handwritten original signed by Gandhi, CWMG, Vol. XVI)

The Ashram,
Sabarmati,
14 January 1920

Dear Gurudev,

I had no idea up to today that the Gujarat Literary Conference had not met at the time it was expected to. The chief organiser Dr. Hari Prasad, however, tells me that, as one of the reasons for your inability to attend was the shortness of notice given to you, it was decided to postpone the holding of the Conference to Easter. It could be done without violating any canon of propriety as the Conference is not an annual fixture meeting at an appointed time. I know that you would come if your health and other considerations make it possible for you to accept the invitation and I sincerely hope that the capital of Gujarat will have the honour of receiving you during Easter.

Yours sincerely,
M.K. Gandhi

11. Gandhi on arrangements for Tagore's reception

(Copy from original letter, not in Gandhi's hand, but signed by him. The words "with all the appointments" and the postscript are in Gandhi's own hand.)

The Ashram,
Sabarmati,
11 March 1920

Dear Gurudev,

I have not been able before now to acknowledge your two telegrams, one addressed at Benares and redirected here and the other addressed here. We are all deeply grateful to you for your acceptance of the invitation. Every effort is being made not to overload you with engagements or *tamashas*. Will you please let me know, if necessary by wire, how long you will be able to give to Gujarat and whether you could visit one or two important centres. The second question is regarding your residence. Will you put up at the Ashram? Nothing would delight me more than to have you at the Ashram. I am most anxious that you should give the benefit of your presence to the many at the Ashram who claim to have been your pupils. Apart from the Gujrati boys and girls and the Sindhi lad Girdhar whom you may recall, Manindra is here still and Saraladevi's son Deepak is also at the Ashram. It is situated about four miles from the centre of Ahmedabad and stands on a ridge on the bank of the Sabarmati.

You can, then, either stay at the Ashram or at a private Bungalow in Ahmedabad with all the appointments. I need not say that your health and comfort are the primary consideratior. and your wishes will be faithfully carried out. Will you please also let me know any special arrangements or things you will desire.

Yours sincerely,
M.K. Gandhi

_____
*The Parishad lasts three days—2nd April to 4th.

12. Tagore's reflections on non-cooperation and cooperation

(The Calcutta journal Modern Review *of May 1921 carried letters inspired by Gandhi's Non-cooperation movement; addressed to C.F. Andrews, London, 1928)*

I

Your last letter gives wonderful news about our students in Calcutta. I hope that this spirit of sacrifice and willingness to suffer will grow in strength; for to achieve this is an end in itself. This is the true freedom! Nothing is of higher value—be it national wealth, or independence—than disinterested faith in ideals, in the moral greatness of man. The West has its unshakable faith in material strength and prosperity; and therefore however loud grows the cry for peace and disarmament, its ferocity grows louder, gnashing its teeth and lashing its tail in impatience. It is like a fish, hurt by the pressure of the flood, planning to fly in the air. Certainly the idea is brilliant, but it is not possible for a fish to realize.

We, in India, shall have to show to the world, what is that truth, which not only makes disarmament possible but turns it into strength. That moral force is a higher power than brute force, will be proved by the people who are unarmed. Life, in its higher development, has thrown off its tremendous burden of armour and a prodigious quantity of flesh; till man has become the conqueror of the brute world. The day is sure to come, when the frail man of spirit, completely unhampered by arms and air fleets, and dreadnoughts will prove that the meek is to inherit the earth. It is in the fitness of things, that Mahatma Gandhi, frail in body and devoid of all material resources, should call up the immense power of the meek, that has been lying waiting in the heart of the destitute and insulted humanity of India. The destiny of India has chosen for its ally, *Narayan*, and not the *Narayansena*—the power of soul and not that of muscle. And she is to raise the history of man, from the muddy level of physical conflict to the higher moral altitude. What is *swaraj*! It is *maya*, it is like a mist, that will vanish leaving no stain on the radiance of the Eternal. However we may delude ourselves with the phrases learnt from the West, *Swaraj* is not our objective.

Our fight is a spiritual fight, it is for Man. We are to emancipate Man from the meshes that he himself has woven round him,—these organisations of National Egoism. The butterfly will have to be persuaded that the freedom of the sky is of higher value than the shelter of the cocoon. If we can defy the strong, the armed, the wealthy, revealing to the world power of the immortal spirit, the whole castle of the Giant Flesh will vanish in the void. And then Man will find his *swaraj*. We, the famished, ragged ragamuffins of the East, are to win freedom for all Humanity. We have no word for Nation in our language. When we borrow this word from other people, it never fits us. For we are to make our league with *Narayan*, and our victory will not give us anything but victory itself; victory for God's world. I have seen the West; I covet not the unholy feast, in which she revels every moment, growing more and more bloated and red and dangerously delirious. Not for us, is this mad orgy of midnight, with lighted torches, but awakenment in the serene light of morning.

II

Lately I have been receiving more and more news and newspaper cuttings from India, giving rise in my mind to a painful struggle that presages a period of suffering which is waiting for me. I am striving with all my power to tune my mood of mind to be in accord with the great feeling of excitement sweeping across my country. But deep in my being why is there this spirit of resistance maintaining its place in spite of my strong desire to remove it? I fail to find a clear answer and through my gloom of dejection breaks out a smile and a voice saying, "Your place is on the seashore of worlds with children; there is your peace, and I am with you there."

And this is why lately I have been playing with inventing new metres. These are merest nothings that are content to be borne away by the current of time, dancing in the sun and laughing as they disappear. But while I play the whole creation is amused, for are not flowers and leaves never ending experiments in metre? Is not my God an eternal waster of time? He flings stars and planets in the whirlwind of changes, he floats paper boats of ages, filled with his fancies, on the rushing stream of appearance. When I tease him and beg him to allow me to remain his little follower and accept a few trifles of mine as the cargo of his playboat he smiles and I trot behind him catching the hem of his robe.

But where am I among the crowd, pushed from behind, pressed from all sides? And what is this noise about me? If it is a song, then my own *sitar* can catch the tune and I join in the chorus, for I am a singer. But if it is a shout, then my voice is wrecked and I am lost in bewilderment. I have been trying all these days to find in it a melody, straining my ear, but the idea of non-cooperation with its mighty volume of sound does not sing to me, its congregated menace of negations shouts. And I say to myself, "If you cannot keep step with your countrymen at this great crisis of their history, never say that you are right and the rest of them wrong; only give up your role as a soldier, go back to your corner as a poet, be ready to accept popular derision and disgrace".

R, in support of the present movement, has often said to me that passion for rejection is a stronger power in the beginning than the acceptance of an ideal. Though I know it to be a fact, I cannot take it as a truth. We must choose our allies once for all, for they stick to us even when we would be glad to be rid of them. If we once claim strength from intoxication, then in the time of reaction our normal strength is bankrupt, and we go back again and again to the demon who lends us resources in a vessel whose bottom it takes away.

Brahma-vidya (the cult of Brahma, the Infinite Being) in India has for its object *mukti*, emancipation, while Buddhism has *nirvana*, extinction. It may be argued that both have the same idea in different names. But names represent attitudes of mind, emphasise particular aspects of truth. *Mukti* draws our attention to the positive, and *nirvana* to the negative side of truth.

Buddha kept silence all through his teachings about the truth of the *Om*, the everlasting yes, his implication being that by the negative path of destroying the self we naturally reach that truth. Therefore he emphasised the fact of *dukkha* (misery) which had to be avoided and the *Brahma-vidya* emphasised the fact of *ananda*, joy, which had to be attained. The latter cult also needs for its fullfilment the discipline of self-abnegation, but it holds before its view the idea of Brahma, not only at the end but all through the process of realisation. Therefore, the idea of life's training was different in the Vedic period from that of the Buddhistic. In the former it was the purification of life's joy, in the latter it was the eradication of it. The abnormal type of asceticism to which Buddhism gave rise in India revelled in celibacy and mutilation of life in all different forms. But the forest life of the *Brahmana* was not antagonistic to the social life of man, but harmonious with it. It was like our musical instrument *tambura* whose duty is to supply the fundamental notes to the music to save it from straying into discordance. It believed in *anandam*, the music of the soul, and its own simplicity was not to kill it but to guide it.

The idea of non-cooperation is political asceticism. Our students are bringing their offering of sacrifices to what? Not to a fuller education but to non-education. It has at its back a fierce joy of annihilation which at best is asceticism, and at its worst is that orgy of frightfulness in which the human nature, losing faith in the basic reality of normal life, finds a disinterested delight in an unmeaning devastation as has been shown in the late war and

on other occasions which came nearer to us. No, in its passive
moral form is asceticism and in its active moral form is violence.
The desert is as much a form of a *himsa* (malignance) as is the
raging sea in storms, they both are against life.

I remember the day, during the *swadeshi* movement in
Bengal, when a crowd of young students came to see me in the
first floor hall of our Vichitra House. They said to me that if I
would order them to leave their schools and colleges they would
instantly obey. I was emphatic in my refusal to do so, and they
went away angry, doubting the sincerity of my love for my
motherland. And yet long before this popular ebullition of excitement I myself had given a thousand rupees, when I had not five
rupees to call my own, to open a *swadeshi* store and courted
banter and bankruptcy. The reason of my refusing to advise those
students to leave their schools was because the anarchy of a mere
emptiness never tempts me, even when it is resorted to as a
temporary measure. I am frightened of an abstraction which is
ready to ignore living reality. These students were no more
phantoms to me; their life was a great fact to them and to the All.
I could not lightly take upon myself the tremendous responsibility of a mere negative programme for them which would
uproot their life from its soil, however thin and poor that soil
might be.

The great injury and injustice which had been done to those
boys who were tempted away from their career before any real
provision was made, could never be made good to them. Of
course that is nothing from the point of view of an abstraction
which can ignore the infinite value even of the smallest fraction
of reality. I wish I were the little creature Jack whose one mission
is to kill the giant abstraction which is claiming the sacrifice of
individuals all over the world under highly painted masks of
delusion.

I say again and again that I am a poet, that I am not a fighter
by nature. I would give everything to be one with my surroundings. I love my fellow beings and I prize their love. Yet I have been
chosen by destiny to ply my boat there where the current is
against me. What irony of fate is this that I should be preaching
cooperation of cultures between East and West on this side of the
sea just at the moment when the doctrine of non-cooperation is
preached on the other side?

You know that I do not believe in the material civilisation of the West just as I do not believe in the physical body to be the highest truth in man. But I still less believe in the destruction of the physical body, and the ignoring of the material necessities of life. What is needed is establishment of harmony between the physical and spiritual nature of man, maintaining of balance between the foundation and superstructure. I believe in the true meeting of the East and the West. Love is the ultimate truth of soul. We should do all we can, not to outrage that truth, to carry its banner against all opposition. The idea of non-cooperation unnecessarily hurts that truth. It is not our heart fire but the fire that burns out our hearth and home.

III

Things that are stationary have no responsibility and need no law. For death, even the tombstone is a useless luxury. But for a world, which is an ever-moving multitude advancing towards an idea, all its laws must have one principle of harmony. This is the law of creation.

Man became great when he found out this law for himself, the law of co-operation. It helped him to move together, to utilise the rhythm and impetus of the world march. He at once felt that this moving together was not mechanical, not an external regulation for the sake of some convenience. It was what the metre is in poetry, which is not a mere system of enclosure for keeping ideas from running away in disorder, but for vitalising them, making them indivisible in a unity of creation.

So far this idea of co-operation has developed itself into individual communities within the boundaries of which peace has been maintained and varied wealth of life produced. But outside these boundaries the law of co-operation has not been realised. Consequently the great world of man is suffering from ceaseless discordance. We are beginning to discover that our problem is world-wide and no one people of the earth can work out its salvation by detaching itself from the others. Either we shall be saved together, or drawn together into destruction.

This truth has ever been recognised by all the great personalities of the world. They had in themselves the perfect consciousness of the undivided spirit of man. Their teachings were against tribal exclusiveness, and thus we find that Buddha's India transcended geographical India and Christ's religion broke through the bonds of Judaism.

Today, at this critical moment of the world's history cannot India rise above her limitations and offer the great ideal to the world that will work towards harmony and co-operation between the different peoples of the earth! Men of feeble faith will say that India requires to be strong and rich before she can raise her voice for the sake of the whole world. But I refuse to believe it. That the measure of man's greatness is in his material resources is a gigantic illusion casting its shadow over the present day world, — it is an insult to man. It lies in the power of the materially weak to save the world from this illusion and India, in spite of her penury and humiliation, can afford to come to the rescue of humanity.

The freedom of unrestrained egoism in the individual is licence and not true freedom. For his truth is in that which is universal in him. Individual human races also attain true freedom when they have the freedom of perfect revelation of Man and not that of their aggressive racial egoism. The idea of freedom which prevails in modern civilisation is superficial and materialistic. Our revolution in India will be a true one when its forces will be directed against this crude idea of liberty.

The sunlight of love has the freedom that ripens the wisdom of immortal life, but passions' fire can only forge fetters for ourselves. The spiritual Man has been struggling for its emergence into perfection, and all true cry of freedom is for this emancipation. Erecting barricades of fierce separateness in the name of national necessity is offering hindrance to it, therefore in the long run building a prison for the nation itself. For the only path of deliverance for nations is in the ideal humanity.

Creation is an endless activity of God's freedom; it is an end in itself. Freedom is true when it is a revelation of truth. Man's freedom is for the revelation of the truth of Man which is struggling to express itself. We have not yet fully realised it. But those people who have faith in its greatness, who acknowledge its sovereignty, and have the instinctive urging in their heart to break down obstructions, are paving the way for its coming.

India ever has nourished faith in the truth of spiritual man for whose realisation she has made innumerable experiments, sacrifices and penance, some verging on the grotesque and the abnormal. But the fact is, she has never ceased in her attempt to find it even though at the tremendous cost of material success.

Therefore I feel that the true India is an idea and not a mere geographical fact. I have come into touch with this idea in far away places of Europe and my loyalty was drawn to it in persons who belonged to different countries from mine. India will be victorious when this idea wins victory,—the idea of *'Purusham mahantam aditya-varnam tamasah parastat'*, the Infinite Personality whose light reveals itself through the obstruction of darkness. Our fight is against this darkness, our object is the revealment of the light of this Infinite Personality in ourselves. This Infinite Personality of man is not to be achieved in single individuals, but in one grand harmony of all human races. The darkness of egoism which will have to be destroyed is the egoism of the People. The idea of India is against the intense consciousness of the separateness of one's own people from others, and which inevitably leads to ceaseless conflicts. Therefore my one prayer is: let India stand for the *cooperation* of all peoples of the world. The spirit of rejection finds its support in the consciousness of separateness, the spirit of acceptance in the consciousness of unity.

India has ever declared that Unity is Truth, and separateness is *maya*. This unity is not a zero, it is that which comprehends all and therefore can never be reached through the path of negation. Our present struggle to alienate our heart and mind from those of the West is an attempt at spiritual suicide. If in the spirit of national vain-gloriousness we shout from our house-tops that the West has produced nothing that has an infinite value for man, then we but create a serious cause of doubt about the worth of any product of the Eastern mind. For it is the mind of Man in the East and West which is ever approaching Truth in her different aspects from different angles of vision; and if it can be true that the standpoint of the West has betrayed it into an utter misdirection, then we can never be sure of the standpoint of the East. Let us be rid of all false pride and rejoice at any lamp being lit at any corner of the world, knowing that it is a part of the common illumination of our house.

The other day I was invited to the house of a distinguished artcritic of America who is a great admirer of old Italian art. I questioned him if he knew anything of our Indian pictures and brusquely said that most probably he would "hate them". I suspected he had seen some of them and hated them. In retaliation I could have said something in the same language about the Western art. But I am proud to say it was not possible for me. For I always try to understand the Western art and never to hate it. Whatever we understand and enjoy in human products instantly becomes ours wherever they might have their origin. I should feel proud of my humanity when I can acknowledge the poets and artists of other countries as mine own. Let me feel with unalloyed gladness that all the great glories of man are mine.

Therefore, it hurts me deeply when the cry of rejection rings loud against the West in my country with the clamour that the Western education can only injure us. It cannot be true. What has caused the mischief is the fact that for a long time we have been out of touch with our own culture and therefore the Western culture has not found its prospective in our life very often found a wrong prospective giving our mental eye a squint. When we have the intellectual capital of our own, the commerce of thought with the outer world becomes natural and fully profitable. But to say that such commerce is inherently wrong, is to encourage the worst form of provincialism, productive of nothing but intellectual indigence. The West has misunderstood the East which is at the root of the disharmony that prevails between them, but will it mend the matter if the East in her turn tries to misunderstand the West? The present age has powerfully been possessed by the West; it has only become possible because to her is given some great mission for man. We from the East have to come to her to learn whatever she has to teach us; for by doing so we hasten the fullfilment of this age. We know that the East also has her lessons to give and she has her own responsibility of not allowing her light to be extinguished, and the time will come when the West will find leisure to realise that she has a home of hers in the East where her food is and her rest.

Rabindranath Tagore

The last meeting: Tagore and Gandhi at the cottage `Shyamalee' in Santiniketan, Kasturba is seated next to Gandhi, 1940

Mahatma Gandhi with the teachers at Sriniketan, 1940

Mahatma Gandhi and Kasturba: felicitation by students of the school in Visva-Bharati (probably in 1940)

At a reception to Mahatma Gandhi and Kasturba in Santiniketan, 1940

13. Gandhi's reactions to Tagore's views

(Gandhi's Young India *of 1 June 1921, carried a reply to the Poet's musings, under the heading 'English Learning')*

Elsewhere the reader will see my humble endeavour in reply to Dr. Tagore's criticism of Non-cooperation. I have since read his letter to the Manager of Santiniketan. I am sorry to observe that the letter is written in anger and in ignorance of facts. The Poet was naturally incensed to find that certain students in London would not give a hearing to Mr. Pearson, one of the truest of Englishmen, and he became equally incensed to learn that I had told our women to stop English studies. The reasons for my advice, the Poet evidently inferred for himself.

How much better it would have been, if he had not imputed the rudeness of the students to Non-cooperation, and had remembered that Non-cooperators worship Andrews, honour Stokes, and gave a most respectful hearing to Messrs. Wedgwood Benn, Spoor and Holford Knight at Nagpur, that Maulana Mahomed Ali accepted the invitation to tea of an English official when he invited him as a friend, that Hakim Ajmalkhan, a staunch Non-cooperator, had the portraits of Lord and Lady Hardinge unveiled in his Tibbia College and had invited his many English friends to witness the ceremony. How much better it would have been, if he had refused to allow the demon doubt to possess him for one moment, as to the real and religious character of the present movement, and had believed that the movement was altering the meaning of old terms, nationalism and patriotism, and extending their scope.

If he, with a poet's imagination, had seen that I was incapable of wishing to cramp the mind of the Indian women, and I could not object to English learning as such, and recalled the fact that throughout my life I had fought for the fullest liberty for women, he would have been saved the injustice which he has done me, and which, I know, he would never knowingly do to an avowed enemy.

The Poet does not know perhaps that English is today studied because of its commercial and so-called political value. Our boys think, and rightly in the present circumstances, that without English they cannot get Government service. Girls are

taught English as a passport to marriage. I know several instances
of women wanting to learn English so that they may be able to
talk to Englishmen in English. I know husbands who are sorry
that their wives cannot talk to them and their friends in English.
I know families in which English is being *made* the mother tongue.
Hundreds of youths believe that without a knowledge of English
freedom for India is practically impossible. The canker has so
eaten into the society that, in many cases, the only meaning of
Education is a knowledge of English.

All these are for me signs of our slavery and degradation.
It is unbearable to me that the vernaculars should be crushed and
starved as they have been. I cannot tolerate the idea of parents
writing to their children, or husbands writing to their wives, not
in their own vernaculars, but in English. I hope I am as great a
believer in free air as the great Poet. I do not want my house to
be walled in on all sides and my windows to be stuffed.

I want the cultures of all the lands to be blown about my
house as freely as possible. But I refuse to be blown off my feet
by any. I refuse to live in other people's houses as an interloper,
a beggar or a slave. I refuse to put the unnecessary strain of
learning English upon my sisters for the sake of false pride or
questionable social advantage. I would have our young men and
young women with literary tastes to learn as much of English and
other world-languages as they like, and then expect them to give
the benefits of their learning to India and to the world, like a Bose,
a Roy or the Poet himself.

But I would not have a single Indian to forget, neglect or be
ashamed of his mother-tongue, or to feel that he or she cannot
think or express the best thoughts in his or her own vernacular.
Mine is not a religion of the prison house. It has room for the least
among God's creation. But it is proof against insolence, pride of
race, religion or colour. I am extremely sorry for the Poet's
misreading of this great movement or reformation, purification
and patriotism spelt humanity. If he will be patient, he will find
no cause for sorrow or shame for his countrymen. I respectfully
warn him against mistaking its excrescences for the movement
itself. It is as wrong to judge Non-cooperation by the students'
misconduct in London or Malegaon's in India, as it would be to
judge Englishmen by the Dyers or the O'Dwyers.

                                                          M.K. Gandhi

14. The Poet's anxiety

(Young India of 1 June 1921 also carried another reply to Tagore from Gandhi on cooperation and non-cooperation vis-a-vis the students.)

The Poet of Asia, as Lord Hardinge called Dr. Tagore, is fast becoming, if he has not already become, the Poet of the world. Increasing prestige has brought to him increasing responsibility. His greatest service to India must be his poetic interpretation of India's message to the world. The Poet is, therefore, sincerely anxious that India should deliver no false or feeble message in her name. He is naturally jealous of his country's reputation. He says he has striven hard to find himself in tune with the present movement. He confesses that he is baffled. He can find nothing for his lyre in the din and the bustle of Non-cooperation. In three forceful letters, he has endeavoured to give expression to his misgivings, and he has come to the conclusion that Non-cooperation is not dignified enough for the India of his vision, that it is a doctrine of negation and despair. He fears that it is a doctrine of separation, exclusiveness, narrowness and negation.

No Indian can feel anything but pride in the Poet's exquisite jealousy of India's honour. It is good that he should have sent to us his misgivings in language at once beautiful and clear.

In all humility, I shall endeavour to answer the Poet's doubts. I may fail to convince him or the reader who may have been touched by his eloquence, but I would like to assure him and India that Non-cooperation in conception is not any of the things he fears, and he need have no cause to be ashamed of his country for having adopted Non-cooperation. If, in actual application, it appears in the end to have failed, it will be no more the fault of the doctrine, than it would be of Truth, if those who claim to apply it in practice do not appear to succeed. Non-cooperation may have come in advance of its time. India and the world must then wait, but there is no choice for India save between violence and Non-cooperation.

Nor need the Poet fear that Non-cooperation is intended to erect a Chinese wall between India and the West. On the contrary, Non-cooperation is intended to pave the way to real, honourable and voluntary co-operation based on mutual respect and trust.

The present struggle is being waged against compulsory co-operation, against one-sided combination, against the armed imposition of modern methods of exploitation, masquerading under the name of civilisation.

Non-cooperation is a protest against an unwitting and unwilling participation in evil.

The Poet's concern is largely about the students. He is of the opinion that they should not have been called upon to give up Government schools before they had other schools to go to. Here I must differ from him. I have never been able to make a fetish of literary training. My experience has proved to my satisfaction that literary training by itself adds not an inch to one's moral height and that character-building is independent of literary training. I am firmly of opinion that the Government schools have unmanned us; rendered us helpless and Godless. They have filled us with discontent, and providing no remedy for the discontent, have made us despondent. They have made us what we were intended to become — clerks and interpreters. A Government builds its prestige upon the apparently voluntary association of the governed. And if it was wrong to cooperate with the Government in keeping us slaves, we were bound to begin with those institutions in which our association appeared to be most voluntary. The youth of a nation are its hope. I hold that, as soon as we discovered that the system of Government was wholly, or mainly evil, it became sinful for us to associate our children with it.

It is no argument against the soundness of the proposition laid down by me that the vast majority of the students went back after the first flush of enthusiasm. Their recantation is proof rather of the extent of our degradation than of the wrongness of the step. Experience has shown that the establishment of national schools has not resulted in drawing many more students. The strongest and the truest of them came out without any national schools to fall back upon, and I am convinced that these first withdrawals are rendering service of the highest order.

But the Poet's protest against the calling out of the boys is really a corollary to his objection to the very doctrine of Non-cooperation. He has a horror of everything negative. His whole soul seems to rebel against the negative commandments of religion. I must give his objection in his own inimitable language.

"R, in support of the present movement has often said to me that passion for rejection is a stronger power in the beginning than the acceptance of an ideal. Though I know it to be a fact, I cannot take it as a truth... *Brahma-vidya* in India has for its object *mukti* (emancipation), while Buddhism has *nirvana* (extinction), negative side of truth... Therefore, he (Buddha) emphasised the fact of *dukkha* (misery) which had to be avoided and the *Brahma-vidya* emphasised the fact of *anand* (joy) which had to be attained." In these and kindred passages, the reader will find the key to the Poet's mentality. In my humble opinion, rejection is as much an ideal as the acceptance of a thing. It is as necessary to reject untruth as it is to accept truth. All religions teach that two opposite forces act upon us and that the human endeavour consists in a series of eternal rejections and acceptances. Non-cooperation with evil is as much a duty as co-operation with good. I venture to suggest that the Poet has done an unconscious injustice to Buddhism in describing *nirvana* as merely a negative state. I make bold to say that *mukti* (emancipation) is as much a negative state as *nirvana*. Emancipation from or extinction of the bondage of the flesh leads to *ananda* (eternal bliss). Let me close this part of my argument by drawing attention to the fact that the final word of the *Upanishads* (*Brahma-vidya*) is *Not*. *Neti* was the best description the authors of the *Upanishads* were able to find for *Brahma*.

I, therefore, think that the Poet has been unnecessarily alarmed at the negative aspect of Non-cooperation. We had lost the power of saying 'no'. It had become disloyal, almost sacrilegious to say 'no' to the Government. This deliberate refusal to co-operate is like the necessary weeding process that a cultivator has to resort before he sows. Weeding is as necessary to agriculture as sowing. Indeed, even whilst the crops are growing, the weeding fork, as every husbandman knows, is an instrument almost of daily use. The nation's Non-cooperation is an invitation to the Government to co-operate with it on its own terms as is every nation's right and every good government's duty. Non-cooperation is the nation's notice that it is no longer satisfied to be in tutelage. The nation had taken to the harmless (for it), natural and religious doctrine of Non-cooperation in the place of the unnatural and irreligious doctrine of violence. And if India is ever to attain the *swaraj* of the Poet's dream, she will do so only by

Non-violent Non-cooperation. Let him deliver his message of peace to the world, and feel confident that India, through her Non-cooperation, if she remains true to her pledge, will have exemplified his message. Non-cooperation is intended to give the very meaning to patriotism that the Poet is yearning after. An India prostrate at the feet of Europe can give no hope to humanity. An India awakened and free has a message of peace and goodwill to a groaning world. Non-cooperation is designed to supply her with a platform from which she will preach the message.

M.K. Gandhi

15. The Call Of Truth

(This long rejoinder from Tagore to Gandhi originally appeared in Pravasee *in Bengali and later in* Modern Review *in English. The original is reproduced in Volume XXIV of the* Collected Works of Rabindranath Tagore)

Parasites have to pay for their readymade victuals by losing the power of assimilating food in natural form. In the history of man, this same sin of laziness has always entailed degeneracy. Man becomes parasitical, not only when he fattens on others' toil, but also when he becomes rooted to a particular set of outside conditions and allows himself helplessly to drift along the stream of things as they are; for the outside is alien to the inner self, and if the former be made indispensable by sheer habit, man acquires parasitical characteristics, and becomes unable to perform his true function of converting the impossible into the possible.

In this sense all the lower animals are parasites. They are carried along by their environment; they live or die by natural selection; they progress or retrogress as nature may dictate. Their mind has lost the power of growth. The bees, for millions of years, have been unable to get beyond the pattern of their hive. For that reason, the form of their cell has attained a certain perfection, but their mentality is confined to the age-long habits of their hive-life and cannot soar out of its limitations. Nature has developed a cautious timidity in the case of her lower types of life; she keeps them tied to her apron strings and has stunted their minds, lest they should stray into dangerous experiments.

But Providence displayed a sudden accession of creative courage when it came to man; for his inner nature has not been tied down, though outwardly the poor human creature has been left naked, weak and defenceless. In spite of these disabilities, man in the joy of his inward freedom has stood up and declared: "I shall achieve the impossible". That is to say, he has consistently refused to submit to the rule of things as they always have been, but is determined to bring about happenings that have never been before. So when, in the beginning of his history, man's lot was thrown in with monstrous creatures, tusked and taloned, he did not, like the deer, simply take refuge in flight, nor, like the tortoise, take refuge in biding, but set to work with flints to make even more efficient weapons. These, moreover, being the creation of his own inner faculties, were not dependent on natural selection, as were those of the other animals, for their developments. And so man's instruments progressed from flint to steel. This shows that man's mind has never been helplessly attached to his environment. What came to his hand was brought under his thumb. Not content with the flint on the surface, he delved for the iron beneath. Not satisfied with the easier process of chipping flints, he proceeded to melt iron ore and hammer it into shape. That which resisted more stubbornly was converted into a better ally. Man's inner nature not only finds success in its activity, but there it also has its joy. He insists on penetrating further and further into the depths, from the obvious to the hidden, from the easy to the difficult, from parasitism to self-determination, from the slavery of his passions to the mastery of himself. That is how he has won.

But if any section of mankind should say, "The flint was the weapon of our revered forefathers; by departing from it we destroy the spirit of the race", then they may succeed in preserving what they call their race, but they strike at the root of the glorious tradition of humanity which was theirs also. And we find that those, who have steadfastly stuck to their flints, may indeed have kept safe their pristine purity to their own satisfaction, but they have been outcasted by the rest of mankind, and so have to pass their lives slinking away in jungle and cave. They are, as I say, reduced to a parasitic dependence on outside nature, driven along blindfold by the force of things as they are. They have not achieved *swaraj* in their inner nature, and so are deprived of *swaraj* in the outside world as well. They have ceased to be even aware, that it is man's true function to make the impossible into the possible by dint of his own powers; that it is not for him to be confined merely to what has happened before; that he must progress towards what ought to be by rousing all his inner powers by means of the force of his soul.

Thirty years ago I used to edit the *Sadhana* magazine and there I tried to say this same thing. Then English-educated India was frightfully busy begging for its rights. And I repeatedly endeavoured to impress on my countrymen, that man is not under any necessity to beg for rights from others, but must create them for himself; because man lives mainly by his inner nature, and there he is the master. By dependence on acquisition from the outside, man's inner nature suffers loss. And it was my contention, that man is not so hard oppressed by being deprived of his outward rights as he is by the constant bearing of the burden of prayers and petitions.

Then when the *Bangadarshan* magazine came into my hands, Bengal was beside herself at the sound of the sharpening of the knife for her partition. The boycott of Manchester, which was the outcome of her distress, had raised the profits of the Bombay mill-owners to a super-foreign degree. And I had then to say: "This will not do, either; for it is also of the outside. Your main motive is hatred of the foreigner, not love of country." It was then really necessary for our countrymen to be made conscious of the distinction, that the Englishman's presence is an external acci-dent,—mere *maya*—but that the presence of our country is an internal fact which is also an eternal truth. *Maya* looms with an exaggerated importance, only when we fix our attention exclu-sively upon it, by reason of some infatuation—be it of love or of hate. Whether in our passion we rush to embrace it, or attack it; whether we yearn for it, or spurn it; it equally fills the whole field of our blood-shot vision.

Maya is like the darkness. No steed, however swift, can carry us beyond it; no amount of water can wash it away. Truth is like a lamp; even as it is lit, *maya* vanishes. Our *shastras* tell us that Truth, even when it is small, can rescue us from the terror which is great. Fear is the atheism of the heart. It cannot be overcome from the side of negation. If one of its heads be struck off, it breeds like the monster of the fable, a hundred others. Truth is positive; it is the affirmation of the soul. If even a little of it be roused, it attacks negation at the very heart and overpowers it wholly.

Alien government in India is a veritable chameleon. Today it comes in the guise of the Englishman; tomorrow perhaps as some other foreigner; the next day, without abating a jot of its virulence, it may take the shape of our own countrymen. However determinedly we may try to hunt this monster of foreign dependence with outside lethal weapons, it will always elude our pursuit by changing its skin, or its colour. But if we can gain within us the truth called our country, all outward *maya* will vanish of itself. The declaration of faith that my country *is* there, to be realised, has to be attained by each one of us. The idea that our country is ours, merely because we have been born in it, can only be held by those who are fastened, in a parasitic existence, upon the outside world. But the true nature of man is his inner nature, with its inherent powers. Therefore, that only can be a man's true country, which he can help to create by his wisdom and will, his love and his actions. So in 1905, I called upon my countrymen to create their country by putting forth their own powers from within. For the act of creation itself is the realization of truth.

The Creator gains Himself in His universe. To gain one's own country means to realize one's own soul more fully expanded within it. This can only be done when we are engaged in building it up with our service, our ideas and our activities. Man's country being the creation of his own inner nature, when his soul thus expands within it, it is more truly expressed, more fully realised. In my paper called *Swadeshi Samaj*, written in 1905, I discussed at length the ways and means by which we could make the country of our birth more fully our own. Whatever may have been the shortcomings of my words then uttered, I did not fail to lay emphasis on the truth, that we must win our country, not from some foreigner, but from our own inertia, our own indifference. Whatever be the nature of the boons we may be seeking for our country at the door it only makes our inertia more densely inert. Any public benefit done by the alien Government goes to their credit not to ours. So whatever outside advantage such public benefit might mean for us, our country will only get more and more completely lost to us thereby. That is to say, we shall have to pay out in soul value for what we purchase as material advantage. The *Rishi* has said: "The son is dear, not because we desire a son, but because we desire to realise our own soul in him". It is the same with our country. It is dear to us, because it is the expression of our own soul. When we realise this, it will become impossible for us to allow our service of our country to wait on the pleasure of others.

These truths, which I then tried to press on my countrymen, were not particularly new, nor was there anything therein which need have grated on their ears; but, whether anyone else remembers it or not, I at least am not likely to forget the storm of indignation which I roused. I am not merely referring to the hooligans of journalism whom it pays to be scurrilous. But even men of credit and courtesy were unable to speak of me in restrained language.

There were two root causes of this. One was anger, the second was greed.

Giving free vent to angry feelings is a species of self-indulgence. In those days there was practically nothing to stand in the way of the spirit of destructive revel, which spread all over the country. We went about picketing, burning, placing thorns in the path of those whose way was not ours, acknowledging no restraints in language or behaviour,—all in the frenzy of our wrath. Shortly after it was all over, a Japanese friend asked me: "How is it you people cannot carry on your work with calm and deep determination? This wasting of energy can hardly be of assistance to your object." I had no help but to reply: "When we have the gaining of the object clearly before our minds, we can be restrained, and concentrate our energies to serve it; but when it is a case of venting our anger, our excitement rises and rises till it drowns the object and then we are spend-thrift to the point of bankruptcy." However that may be, there were my countrymen encountering, for the time being, no check to the overflow of their outraged feelings. It was like a strange dream. Everything seemed possible. Then all of a sudden it was my misfortune to appear on the scene with my doubts and my attempts to divert the current into the path of self-determination. My only success was in diverting their wrath on to my own devoted head.

Then there was our greed. In history, all people have won valuable things by pursuing difficult paths. We had hit upon the device of getting them cheap, not even through the painful indignity of supplication with folded hands, but by proudly conducting our beggary in threatening tones. The country was in ecstasy at the ingenuity of the trick. It felt like being at a reduced price sale. Everything worth having in the political market was ticketed at half-price. Shabby-genteel mentality is so taken up with low prices that it has no attention to spare for quality and feels inclined to attack anybody who has the hardihood to express doubts in that regard. It is like the man of worldly piety who believes that the judicious expenditure of coin can secure, by favour of the priest, a direct passage to heaven. The dare devil who ventures to suggest that not heaven but dreamland is likely to be his destination must beware of a violent end.

Anyhow, it was the outside *maya* which was our dream and our ideal in those days. It was a favourite phrase of one of the leaders of the time that we must keep one hand at the feet and the other at the throat of the Englishman,—that is to say, with no hand left free for the country! We have since perhaps got rid of this ambiguous attitude. Now we have one party that has both hands raised to the foreigner's throat, and another party which has both hands down at his feet; but whichever attitude it may be, these methods still appertain to the outside *maya*. Our unfortunate minds keep revolving round and round the British Government, now to the left, now to the right; our affirmations and denials alike are concerned with the foreigners.

In those days, the stimulus from every side was directed towards the heart of Bengal. But emotion by itself, like fire only consumes its fuel and reduces it to ashes; it has no creative power. The intellect of man must busy itself, with patience, with skill, with foresight, in using this fire to melt that which is hard and difficult into the object of its desire. We neglected to rouse our intellectual forces, and so were unable to make use of this surging emotion of ours to create any organisation of permanent value. The reason of our failure, therefore, was not in anything outside, but rather within us. For a long time past we have been in the habit, in our life and endeavour, of setting apart one place for our emotions and another for our practices. Our intellect has all the time remained dormant, because we have not dared to allow it scope. That is why, when we have to rouse ourselves to action, it is our emotion which has to be requisitioned, and our intellect has to be kept from interfering by the hypnotism of some magical formula,—that is to say we hasten to create a situation absolutely inimical to the free play of our intellect.

The loss which is incurred by this continual deadening of our mind cannot be made good by any other contrivance. In our desperate attempts to do so we have to invoke the magic of *maya* and our impotence jumps for joy at the prospect of getting hold of Alladin's lamp. Of course everyone has to admit that there is nothing to beat Alladin's lamp, its only inconvenience being that it beats one to get hold of. The unfortunate part of it is that the person, whose greed is great, but whose powers are feeble, and who has lost all confidence in his own intellect, simply will not allow himself to dwell on the difficulties of bespeaking the services of some genie of the lamp. He can only be brought to exert himself at all by holding out the speedy prospect of getting at the wonderful lamp. If any one attempts to point out the futility of his hopes, he fills the air with wailing and imprecation, as at a robber making away with his all.

In the heat of the enthusiasm of the partition days, a band of youths attempted to bring about the millenium through political revolution. Their offer of themselves as the first sacrifice to the fire which they had lighted makes not only their own country, but other countries as well, bare the head to them in reverence. Their physical failure shines forth as the effulgence of spiritual glory. In the midst of the supreme travail, they realised at length that the way of bloody revolution is not the true way; that where there is no politics, a political revolution is like taking a short cut to nothing; that the wrong way may appear shorter, but it does not reach the goal, and only grievously hurts the feet. The refusal to pay the full price for a thing leads to the loss of the price without the gain of the thing. These impetuous youths offered their lives as the price of their country's deliverance; to them it meant the loss of their all but alas! the price offered on behalf of the country was insufficient. I feel sure that those of them who still survive must have realised by now, that the country must be the creation of all its people, not of one section alone. It must be the expression of all their forces of heart, mind and will.

This creation can only be the fruit of that *yoga*, which gives outward form to the inner faculties. Mere political or economical *yoga* is not enough; for that all the human powers must unite.

When we turn our gaze upon the history of other countries, the political steed comes prominently into view; on it seems to depend wholly the progress of the carriage. We forget that the carriage also must be in a fit condition to move; its wheels must be in agreement with one another and its parts well fitted together; with which not only have fire and hammer and chisel been busy but much thought and skill and energy have also been spent in the process. We have seen some countries which are externally free and independent; when however, the political carriage is in motion, the noise which it makes arouses the whole neighbourhood from slumber and the jolting produces aches and pains in the limbs of the helpless passengers. It comes to pieces in the middle of the road, and it takes the whole day to put it together again with the help of ropes and strings. Yet however loose the screws and however crooked the wheels, still it is a vehicle of some sort after all. But for such a thing as is our country — a mere collection of jointed logs, that not only have no wholeness amongst themselves, but are contrary to one another — for this to be dragged along a few paces by the temporary pull of some common greed or anger, can never be called by the name of political progress. Therefore, is it not, in our case, wiser to keep for the moment our horse in the stable and begin to manufacture a real carriage?

From the writings of the young men, who have come back out of the valley of the shadow of death, I feel sure some such thoughts must have occurred to them. And so they must be realising the necessity of the practice of *yoga* as of primary importance;—that from which is the union in a common endeavour of all the human faculties. This cannot be attained by any outside blind obedience, but only by the realisation of self in the light of intellect. That which fails to illumine the intellect, and only keeps it in the obsession of some delusion, is its greatest obstacle.

The call to make the country our own by dint of our own creative power, is a great call. It is not merely inducing the people to take up some external mechanical exercise; for man's life is not in making cells of uniform pattern like the bee, nor in incessant weaving of webs like the spider; his greatest powers are within, and on these are his chief reliance. If by offering some allurement we can induce man to cease from thinking, so that he may go on and on with some mechanical piece of work, this will only result in prolonging the sway of *maya*, under which our country has all along been languishing. So far, we have been content with surrendering our greatest right—the right to reason and to judge for ourselves—to the blind forces of *shastric* injunctions and social conventions. We have refused to cross the seas, because Manu has told us not to do so. We refuse to eat with the Mussalman, because prescribed usage is against it. In other words, we have systematically pursued a course of blind routine and habit, in which the mind of man has no place. We have thus been reduced to the helpless condition of the master who is altogether dependent on his servant. The real master, as I have said, is the internal man; and he gets into endless troubles, when he becomes his own servant's slave—a mere automaton, manufactured in the factory of servitude. He can then only rescue himself from one master by surrendering himself. Similarly, he who glorifies inertia by attributing to it a fanciful purity, becomes, like it, dependent on outside impulses, both for rest and motion. The inertness of mind, which is the basis of all slavery, cannot be got rid of by a docile, submission to being hoodwinked, nor by going through the motions of a wound-up mechanical doll.

The movement, which has now succeeded the *swadeshi* agitation, is ever so much greater and has moreover extended its influence all over India. Previously, the vision of our political leaders had never reached beyond the English-knowing classes, because the country meant for them only that bookish aspect of it which is to be found in the pages of the Englishman's history. Such a country was merely a mirage born of vapourings in the English language, in which litted about thin shades of Burke and Gladstone, Mazzini and Garibaldi. Nothing resembling self-sacrifice or true feeling for their countrymen was visible. At this juncture, Mahatma Gandhi came and stood at the cottage door of the destitute millions, clad as one of themselves, and talking to them in their own language. Here was the truth at last, not a mere quotation out of a book. So the name of Mahatma, which was given to him, is his true name. Who else has felt so many men of India to be of his own flesh and blood? At the touch of Truth the pent-up forces of the soul are set free. As soon as true love stood at India's door, it flew open; all hesitation and holding back vanished. Truth awakened truth.

Stratagem in politics is a barren policy—this was a lesson of which we were sorely in need. All honour to the Mahatma, who made visible to us the power of Truth. But reliance on tactics is so ingrained in the cowardly and the weak, that in order to eradicate it, the very skin must be sloughed off. Even to-day, our worldly-wise men cannot get rid of the idea of utilising the Mahatma at a secret and more ingenious move in their political gamble. With their minds corroded by untruth, they cannot understand what an important thing it is that the Mahatma's supreme love should have drawn forth the country's love. The thing that has happened is nothing less than the birth of freedom. It is the gain by the country of itself. In it there is no room for any thought, as to where the Englishman is, or is not. This love is self-expression. It is pure affirmation. It does not argue with negation: it has no need for argument.

Some notes of the music of this wonderful awakening of India by love, floated over to me across the seas. It was a great joy to me to think that the call of this festivity of awakening would come to each one of us; and that the true *shakti* of India's spirit, in all its multifarious variety, would at last find expression. This thought came to me because I have always believed that in such a way India would find its freedom. When Lord Buddha voiced forth the truth of compassion for all living creatures, the man-hood of India was roused and poured itself forth in science and art and wealth of every kind. True in the matter of political unification the repeated attempts that were then made as often failed; nevertheless India's mind had awakened into freedom from its submergence in sleep, and its overwhelming force would brook no confinement within the petty limits of country. It overflowed across ocean and desert, scattering its wealth of the spirit over every land that it touched. No commercial or military exploiter, to-day has ever been able to do anything like it. Whatever land these exploiters have touched has been agonised with sorrow and insult, and the fair face of the world has been scared and disfigured. Why? Because not greed but love is true. When love gives freedom it does so at the very centre of our life. When greed seeks unfettered power, it is forcefully impatient. We saw this during the partition agitation. We then compelled the poor to make sacrifices, not always out of the inwardness of love, but often by outward pressure. That was because greed is always seeking for a particular result within a definite time. But the fruit which love seeks is not of today or tomorrow, nor for a time only: it is sufficient unto itself.

So, in the expectation of breathing the buoyant breezes of this new found freedom, I came home rejoicing. But what I found in Calcutta when I arrived depressed me. An oppressive atmosphere seemed to burden the land. Some outside compulsion seemed to be urging one and all to talk in the same strain, to work at the same mill. When I wanted to inquire, to discuss, my well-wishers clapped their hands over my lips, saying: "Not now, not now". To-day, in the atmosphere of the country, there is a spirit of persecution, which is not that of armed force, but something still more alarming, because it is invisible. I found, further, that those who had their doubts as to the present activities, if they happened to whisper them out, however cautiously, however guardedly, felt some admonishing hand clutching them within. There was a newspaper which one day had the temerity to disapprove, in a feeble way, of the burning of cloth. The very next day, the editor was shaken out of his balance by the agitation of his readers. How long would it take for the fire which was burning cloth to reduce his paper to ashes? The sight that met my eye was, on the one hand people immensely busy; on the other, intensely afraid. What I heard on every side was, that reason, and culture as well, must be closured. It was only necessary to cling to an unquestioning obedience. Obedience to whom? To some *mantra*, some unreasoned creed!

And why this obedience? Here again comes that same greed, our spiritual enemy. There dangles before the country the bait of getting a thing of inestimable value dirt cheap and in double-quick time. It is like the *faqir* with his goldmaking trick. With such a lure men cast so readily to the winds their independent judgement and wax so mightly wroth with those who will not do likewise. So easy is to overpower, in the name of outside freedom the inner freedom of man. The most deplorable part of it is that so many do not even honestly believe in the hope that they swear by. "It will serve to make our countrymen do what is necessary"—say they. Evidently, according to them, the India which once declared: "In truth is Victory, not in untruth"—that India would not have been fit for *swaraj*.

Another mischief is that the gain, with the promise of which obedience is claimed, is indicated by name, but is not defined, just as when fear is vague it becomes all the more strong, so the vagueness of the lure makes it all the more tempting; inasmuch as ample room is left for each one's imagination to shape it to his taste. Moreover there is no driving it into a corner because it can always shift from one shelter to another. In short, the object of the temptation has been magnified through its indefiniteness while the time and method of its attainment have been made too narrowly definite. When the reason of man has been overcome in this way, he easily consents to give up all legitimate questions and blindly follows the path of obedience. But can we really afford to forget so easily that delusion is at the root of all slavery —that all freedom means freedom from *maya*? What if the bulk of our people have unquestioningly accepted the creed, that by means of sundry practices *swaraj* will come to them on a particular date in the near future and are also ready to use their clubs to put down all further argument,—that is to say, they have surrendered the freedom of their own minds and are prepared to deprive other minds of their freedom likewise,—is not this by itself a reason for profound misgiving? We were seeking the exorciser to drive out this very ghost; but if the ghost itself comes in the guise of exorciser then the danger is only heightened.

The Mahatma has won the heart of India with his love; for that we have all acknowledged his sovereignty. He has given us a vision of the *shakti* of Truth; for that our gratitude to him is unbounded. We read about Truth in books: we talk about it: but it is indeed a red-letter day, when we see it face to face. Rare is the moment, in many a long year, when such good fortune happens. We can make and break Congresses every other day. It is at any time possible for us to stump the country preaching politics in English. But the golden rod, which can awaken our country in Truth and Love is not a thing which can be manufactured by the nearest goldsmith. To the weilder of that rod our profound salutation! But if having seen Truth, our belief in it is not confirmed, what is the good of it all? Our mind must acknowledge the Truth of the intellect, just as our heart does the Truth of love. No Congress or other outside institution succeeded in touching the heart of India. It was roused only by the touch of love. Having had such a clear vision of this wonderful power of Truth, are we to cease to believe in it, just where the attainment of *swaraj* is concerned? Has the Truth, which was needed in the process of awakenment, to be got rid of in the process of achievement?

Let me give an illustration. I am in search of a *vina* player. I have tried East and I have tried West, but have not found the man of my quest. They are all experts, they can make the strings resound to a degree, they command high prices, but for all their wonderful execution they can strike no chord in my heart. At last I come across one whose very first notes melt away the sense of oppression within. In him is the fire of the *shakti* of joy which can light up all other hearts by its touch. His appeal to me is instant and I hail him as Master. I then want a *vina* made. For this, of course are required all kinds of material and a different kind of science. If, finding me to be lacking in the means my master should be moved to pity and say: "Never mind, my son do not go to the expense in workmanship and time which a *vina* will require. Take rather this simple string tightened across a piece of wood and practise on it. In a short time you will find it to be as good as a *vina*." Would that do? I am afraid not. It would, in fact, be a mistaken kindness for the master thus to take pity on my circumstances. Far better if he were to tell me plainly that such things cannot be had cheaply. It is he who should teach me that merely one string will not serve for a true *vina*, that the materials required are many and various; that the lines of its moulding must be shapely and precise; that if there be anything faulty, it will fail to make good music, so that all laws of science and technique of art must be rigorously and intelligently followed. In short the true function of the master player should be to evoke a response from the depths of our heart, so that we may gain the strength to wait and work till the true end is achieved.

From our master, the Mahatma—may our devotion to him never grow less!—we must learn the truth of love in all its purity, but the science and art of building up *swaraj* is a vast subject. Its pathways are difficult to traverse and take time. For this task, aspiration and emotion must be there, but no less must study and thought be there likewise. For it, the economist must think, the mechanic must labour, the educationist and statesman must teach and contrive. In a word, the mind of the country must exert itself in all directions. Above all, the spirit of Inquiry throughout the whole country must be kept intact and untrammelled, its mind not made timid or inactive by compulsion open or secret.

We know from past experience that it is not any and every call to which the country responds. It is because no one has yet been able to unite in *yoga* all the forces of the country in the work of its creation, that so much time has been lost over and over again. And we have been kept waiting and waiting for him who has the right and the power to make the call upon us. In the old forests of India, our *gurus*, in the fullness of their vision of the truth had sent forth such a call saying: "As the rivers flow on their downward course, as the months flow on to the year, so let all seekers after Truth come from all sides". The initiation into Truth of that day has borne fruit, undying to this day, and the voice of its message still rings in the ears of the world.

Why should not our *guru* of today, who would lead us on the paths of *karma*, send forth such a call? Why should he not say: "Come ye from all sides and be welcome. Let all the forces of the land be brought into action, for then alone shall the country awake. Freedom is in complete awakening, in full self-expression." God has given the Mahatma the voice that can call, for in him there is the Truth. Why should this not be our long awaited opportunity?

But his call came to one narrow field alone. To one and all he simply says: "Spin and weave, spin and weave". Is this the call: "Let all seekers after Truth come from all sides"? Is this the call of the New Age to new creation? When nature called to the Bee to take refuge in the narrow life of the hive, millions of bees responded to it for the sake of efficiency, and accepted the loss of sex in consequence. But this sacrifice by way of self-atrophy led to the opposite of freedom. Any country, the people of which can agree to become neuters for the sake of some temptation, or command, carries within itself its own prison-house. To spin is easy, therefore for all men it is an imposition hard to bear. The call to the case efficiency is well enough for the Bee. The wealth of power, that is Man's, can only become manifest when his utmost is claimed.

Sparta tried to gain strength by narrowing herself down to a particular purpose, but she did not win. Athens sought to attain perfection by opening herself out in all her fullness, and she did win. Her flag of victory still flies at the masthead of man's civilisation. It is admitted that European military camps and

factories are stunting man, that their greed is cutting man down
to the measure of their own narrow purpose, that for these
reasons joylessness darkly lowers over the West. But if man be
stunted by big machines, the danger of his being stunted by small
machines must not be lost sight of. The *charkha* in its proper place
can do no harm but will rather do much good. But where, by
reasoned failure to acknowledge the differences in man's temperament it is in the wrong place, there thread can only be spun at
the cost of a great deal of the mind itself. Mind is no less valuable
than cotton thread.

Some are objecting: "We do not propose to curb our minds
for ever, but only for a time". But why should it be even for a
time? Is it because within a short time spinning will give us
swaraj? But where is the argument for this? *swaraj* is not concerned with our apparel only — it cannot be established on cheap
clothing; its foundation is in the mind, which, with its diverse
powers and its confidence in those powers, goes on all the time
creating *swaraj* for itself. In no country in the world is the building
up of *swaraj* completed. In some part or other of every nation,
some lurking greed or illusion still perpetuates bondage. And the
root of such bondage is always within the mind. Where then I ask
again, is the argument, that in our country *swaraj* can be brought
about by everyone engaging for a time in spinning? A mere
statement, in lieu of argument, will surely never do. If once we
consent to receive fate's oracles from human lips, that will add
one more to the torments of our slavery, and not the least one
either. If nothing but oracles will serve to move us, oracles will
have to be manufactured morning, noon and night, for the sake
of urgent needs, and all other voices would be defeated. Those for
whom authority is needed in place of reason, will invariably
accept despotism in place of freedom. It is like cutting at the root
of a tree while pouring water on the top. This is not a new thing
I know. We have enough of magic in the country—magical
revelation, magical healing, and all kinds of divine intervention
in mundane affairs. That is exactly why I am so anxious to re-
instate reason on its throne. As I have said before, God himself
has given the mind sovereignty in the material world. And I say
today that only those will be able to get and keep *swaraj* in the
material world who have realised the dignity of self-reliance and
self-mastery in the spiritual world, those whom no temptation,

no delusion, can induce to surrender the dignity of intellect into the keeping of others.

Consider the burning of cloth, heaped up before the very eyes of our motherland shivering and ashamed in her nakedness. What is the nature of the call to do this? Is it not another instance of a magical formula? The question of using or refusing cloth of a particular manufacture belongs mainly to economic science. The discussion of the matter by our countrymen should have been in the language of economics. If the country has really come to such a habit of mind that precise thinking has become impossible for it, then our very first fight should be against such a fatal habit, to the temporary exclusion of all else if need be. Such a habit would clearly be the original sin from which all our ills are flowing. But far from this, we take the course of confirming ourselves in it by relying on the magical formula that foreign cloth is 'impure'. Thus economics is bundled out and a fictitious moral dictum dragged into its place.

Untruth is impure in any circumstances, not merely because it may cause us material loss, but even when it does not; for it makes our inner nature unclean. This is a moral law and belongs to a higher plane. But if there be anything wrong in wearing a particular kind of cloth that would be an offence against economics, or hygiene, or aesthetics, but certainly not against morality. Some urge that any mistake which brings sorrow to body or mind is a moral wrong. To which I reply that sorrow follows in the train of every mistake. A mistake in geometry may make a road too long, or a foundation weak, or a bridge dangerous. But mathematical mistakes cannot be cured by moral maxims. If a student makes a mistake in his geometry problem and his exercise book is torn up in consequence the problem will nevertheless remain unsolved until attacked by geometrical methods. But what if the schoolmaster comes to the conclusion that unless the exercise books are condemned and destroyed, his boys will never realise the folly of their mistakes? If such conclusion be well-founded, then I can only repeat that the reformation of such moral weakness of these particular boys should take precedence over all other lessons, otherwise there is no hope of their becoming men in the future.

The command to burn our foreign clothes has been laid on us. I, for one, am unable to obey it. Firstly, because I conceive it to be my very first duty to put up a valiant fight against this terrible habit of blindly obeying orders, and this fight can never be carried on by our people being driven from one injunction to another. Secondly, I feel that the clothes to be burnt are not mine, but belong to those who most sorely need them. If those who are going naked should have given us the mandate to burn, it would, at least, have been a case of self-immolation and the crime of incendiarism would not lie at our door. But how can we expiate the sin of the forcible destruction of clothes which might have gone to women whose nakedness is actually keeping them prisoners unable to stir out of the privacy of their homes?

I have said repeatedly and must repeat once more that we cannot afford to lose our mind for the sake of any external gain. Where Mahatma Gandhi has declared war against the tyranny of the machine which is oppressing the whole world, we are all enrolled under his banner. But we must refuse to accept as our ally the illusion-haunted magic-ridden slave mentality that is at the root of all the poverty and insult under which our country groans. Here is the enemy itself on whose defeat alone *swaraj* within and without can come to us.

The time, moreover, has arrived when we must think of one thing more, and that is this. The awakening of India is a part of the awakening of the world. The door of the New Age has been flung open at the trumpet blast of a great war. We have read in the *Mahabharata* how the day of self-revelation had to be preceded by a year of retirement. The same has happened in the world today. Nations had attained nearness to each other without being aware of it, that is to say, the outside fact was there, but it had not penetrated into the mind. At the shock of the war, the truth of it stood revealed to mankind. The foundation of modern, that is Western, civilisation was shaken; and it has become evident that the convulsion is neither local nor temporary but has traversed the whole earth and will last until the shocks between man and man, which have extended from continent to continent, can be brought to rest, and a harmony be established.

From now onward, any nation which takes an isolated view of its own country will run counter to the spirit of the New Age, and know no peace. From now onward, the anxiety that each country has for its own safety must embrace the welfare of the world. For some time the working of the new spirit has occasionally shown itself even in the Government of India, which has had to make attempts to deal with its own problems in the light of the world problem. The war has torn away a veil from before our minds. What is harmful to the world, is harmful to each one of us. This was a maxim which we used to read in books. Now mankind has seen it at work and has understood that wherever there is injustice, even if the external right of possession is there, the true right is wanting. So that it is worthwhile even to sacrifice some outward right in order to gain the reality. This immense change, which is coming over the spirit of man raising it from the petty to the great is already at work even in Indian politics. There will doubtless be imperfections and obstacles without number. Self-interest is sure to attack enlightened interest at every step. Nevertheless it would be wrong to come to the decision that the working of self-interest alone is honest, and the larger-hearted striving is hypocritical.

After sixty years of self-experience, I have found that out and out hypocrisy is an almost impossible achievement, so that the pure hypocrite is a rarity indeed. The fact is, that the character of man has always more or less of duality in it. But our logical faculty, the trap-door of our mind, is unable to admit opposites together. So when we find the good with the bad, the former is promptly rejected as spurious. In the universal movement, as it becomes manifest in different parts of the world, this duality of man's character cannot but show itself. And whenever it does, if we pass judgment from past experience, we are sure to pronounce the selfish part of it to be the real thing; for the spirit of division and exclusion did in fact belong to the past age. But if we come to our judgment in the light of future promise, then shall we understand the enlightened large-heartedness to be the reality and the counsel which will unite each to each to be the true wisdom.

I have condemned, in unsparing terms, the present form and scope of the League of Nations and the Indian Reform Councils. I therefore feel certain that there will be no misunderstanding when I state that, even in these, I find signs of the Time Spirit, which is moving the heart of the West. Although the present form is unacceptable, yet there is revealed an aspiration, which is towards the Truth, and this aspiration must not be condemned. In this morning of the world's awakening, if in only

our own national striving there is no response to its universal
aspiration, that will betoken the poverty of our spirit. I do not say
for a moment that we should belittle the work immediately to
hand. But when the bird is roused by the dawn, all its awakening
is not absorbed in its search for food. Its wings respond
unweariedly to the call of the sky, its throat pours forth for songs,
for joy of the new light. Universal humanity has sent us its call
today. Let our mind respond in its own language for response is
the only true sign of life. When of old we were immersed in the
politics of dependence on others, our chief business was the
compilation of others' short-comings. Now that we have decided
to dissociate our politics from dependence, are we still to establish and maintain it on the same recital of others' sins? The state
of mind so engendered will only raise the dust of angry passion,
obscuring the greater world from our vision, and urge us more
and more to take futile short cuts for the satisfaction of our
passions. It is a sorry picture of India, which we shall display if
we fail to realise for ourselves the greater India. This picture
will have no light. It will have in the foreground only the business
side of our aspiration. Mere business talent, however, has
never created anything.

In the West, a real anxiety and effort of their higher mind to
rise superior to business considerations, is beginning to be seen.
I have come across many there whom this desire has imbued with
the true spirit of the *sannyasin*, making them renounce their
home-world in order to achieve the unity of man, by destroying
the bondage of nationalism; men who have within their own soul
realised the *Advaita* of humanity. Many such have I seen in
England who have accepted persecution and contumely from
their fellow countrymen in their struggles to free other people
from the oppression of their own country's pride of power. Some
of them are amongst us here in India. I have seen *sannyasins* too
in France—Romain Rolland for one, who is an outcast from his
own people. I have also seen them in the minor countries of
Europe. I have watched the faces of European students all aglow
with the hope of a united mankind, prepared manfully to bear all
the blows, cheerfully to submit to all the insults, of the present age
for the glory of the age to come. And are we alone to be content
with telling the beads of negation, harping on others' faults and
proceeding with the erosion of *swaraj* on a foundation of quarrel-

someness? Shall it not be our first duty in the dawn to remember Him, who is One, who is without distinction of class or colour, and who with his varied *shakti* makes true provision for the inherent need of each and every class; and to pray to the Giver of Wisdom to unite us all in right understanding:—

> *Yo ekovarno vahudha shakti yogat*
> *Varnanekan nihitarthodadhati*
> *Vichaiti chante vishwamadau*
> *Sa no buddhya subhaya samyunaktu!*

Rabindranath Tagore

16. The Great Sentinel

(The following article by Gandhi on Tagore and his criticism appeared in Young India *of 13 October 1921. It was in reply to 'The Call of Truth')*

The Bard of Santiniketan has contributed to the *Modern Review* a brilliant essay on the present movement. It is a series of word pictures which he alone can paint. It is an eloquent protest against authority, slave mentality or whatever description one gives of blind acceptance of a passing mania whether out of fear or hope. It is a welcome and wholesome reminder to all workers that we must not be impatient, we must not impose authority no matter how great. The poet tells us summarily to reject anything and everything that does not appeal to our reason or heart. If we would gain *swaraj* we must stand for Truth as we know it, at any cost. A reformer, who is enraged because his message is not accepted must retire to the forest to learn how to watch, wait and pray. With all this one must heartily agree, and the Poet deserves the thanks of his countrymen for standing up for Truth and Reason. There is no doubt that our last state will be worse than our first, if we surrender our reason into somebody's keeping. And I would feel extremely sorry to discover that the country had unthinkingly and blindly followed all I had said or done. I am quite conscious of the fact that blind surrender to love is often more mischievous than a forced surrender to the lash of the tyrant. There is hope for the slave of the brute, none for that of love. Love is needed to strengthen the weak, love becomes tyrannical when it exacts obedience from an unbeliever. To mutter a *mantra* without knowing its value is unmanly. It is good, therefore, that the Poet has invited all who are slavishly *mimicking* the call of the *charkha* boldly to declare their revolt. His essay serves as a warning to us all who in our impatience are betrayed into intolerance or even violence against those who differ from us. I regard the Poet as a sentinel warning us against the approaching enemies called Bigotry, Lethargy, Intolerance, Ignorance, Inertia and other members of that brood.

But whilst I agree with all that the Poet has said as of the necessity of watchfulness lest we cease to think, I must not be understood to endorse the proposition that there is any such blind obedience on a large scale in the country today. I have again and again appealed to reason, and let me assure him that if happily the country has come to believe in the spinning wheel as the giver of plenty, it has done so after laborious thinking, after great hesitation. I am not sure that even now educated India has assimilated the truth underlying the *charkha*. He must not mistake the surface dirt for the substance underneath. Let him go deeper and see for himself whether the *charkha* has been accepted from blind faith or from reasoned necessity.

I do indeed ask the poet and the sage to spin the wheel as a sacrament. When there is war, the poet lays down the lyre, the lawyer his law reports, the schoolboy his books. The poet will sing the true note after the war is over, the lawyer will have occasion to go to his law books when people have time to fight among themselves. When a house is on fire, *all* the inmates go out, and each one takes up a bucket to quench the fire. When all about me are dying for want of food, the only occupation permissible to me is to feed the hungry. It is my conviction that India is a house on fire because its manhood is being daily scorched, it is dying of hunger because it has no work to buy food with. Khulna is starving not because the people cannot work, but because they have no work. The Ceded Districts are passing successively through a fourth famine. Orissa is a land suffering from chronic famines. Our cities are *not* India. India lives in her seven and a half lacs of villages, and the cities live upon the villages. They do not bring their wealth from other countries. The city people are brokers and commission agents for the big houses of Europe, America and Japan. The cities have cooperated with the latter in the bleeding process that has gone on for the past two hundred years. It is my belief based on experience, that India is daily growing poorer. The circulation about her feet and legs has almost stopped. And if we do not take care, she will collapse altogether.

To a people famishing and idle, the only acceptable form in which God can dare appear is work and promise of food as wages. God created man to work for his food, and said that those who ate without work were thieves. Eighty percent of India are compulsorily thieves half the year. Is it any wonder if India has become one vast prison? Hunger is the argument that is driving India to the spinning wheel. The call of the spinning wheel is the noblest of all. Because it is the call of love. And love is *swaraj*. The spinning wheel will 'curb the mind' when the time is spent on necessary physical labour can be said to do so. We must think of millions who are today less than animals, who are almost in a dying state. The spinning wheel is the reviving draught for the millions of our dying countrymen and country-women. 'Why should I who have no need to work for food, spin?' may be the question asked. Because I am eating what does not belong to me. I am living on the spoilation of my countrymen. Trace the course of every pice that finds its way into your pocket, and you will realise the truth of what I write. *Swaraj* has no meaning for the millions if they do not know to employ their enforced idleness. The attainment of this *swaraj* is possible within a short time and it is so possible only by the revival of the spinning wheel.

I do want growth. I do want self-determination, I do want freedom, but I want all these for the soul. I doubt if the steel age is an advance upon the flint age. I am indifferent. It is the evolution of the soul to which the intellect and all our faculties have to be devoted. I have no difficulty in imagining the possibility of a man armoured after the modern style making some lasting and new discovery for mankind, but I have less difficulty in imagining the possibility of a man having nothing but a bit of flint and a dail for lighting his path or his matchlock ever singing new hymns of praise and delivering to an aching world a message of peace and goodwill upon earth. A plea for the spinning wheel is a plea for recognising the dignity of labour.

I claim that in losing the spinning wheel we lost our left lung. We are therefore suffering from galloping consumption.

The restoration of the wheel arrests the progress of the fell disease. There are certain things which all must do in all climes. The spinning wheel is the thing which all must turn in the Indian clime for the transition stage at any rate and the vast majority must for all time.

It was our love of foreign cloth that ousted the wheel from its position of dignity. Therefore I consider it a sin to wear foreign cloth. I must confess that I do not draw a sharp or any distinction between economics and ethics. Economics that hurt the moral well being of an individual or a nation are immoral and therefore sinful. Thus the economics that permit one country to prey upon another are immoral. It is sinful to buy and use articles made by sweated labour. It is sinful to eat American wheat and let my neighbour the grain dealer starve for want of custom. Similarly it is sinful for me to wear the latest finery of Regent Street, when I know that if I had but worn the things woven by the neighbouring spinners and weavers, that would have clothed me, and fed and clothed them. On the knowledge of my sin bursting upon me, I must consign the foreign garments to the flames and thus purify myself, and thenceforth rest content with the rough *khadi* made by my neighbours. On knowing that my neighbours may not having given up the occupation, take kindly to the spinning wheel, I must take it up myself and thus make it popular.

I venture to suggest to the Poet that the clothes I ask him to burn must be and are his. If they had to his knowledge belonged to the poor or the ill-clad, he would long ago have restored to the poor what was theirs. In burning *my* foreign clothes I burn my shame. I must refuse to insult the naked by giving them clothes they do not need, instead of giving them work which they sorely need. I will not commit the sin of becoming their patron, but on learning that I had assisted in impoverishing them, I would give them a privileged position and give them neither crumbs nor cast off clothing but the best of my food and clothes and associate myself with them in work.

Nor is the scheme of Non-cooperation or *swadeshi* an exclusive doctrine. My modesty has prevented me from declaring from the house top that the message of Non-cooperation, Non-violence and *swadeshi,* is a message to the world. It must fall flat, if it does not bear fruit in the soil where it has been delivered. At the present moment India has nothing to share with the world save her degradation, pauperism and plagues. Is it her ancient *shastras* that we should send to the world? Well they are printed in many editions, and an incredulous and idolatrous world refuses to look at them, because we, the heirs and custodians, do not live them. Before, therefore, I can think of sharing with the world, I must possess. Our Non-cooperation is neither with the English nor with the West. Our Non-cooperation is with the system the English have established, with the material civilisation and its attendant greed and exploitation of the weak. Our Non-cooperation is a retirement within ourselves. Our Non-cooperation is a refusal to co-operate with the English administrators on their own terms. We say to them, 'Come and co-operate with us on our terms, and it will be well for us, for you and the world.' We must refuse to be lifted off our feet. A drowning man cannot save others. In order to be fit to save others, we must try to save ourselves. Indian nationalism is not exclusive, nor aggressive, nor destructive. It is health giving, religious and therefore humanitarian. India must learn to live before she can aspire to die for humanity. The mice which helplessly find themselves between the cat's teeth acquire no merit from their enforced sacrifice.

True to his poetical instinct the Poet lives for the morrow and would have us do likewise. He presents to our admiring gaze the beautiful picture of the birds early in the morning singing hymns of praise as they soar into the sky. These birds had their day's food and soared with rested wings in whose veins new blood had flown during the previous night. But I have had the pain of watching birds who for want of strength could not be coaxed even into a flutter of their wings. The human bird under the Indian sky gets up weaker than when he pretended to retire. For millions it is an eternal vigil or an eternal trance. It is an indescribably painful state which has to be experienced to be realised. I have found it impossible to soothe suffering patients with a song from Kabir. The hungry millions ask for one poem—invigorating food. They cannot be given it. They must earn it. And they can earn only by the sweat of their brow.

Niyatham kuru karmathvam karmajyaayohyakarmanah:

. . . .

Yagnyaarthaath karmanonyathra lokoyam karmabandhanah: (8)
Thadarttham karma Kountheya mukthasanga: samachara   (9)
Saha yagnaah: prajaah srishtva purovaacha prajaapathihi:

Arena prasavishyaddvamesha Voasthishtakaamaddhuk   (10)
Devaanbhaavayathaanena the devaabhaavayanthu vah:
Parasparam bhaavayanthah: sreyah: paramavaapsyattha   (11)
Ishtaanbhogaanhivodevaa daasyanthe yagnyabhaavithaah:
Thairdattaanapradayaibhyo yo bhungthe sthena eva sah: (12)
Yagnasishtaasinah: santho mutchyamte sarvakilbishaii:
Bhujamthe the thvagham paapaa ye pachanthyaathmakaranaath   (13)
Annaathbhavanthi dhuthaani parjanyaadannrsambhavah:
Yagnyaathbhavathi parajanyo yagnah: karmasamudbhavah: (14)
Karma brahmoobhavam viddhi brahmaaksharasamudbhavam
Thasmaathsarvagatham brahma nithyma yagne prathishtitham   (15)
Evam pravarthitham chakram naanuvarthayathiiha yah:
Aghaayurindriyaaraamo mogham paarttha sa jiivathi   (16)

Gita (Chapter III)

In these verses is contained for me the whole truth of the spinning wheel as an indispensable sacrament for the India of to-day. If we will take care of to day, God will take care of the morrow.

M.K. Gandhi

PART II

1923–1928

1923–1928

Notes on Documents

Upon Gandhi's release from imprisonment in February 1924, in fact on the day of his release, Tagore sent him a cable, "we rejoice" and followed this with a letter proposing to send their mutual friend C.F. Andrews to Pune to meet Gandhi. (Document 1, 2). Gandhi was at the Sassoon Hospital—the name is misspelt in the cable—to undergo appendectomy. Tagore seems to have invited Gandhi to Santiniketan, for Gandhi acknowledges that (Document 3): it is not known whether the invitation was through some personal emissary or by letter—no letter is traceable.

Soon after this, in late 1925, Tagore resumed his debate with Gandhi— a debate which he had suspended while Gandhi was in prison. Tagore published in a Bengali literary journal *Sabuj-Patra* an article entitled '*Charkha*' which was promptly translated into English under the title 'The Cult of the *Charkha*' in the *Modern Review* in September 1925 (Document 6). Next month he wrote '*Swaraj-Sadhan*' in the same Bengali journal, and this too appeared in the *Modern Review* (Document 7). Gandhi considered a reply for quite some time till November 1925 when he wrote the essay 'The Poet and the *Charkha*' and again in March 1926 'The Poet and the Wheel' in *Young India* (Documents 6, 7).

It appears that in some circles Gandhi's reference to Tagore as "Sir Rabindranath" and his allusion to "jealousy" caused surprise and dismay. Documents 4 and 5 relate to this. By themselves the letters do not tell the tale; it is equally unedifying to read in the *Collected Works of Mahatma Gandhi* (XXIX, p.376): "I am thankful for your sweet letter. It has given me much relief. M.K. Gandhi." To understand what this letter is about one has to read Tagore's letter (Document 4) which Gandhi thus acknowledges. And further, Tagore's letter is itself an acknowledgement of Gandhi's letter to Vidhusekhar Sastry. It transpires that Gandhi, upon learning of the dismay caused by his

reference to "Sir Rabindranath" etc., wrote to Sastry, the doyen
of the Santiniketan Faculty, a word of explanation in the hope that
it would be conveyed to Tagore. "I can but explain my position
and ask every friend in Shantiniketan [sic: Gandhi always preferred this spelling contrary to the habit of Santiniketanis] to
accept my explanation.... And will you get an assurance from the
Poet that he at least did not misunderstand me?" (Gandhi to
Shastri Mahashay, 21 Dec. 1925, CWMG, XXIX, p.341). Gandhi's
explanation was that "Sir Rabindranath" was written automatically without forethought, and that "he had not renounced the
title but had asked to be relieved of it. He was not so relieved."
Thus no taunt was intended. "As to jealousy let R. Babu
[Ramananda Chatterjee] and the other friends know that not one
but several Bengali friends and some Gujarati friends and even
others mentioned the matter in that light. Let me also add that I
tried to disabuse them of the prejudice." Upon seeing this letter
of explanation Tagore hastily wrote to Gandhi (Document 4) that
he could take a knock or two if Gandhi thought that was needed
"in the cause of what you think as truth." It is to this that Gandhi
responds when he writes about Tagore's sweet letter which
brought him "much relief." (Document 5; or CWMG, XXIX,
p.376).

A few weeks after this Gandhi answered a correspondent in
Young India who had asked about the "many matters" on which
Dr. Tagore and Mr. Gandhi differed. "I have not differed from
Dr. Tagore in many matters. There are certainly differences of
opinion between us in some matters. It would be strange if there
were none.... Indeed the friendship between us is all the richer
and truer for the intellectual differences between us." (Young
India, 25 February 1926).

EDITOR

1. Tagore's telegram after Gandhi's release from prison

Santiniketan,
5.2.1924

To: Mahatma Gandhi Sasoon hospital Poona
    We Rejoice

Rabindranath

2. Tagore sends Andrews to Gandhi

Santiniketan,
20 February 1924

Dear Mahatmaji,

I do not want to dwell upon my joy at the fact of your freedom from imprisonment but I cannot remain silent and inactive when I feel great anxiety at the unbounded prospect of freedom which other people have in wrecking your health and peace of mind. All I can do to serve you in this crisis is to send Charlie to keep you company and help you as only he knows how to do with love,

Rabindranath Tagore

3. Gandhi plans a visit to Santiniketan

(The original letter in Gandhi's own hand is on a postcard bearing the postmark: "Dadar, 18 May 25".)

18.5.25

Dear Gurudev,

Nepal Babu has sent me your very kind and cordial note. I do want to pass a day or two at Bolpur. I would not think of your leaving Bolpur to meet me. I know the delicate state of your health. I shall inform you of the date when I can come.

I am
Yours,
M.K. Gandhi

4. Tagore on his personal relationship with Gandhi

(A handwritten copy of the letter)

Santiniketan,
Bengal, India
27 December 1925

Dear Mahatmaji,

I have seen the letter you have written to our Shastrimahashaya. It is full of your noble spirit. You have my assurance that even if you ever hit me hard in the cause of what you think as truth our personal relationships based upon mutual respect will bear that strain and will remain uninjured.

With Namaskar

Rabindranath Tagore
(in Bengali)

5. Gandhi's letter of acknowledgement

(The original letter is in Gandhi's own hand)

Sabarmati,
3:1:26

Dear Gurudev,

I am thankful for your sweet letter. It has given me much relief.

Yours sincerely,
M.K. Gandhi

6. Tagore's essay, 'The Cult of the Charkha'

(Tagore's contribution to the controversy on 'The Cult of the Charkha', which appeared in Modern Review *on September 1925)*

Acharya Prafulla Chandra Ray has marked me with his censure in printer's ink, for that I have been unable to display enthusiasm in the turning of the *charkha*. But, because it is impossible for him to be pitiless to me even when awarding punishment, he has provided me with a companion in my ignominy in the illustrious person of Acharya Brajendra Nath Seal. That has taken away the pain of it and also given me fresh proof of the eternal human truth, that we are in agreement with some people and with some others we are not. It only proves that while creating man's mind, God did not have for his model the spider mentality doomed to a perpetual conformity in its production of web and that it is an outrage upon human nature to force it through a mill and reduce it to some stardardised commodity of uniform size and shape and purpose.

When in my younger days I used to go boating on the river, the boatmen of Jagannath Ghat would swarm around, each pressing on me the service of his own particular vessel. My selection once made, however, there would be no further trouble; for, if the boats were many so were the passengers, and the places to go to were likewise various. But suppose one of the boats had been specially hall-marked, as the one and only sacred ferry by some dream emanating from the shrine of Tarakeswar, then indeed it would have been difficult to withstand the extortions of its touts, despite the inner conviction of the travellers that though the shore opposite may be one, its landing places are many and diversely situated

Our *shastras* tell us that the divine *shakti* is many-sided so that a host of different factors operate in the work of creation. In death these merge into sameness; for chaos alone is uniform. God has given to man the same many-sided *shakti* for which reason the civilisation of his creation have their divine wealth of diversity. It is God's purpose that in the societies of man the various should be strung together into a garland of unity; while often the mortal providence of our public life, greedy for particular results, seeks to knead them all into a lump of uniformity. That is why we see in the concerns of this world so many identically liveried, machine-made workers, so many marionettes pulled by the same string, and on the other hand, where the human spirit has not been reduced to the coldness of collapse, we also see perpetual rebelliousness against this mechanical mortar pounded homogeneity.

If in any country we find no symptom of such rebellion, if we find its people submissively or contentedly prone on the dust, in dumb terror of some master's bludgeon, or blind acceptance of some *guru's* injunction, then indeed should we know that for such a country, *in extremis*, it is high time to mourn.

In our country, this ominous process of being levelled down into sameness has long been at work. Every individual of every caste has his function assigned to him, together with the obsession into which he has been hypnotised, that, since he is bound by some divine mandate, accepted by his first ancestor, it would be sinful for him to seek relief therefrom. This imitation of the social scheme of ant-life makes very easy the performance of petty routine duties, but specially difficult the attainment of manhood's estate. It imparts skill to the limbs of the man who is a bondsman, whose labour is drudgery; but it kills the mind of a man who is a doer, whose work is creation. So in India, during long ages past, we have the spectacle of only a repetition of that which has gone before.

In the process of this continuous grind India has acquired a distaste for very existence. In dread of the perpetuation of this same grind, through the eternal repetition of births, she is ready to intern all mental faculties in absolute inaction in order to cut at the root of *Karma* itself. For only too well has she realised, in the dreary round of her daily habit the terribleness of this everlasting recapitulation. Moreover, this dreariness is not the only loss sustained by those who have suffered themselves to be reduced to a machinelike existence; for they have also lost all power to combat aggression or exploitation. From age to age, they have been assaulted by the strong, defrauded by the cunning and deluded by the *gurus* to whom their conscience was surrendered. Such a state of abject passivity has become easy because of the teaching that through an immutable decree of providence, they have been set adrift on the sea of Time, upon the raft of monotonous living death, burdened with a vocation that makes no allowance for variation in human nature.

But whatever our *shastras* may or may not have said, this popular conception of the Creator's doing is the very opposite of what he really did do to man at the moment of his creation. Instead of furnishing him with an automatically revolving grindstone—God slipped into his constitution that most lively sprightly thing called Mind. And unless man can be made to get rid of this mind it will remain impossible to convert him into a machine. In so far as the men at the top succeeded in paralysing the people's minds by fear—or greed or hypnotic texts, they succeeded in extorting—from one class of them, only textiles from their looms; from another class, only pots from their wheels; from a third, only oil from their mills. Now when from such persons as these it becomes necessary to demand the application of their mind to any big work on hand, they stand aghast, "Mind!" cry they, "What on earth is that? Why don't you order us what to do and give some text for us to repeat from mouth to mouth and age to age?"

Our mind, in doing duty only as a hedge to prevent the encroachment of living ideas, had been kept evenly clipped short for the purpose. If, in spite of that, in this age of self-assertion, we find mischievous branches trying to make room for the disturbance of the spruceness of the trimming,—if all over minds refuse incessantly to reverberate some one set *mantram*, in the droning chirp of the cicadas of the night,—let no one be annoyed or alarmed; for only because of this does the attainment of *swaraj* become thinkable!

That is why I am not ashamed,—though there is every reason to be afraid,—to admit that the depths of my mind have not been moved by the *charkha* agitation. This may be counted by many as sheer presumption on my part, they may even wax abusive; for swearing is a much needed relief for the feelings when even one stray fish happens to elude the all-embracing net. Still, I cannot help doing that there are others who are in the same plight as myself,—though it is difficult to find them all out. For even where hands are reluctant to work the spindle, mouths are all the more busy spinning its praises.

I am strongly of opinion that all intense pressure of persuasion brought upon the crowd psychology is unhealthy for it. Some strong and wide-spread intoxication of belief among a vast number of men can suddenly produce a convenient uniformity of purpose, immense and powerful. It seems for the moment a miracle of a wholesale conversion; and a catastrophic phenomenon of this nature stuns our rational mind, raising high some hope of easy realisation which is very much like a boom in the business market. The amazingly immediate success is no criterion of its reality,—the very dimension of its triumph having a dangerous effect of producing a sudden and universal eclipse of our judgment. Human nature has its elasticity; and in the name of urgency, it can be forced towards a particular direction far beyond its normal and wholesome limits. But the rebound is sure to follow, and the consequent disillusionment will leave behind it a desert track of demoralisation. We have had our experience of this in the tremendous exultation lately produced by the imaginary easy prospect of Hindu-Muslim unity. And therefore I am afraid of a blind faith on a very large scale in the *charkha*, in the country, which is so liable to succumb to the lure of short cuts when pointed out by a personality about whose moral earnestness they can have no doubt.

Anyhow what I say is this. If, today, poverty has come upon our country, we should know that the root cause is complexly ramified and it dwells within ourselves. For the whole country to fall upon only one of its external symptoms with the application of one and the same remedy will not serve to fight the demon away. If man had been a mindless image of stone, a defect in his features might have been cured with hammer and chisel; but when his shrunken features bespeak vital poverty, the cure must be constitutional, not formal; and repeated hammer strokes upon some one particular external point will only damage that same life still more.

In the days when our country had to bear the brunt of Mughal and Pathan—the little jerry-built edifices of Hindu sovereignty fell to pieces on every side. There was then no dearth of home-spun thread, but that did not serve to bind these into stability. And, yet, in those days there was no economic antagonism between the people and their rulers. The throne of the latter was established on the soil of the country, so that the ripe fruits fell to the ground where the trees stood. Can it then be today— when we have not one or two kings—but a veritable flood of them sweeping away our life-stuffs across the seas away from our motherland, causing it to lose both its fruits and its fertility,—can it be, I say, that the lack of sufficient thread prevents our stemming this current? Is it not rather our lack of vitality, our lack of union?

Some will urge that though in the days of Mughal and Pathan we had not sovereign power, we had at least a sufficiency of food and clothing. When the river is not flowing, it may be possible to bank up little pools in its bed to hold water enough for our needs, conveniently at hand for each. But can such banks guarding our scanty economic resources for local use withstand the shocks which come upon it today from far and near? No longer will it be possible to hide ourselves away from commerce with the outside world. Moreover such isolation itself would be the greatest of deprivations for us. If, therefore, we cannot rouse the forces of our mind, in adequate strength to take our due part in this traffic of exchanging commodities, our grain will continue to be consumed by others, leaving only the chaff as our own portion. In Bengal we have a nursery rhyme which soothes the infant with the assurance that it will get the lollipop if only it twirls its hands. But is it a likely policy to reassure grown up people by telling them that they will get their *swaraj*,—that is to say, get rid of all poverty, in spite of their social habits that are a perpetual impediment and mental habits producing inertia of intellect and will,—by simply twirling away with their hands? No. If we have to get rid of this poverty which is visible outside, it can only be done by rousing our inward forces of wisdom of fellowship and mutual trust which make for cooperation.

But, it may be argued, does not external work react on the mind? It does, only if it has its constant suggestions to our intellect, which is the master, and not merely its commands for our muscles, which are slaves. In this clerk-ridden country, for instance, we all know that the routine of clerkship is not mentally stimulating. By doing the same thing day after day mechanical skill may be acquired; but the mind like a mill-turning bullock will be kept going round and round a narrow range of habit. That is why, in every country man has looked down on work which involves this kind of mechanical repetition. Carlyle may have proclaimed the dignity of labour in his stentorian accents, but a still louder cry has gone up from humanity, age after age, testifying to its indignity. "The wise man sacrifices the half to avert a total loss"—so says our Sanskrit proverb. Rather than die of starvation, one can understand a man preferring to allow his mind to be killed. But it would be a cruel joke to try to console him by talking of the dignity of such sacrifice.

In fact, humanity has ever been beset with the grave problem, how to rescue the large majority of the people from being reduced to the stage of machines. It is my belief that all the civilisations, which have ceased to be, have come by their death when the mind of the majority got killed under some pressure by the minority; for the truest wealth of man is his mind. No amount of respect outwardly accorded, can save man from the inherent ingloriousness of labour divorced from mind. Only those who feel that they have become inwardly small can be belittled by others, and the numbers of the higher castes have ever dominated over those of the lower, not because they have any accidental advantage of power, but because the latter are themselves humbly conscious of their dwarfed humanity. If the cultivation of science by Europe has any moral significance, it is in its rescue of man from outrage by nature, not its use of man as a machine but its use of the machine to harness the forces of nature in man's service. One thing is certain, that the all-embracing poverty which has overwhelmed our country cannot be removed by working with our hands to the neglect of science. Nothing can be more undignified drudgery than that man's knowing should stop dead and his doing go on for ever.

It was a great day for man when he discovered the wheel. The facility of motion thus given to inert matter enabled it to bear much of man's burden. This was but right, for Matter is the true *shudra*; while with his dual existence in body and mind, Man is a *dwija*. Man has to maintain both his inner and outer life. Whatever functions he cannot perform by material means are left as an additional burden on himself, bringing him to this extent down to the level of matter, and making him a *shudra*. Such *shudras* cannot obtain glory by being merely glorified in words.

Thus, whether in the shape of the spinning wheel, or the potter's wheel or the wheel of a vehicle, the wheel has rescued innumerable men from the *shudra's* estate and lightened their burdens. No wealth is greater than this lightening of man's material burdens. This fact man has realised ever more and more, since the time when he turned his first wheel; for his wealth has thereupon gone on compounding itself in ever-increasing rotation, refusing to be confined to the limited advantage of the original *charkha*.

Is there no permanent truth underlying these facts? One aspect of Vishnu's *shakti* is the *Padma*, the beautiful lotus; another is the *Chakra*, the movable discus. The one is the complete ideal of perfection, the other is the process of movement, the ever active power seeking fulfillment. When man attained touch with this moving *shakti* of Vishnu, he was liberated from that inertia which is the origin of all poverty. All divine power is infinite. Man has not yet come to the end of the power of the revolving wheel. So, if we are taught that in the pristine *charkha* we have exhausted all the means of spinning thread, we shall not gain the full favour of Vishnu. Neither will his spouse Lakshmi smile on us. When we forget that science is spreading the domain of Vishnu's *chakra*, those who have honoured the Discus-Bearer to better purpose will spread their dominion over us. If we are wilfully blind to the grand vision of whirling forces, which science has revealed, the *charkha* will cease to have any message for us. The hum of the spinning wheel, which once carried us so long a distance on the path of wealth, will no longer talk to us of progress.

Some have protested that they never preached that only the turning of the *charkha* should be engaged in. But they have not spoken of any other necessary work. Only one means of attaining *swaraj* has been definitely ordered and the rest is a vast silence. Does not such silence amount to a speech stronger than any uttered word? Is not the *charkha* thrust out against the background of this silence into undue prominence? Is it really so big as all that? Has it really the divinity which may enable it to appropriate the single-minded devotion of all the millions of India, despite their diversity of temperament and talent? Repeated efforts, even unto violence and bloodshed, have been made, all the world over, to bring mankind together on the basis of the common worship of a common Deity, but even these have not been successful. Neither has a common God been found, nor a common form of worship. Can it then be expected that, in the shrine of *swaraj*, the *charkha* goddess will attract to herself alone the offerings of every devotee? Surely such expectation amounts to a distrust of human nature, a disrespect for India's people.

In my childhood, I had an up-country servant, called Gopee, who used to tell us how once he went to Puri on a pilgrimage, and was at a loss what fruit to offer to Jagannath, since any fruit so offered could not be eaten by him any more. After repeatedly going over the list of edible fruits known to him he suddenly bethought himself of the tomato (which had very little fascination for him) and the tomato it was which he offered, never having reason to repent of such clever abnegation. But to call upon man to make the easiest of offerings to the smallest of gods is the greatest of insults to his manhood. To ask all the millions of our people to spin the *charkha* is as bad as offering the tomato to Jagannath. I do hope and trust that there are not thirty-three crores of Gopees in India. When man receives the call of the great to make some sacrifice, he is indeed exalted; for then he comes to himself with a start of revelation,—to find that he too has been bearing his hidden resources of greatness.

Our country is the land of rites and ceremonials, so that we have more faith in worshipping the feet of the priest than the Divinity whom he serves. We cannot get rid of the conviction that we can safely cheat our inner self of its claims, if we can but bribe some outside agency. This reliance on outward help is a symptom of slavishness, for no habit can more easily destroy all reliance on self. Only to such a country can come the *charkha* as the emblem of her deliverance and the people dazed into obedience by some spacious temptation go on turning their *charkha* in the seclusion of their corners, dreaming all the while that the car of *swaraj* of itself rolls onward in triumphal progress at every turn of their wheel.

And so it becomes necessary to restate afresh the old truth that the foundation of *swaraj* cannot be based on any external conformity, but only on the internal union of hearts. If a great union is to be achieved, its field must be great likewise. But if out of the whole field of economic endeavour only one fractional portion be selected for special concentration thereon, then we may get home-spun thread, and even genuine *khaddar*, but we shall not have united, in the pursuit of one great complete purpose, the lives of our countrymen.

In India, it is not possible for every one to unite in the realm of religion. The attempt to unite on the political platform is of recent growth and will yet take long to permeate the masses. So that the religion of economics is where we should above all try to bring about this union of ours. It is certainly the largest field available to us; for here high and low, learned and ignorant, and all have their scope. If this field ceases to be one of warfare, if there we can prove, that not competition but cooperation is the real truth, then indeed we can reclaim from the hands of the Evil One an immense territory for the reign of peace and goodwill. It is important to remember, moreover, that this is the ground whereon our village communities had actually practised unity in the past. What if the thread of the old union has snapped? It may again be joined together, for such former practice has left in our character the potentiality of its renewal.

As is livelihood for the individual, so is politics for a particular people,—a field for the exercise of their business instincts of patriotism. All this time, just as business has implied antagonism so has politics been concerned with the self-interest of a pugnacious nationalism. The forging of arms and of false documents has been its main activity. The burden of competitive armaments has been increasing apace, with no end to it in sight, no peace for the world in prospect.

When it becomes clear to man that in the co-operation of nations lies the true interest of each,—for man is established in mutuality—then only can politics become a field for true endeavour. Then will the same means which the individual recognises as moral and therefore true, be also recognised as such by the nations. They will know that cheating, robbery and the exclusive pursuit of self-aggrandisement are as harmful for the purposes of this world as they are deemed to be for those of the next. It may be that the League of Nations will prove to be the first step in the process of this realisation.

Again, just as the present day politics is a manifestation of extreme individualism in nations, so is the process of gaining a livelihood an expression of the extreme selfishness of individuals. That is why man has descended to such depths of deceit and cruelty in his indiscriminate competition. And yet, since man is man, even in his business he ought to have cultivated his human-ity rather than the powers of exploitation. In working for his livelihood he ought to have earned not only his daily bread but also his eternal truth.

When, years ago, I first became acquainted with the principles of cooperation in the field of business, one of the knots of a tangled problem, which had long perplexed my mind seemed to have been unravelled, I felt that the separateness of self-interest, which had so long contemptuously ignored the claims of the truth of man was at length to be replaced by a combination of common interests which would help to uphold that truth, proclaiming that poverty lay in the separation, and wealth in the union of man and man. For myself I had never believed that this original truth of man could find its limit in any region of his activity.

The cooperative principle tells us, in the field of man's livelihood, that only when he arrives at his truth can he get rid of his poverty,—not by any external means. And the manhood of man is at length honoured by the enunciation of this principle. Cooperation is an ideal, not a mere system, and therefore it can give rise to innumerable methods of its application. It leads us into no blind alley; for at every step it communes with our spirit. And so, it seemed to me, in its wake would come, not merely food, but the goddess of plenty herself, in whom all kinds of material food are established in an essential moral oneness.

It was while some of us were thinking of the ways and means of adopting this principle in our institution that I came across the book called *The National Being* written by that Irish idealist, A. E. who has a rare combination in himself of poetry and practical wisdom. There I could see a great concrete realisation of the co-operative living of my dreams. It became vividly clear to me what varied results could flow therefrom, how full the life of man could be made thereby. I could understand how great the concrete truth was in any plane of life, the truth that in separation is bondage, in union is liberation. It has been said in the *Upanishad* that *Brahma* is reason, *Brahma* is spirit but *Anna* also is *Brahma*, which means that food also represents an internal truth, and therefore through it we may arrive at a great realisation, if we travel along the true path.

I know there will be many to tax me with indicating a solution of great difficulty. To give concrete shape to the ideal of cooperation on so vast a scale will involve endless toil in experiment and failure, before at length it may become an accomplished fact. No doubt it is difficult. Nothing great can be got cheap. We only cheat ourselves when we try to acquire things

that are precious with a price that is inadequate. The problem of
our poverty being complex, with its origin in our ignorance and
unwisdom, in the inaptitude of our habits, the weakness of our
character, it can only be effectively attacked by taking in hand
our life as a whole and finding both internal and external
remedies for the malady which afflicts it. How can there be an
easy solution?

There are many who assert and some who believe that
swaraj can be attained by the *charkha*; but I have yet to meet a
person who has a clear idea of the process. That is why there is
no discussion, but only quarreling over the question. If I state that
it is not possible to repel foreign invaders armed with guns and
cannons by the indigenous bow and arrow, there will I suppose
be still some to contradict me asking, 'Why not?' It has already
been said by some, "Would not the foreigners be drowned even
if every one of our three hundred and thirty millions were only
to spit at them?" While not denying the fearsomeness of such a
flood, or the efficacy of such a suggestion, for throwing odium on
foreign military science, the difficulty which my mind feels to be
insuperable is that you can never get all these millions even to spit
in unison. It is too simple for human beings. The same difficulty
applies to the *charkha* solution.

The disappointments, the failures, the recommencements
that Sir Horace Plunkett had to face when he set to work to apply
the cooperative principle in the economic reconstruction of Ireland, are a matter of history. But though it takes time to start a
fire, once alight it spreads rapidly. That is the way with truth as
well. In whatever corner of the earth it may take root, the range
of its seeds is world wide, and everywhere they may find soil for
growth and give of their fruit to each locality. Sir Horace Plunkett's
success was not confined to Ireland alone; he achieved also the
possibility of success for India. If any true devotee of our motherland should be able to eradicate the poverty of only one of her
villages, he will have given permanent wealth to the thirty three
crores of his countrymen. Those who are wont to measure truth
by its size get only an outside view and fail to realise that each
seed, in its tiny vital spark, brings divine authority to conquer the
whole world.

As I am writing this, a friend objects that even though I may
be right in thinking that the *charkha* is not competent to bring us

swaraj, or remove the whole of our poverty, why ignore such virtues as it admittedly possesses? Every farmer, every house-holder, has a great deal of leisure left over after his ordinary work is done; so that if everyone would utilise such spare time in productive work much could be done towards the alleviation of our poverty. Why not glorify the *charkha* as one of the instruments of such a desirable consummation? This reminds me of a similar proposition I have heard before. Most of our people throw away the water in which their rice is boiled. If everyone conserved this nutritious fluid that would go a long way to solve the food problem. I admit there is truth in this contention. The slight change of taste required for eating boiled rice with its water retained should not be very difficult to acquire, in view of the object sought to be gained. Many other similar savings could be effected which are doubtless worth the effort and should be looked upon as a duty. But has any one ever suggested that the conservation of rice-water should be made a plank in the platform of *swaraj* work? And is there no good reason for the omission?

In order to make my point clear, let me take an instance from the case of religion. If a preacher should repeatedly and insistently urge that the drinking of water from any and every well is the cause of the degeneracy of our religion, then the chief objection to his teaching would be its tendency to debase the value of moral action as a factor in religion. No doubt there is the chance of some well or other containing impure water; impure water destroys health; a diseased body begets a diseased mind; and therefore spiritual welfare is in danger. I am not concerned to dispute the truth in all this, yet I must repeat that to give undue value to the comparatively unimportant, lowers the value of the important. And so we find that there are numbers of Hindus who would not hesitate even to kill a Mohamedan if he came to draw water from their own well. If the small be put on an equal footing with the big, it is not content to rest there, but needs must push its way higher up. That is how the injunction: "Thou shalt not drink dubious water" gets the better of the commandment, "Thou shalt not kill". There is no end to the perversions of value which have become habituated to their facile intrusion that no one is surprised to see the *charkha* stalk the land, with uplifted club, in the garb of *swaraj* itself. The *charkha* is doing harm because of the undue prominence, which it has thus usurped whereby it only adds fuel to the smouldering weakness that is eating into our vitals. Suppose some mighty voice should next proclaim that the rice water must not be suffered to enter our councils. Given requisite forcefulness that may lead to the flow of rice water being followed by the flow of human blood, in the sacred name of political purity. If the idea of the impurity of foreign textiles should effect a lodgement in our mind along with the numerous fixed ideas already there, in regard to the impurity of certain food and waters, the Id riots, to which we are accustomed, might pale before the sanguinary strife that may eventually be set ablaze between the so-called unclean lot who may use foreign cloth and those politically pure souls who do not. The danger to my mind is that the contagion of "untouchability", which was hitherto confined to our society, may extend to the economic and political spheres as well.

Some one whispers to me that to combine in *charkha* spinning is cooperation itself. I beg to disagree. If all the higher caste people of the Hindu community combine in keeping their well water undefiled from use of the lower ones this practice in itself does not give it the dignity of Bacteriology. It is a particular action isolated from the comprehensive vision of this science. And therefore while we keep our wells reserved for the cleaner sect, we allow our ponds to get polluted, the ditches round our houses to harbour messengers of death. Those who intimately know Bengal also know that at the time of preparing a special kind of pickle our women take extra precaution in keeping themselves clean. In fact they go through a kind of ceremonial of ablution and other forms of purifications. For such extra care their pickle survives the ravage of time, while their villages are devastated by epidemics. For while there may remain some Pasteur's law invisible at the depth of this pickle-making precaution, the diseased spleens in the neighbourhood make themselves only too evident by their magnitude. The universal application of Pasteur's law in the production of pickle has some similarity to the application of the principle of a cooperation method of livelihood in turning the spinning wheel. It may produce enormous quantity of yarn, but the blind suppression of intellect which guards our poverty in its dark dungeon will remain inviolate. This narrow activity will shed light only upon one detached piece of fact keeping its great background of truth densely dark.

It is extremely distasteful to me to have to differ from Mahatma Gandhi in regard to any matter of principle or method. Not that, from a higher standpoint, there is anything wrong in so doing; but my heart shrinks from it. For what could be a greater joy than to join hands in the field of work with one for whom one has such love and reverence? Nothing is more wonderful to me than Mahatmaji's great moral personality. In him divine providence has given us a burning thunderbolt of *shakti*. May this *shakti* give power to India,—not overwhelm her,—that is my prayer! The difference in our standpoints and temperaments has made the Mahatma look upon Rammohun Roy as a pygmy—while I revere him as a giant. The same difference makes the Mahatma's field of work one which my conscience cannot accept as its own. That is a regret which will abide with me always. It is, however, God's will that man's paths of endeavour shall be various, else why these differences of mentality. How often have any personal feelings of regard strongly urged me to accept at Mahatma Gandhi's hands my enlistment as a follower of the *charkha* cult, but as often have my reason and conscience restrained me, lest I should be a party to the raising of the *charkha* to a higher place than is its due, thereby distracting attention from other more important factors in our task of all-round reconstruction. I feel sure that Mahatma himself will not fail to understand me, and keep for me the same forbearance which he has always had. Acharya Roy, I also believe, has respect for independence of opinion, even when unpopular; so that, although when carried away by the fervour of his own propaganda he may now and then give me a scolding, I doubt not he retains for me a soft corner in his heart. As for my countrymen the public,—accustomed as they are to drown, under the facile flow of their minds, both past services and past disservices done to them,—if today they cannot find it in their hearts to forgive, they will forget tomorrow. Even if they do not,—if for me their displeasure is fated to be permanent, then just as today I have Acharya Seal as my fellow culprit, so tomorrow I may find at my side persons rejected by their own country whose reliance reveals the black unreality of any stigma of popular disapprobation.

Rabindranath Tagore

7. Striving for *Swaraj*

(In the September 1925 issue of Modern Review, *Tagore raised some more questions about* Charkha *and* Swaraj)

Our wise men have warned us, in solemn accents of Sanskrit, to talk away as much as we like, but never to write it down. There are proofs,—many of them,—that I have habitually disregarded this sage advice, following it only when called upon to reply. I have never hesitated to write, whenever I had anything to say, be it in prose or in verse, controversy alone excepted,—for on that my pen has long ceased to function.

Such of our beliefs as become obsessions are hardly ever made up of pure reason,—our temperament, or moods of the moment, mainly go to their fashioning. It is but rarely that we believe, because we have found a good reason. We most often seek reasons because we believe. Only in Science do our conclusions follow upon strict proofs; while the rest of them, under the influence of our attractions and repulsions, keep circling round the centre of our personal predilections. This is all the more true when our belief is the outcome of a desire for some particular result especially when that desire is shared by a large number of our fellow men. In such case no reason needs to be adduced in order to persuade people into a common course,— it being sufficient if such course is fairly easy, and, above all, if the hope is roused of speedy success.

It is some time since the minds of our countrymen have been kept in a state of agitation by the idea that *swaraj* may be easily and speedily attained, in this unsettled atmosphere of popular excitement any attempt at a discussion of pros and cons does but bring down a cyclonic storm, in which it becomes almost hopeless to expect the vessel of reason to make sail for any part of destination. Hitherto, we had always thought that the achievement of *swaraj* was a difficult matter. So, when it came to our ears that, on the contrary, it was extremely easy, and by no means impossible to reach in a very short time, who could have the heart to raise questions or obtrude arguments? Those who were enthusiastic over the prospect of *faqir* turning a copper coin into a gold *mohur*, are able to do so, not because they are lacking in intellect, but because their avidity restrains them from exercising their intelligence.

Anyhow, it was only the other day that our people were beside themselves at the message that *swaraj* was at our very door. Then when the appointed time for its advent had slipped by, it was given out that the disappointment was due to our non-fulfillment of the conditions. But few thereupon paused to consider that it was just in the fulfillment of these conditions that the difficulty lay. Is it not a self-evident truth that we do not have *swaraj* simply because we do not fulfil its conditions? It goes without saying that if Hindu and Moslem should come together in amity and good fellowship, that would be a great step towards its realisation. But the trouble always is, the Hindu and Moslem do not come together. Had their union been real, all the 365 days in the calendar would have been auspicious days for making the venture. True, the announcement of a definite date for the start has an intoxicating effect. But I cannot admit that an intoxicating state makes the journey any easier.

The appointed time has not long gone by, yet the intoxication lingers,—the intoxication which consists in a confusion of haste with speed, in a befogged reliance on one or two narrow paths as the sole means of gaining a vast realisation. Amongst those paths prominently looms the *charkha*.

And so the question has to be raised: What is this *swaraj*? Our political leaders have refrained from giving us any clear explanation of it. As a matter of fact we have the freedom to spin our own thread on our own *charkha*. If we have omitted to avail ourselves of it, that is because the thread so spun cannot compete with the product of the power mill. No doubt it might have been otherwise if the millions of India had devoted their leisure to the *charkha*, thereby reducing the exchange value of home spun thread. But nothing proves the hopelessness of such an expectation more than the fact that those very persons who are wielding their pens in its support are not wielding the *charkha* itself.

The second point is, even if every one of our countrymen should betake himself to spinning thread, that might somewhat mitigate their poverty, but it would not be *swaraj*. What of that? Is the increase of wealth a small thing for a poverty stricken country? What a difference it would make if our cultivators, who improvidently waste their spare time, were to engage in such productive work! Let us concede for the moment that the profitable employment of the surplus time of the cultivator is of the first importance. But the thing is not so simple as it sounds. One who takes up the problem must be prepared to devote precise thinking and systematic endeavour to its solution. It is not enough to say: *Let them spin*.

The cultivator has acquired a special skill with his hands, and a special bent of mind, by dint of consistent application to his own particular work. The work of cultivation is for him the line of least strain. So long as he is working, he is busy with one or other of the operations connected therewith: when he is not so busy, he is not at work. It would be unfair to charge him with laziness on this account. Had the processes of cultivation lasted throughout the year, he also would have been at work from one end of it to the other. It is an inherent defect of all routine toil, such as is the work of cultivation, that it dulls the mind by disuse. In order to be able to go from one habitual round of daily work to a different one, an active mind is required. But this kind of manual labour, like a tram car, runs along a fixed track, and cannot take a different course with any ease, however dire the necessity. To ask the cultivator to spin, is to derail his mind. He may drag on with it for a while, but at the cost of disproportionate effort, and therefore waste of energy.

I have an intimate acquaintance with the cultivators of at least two districts of our province and I know from experience how rigorous for them are the bonds of habit. One of these districts is mainly rice-producing and there the cultivators have to toil with might and main to grow their single crop of rice. Nevertheless in their spare time, they might have realised growing green vegetables round their homesteads. I tried to encourage them to do so, but failed. The very men who willingly sweated over their rice, refused to stir for the sake of vegetables. In the other district the cultivators are busy, all the year round with rice, jute and sugarcane, mustard and other spring crops. Such portions of their holdings as do not bear any of these, are left fallow, without any corresponding remissions of rent. To this same locality come peasants from the North-West, who take up, and pay a good rent for similar waste lands and, raising thereon different varieties of melon, return home with a substantial profit. The producer of jute can by no means be called lazy. I am told there are other places in the world quite as suitable for growing jute, where the farmers nevertheless refuse to undergo the hard-ships of its cultivation. It would seem, therefore, that if Bengal has a monopoly of jute, that is more due to the character of her peasants than of her soil. And yet these hard-working jute cultivators, with the example before their very eyes of the profits made by those up-country melon growers, do not care to follow it in the case of their own fallow holdings by treading a path to which they are unaccustomed.

Therefore, when we are faced with any such problem, the difficulty we have to contend with is how to draw the mind of the people out of its path of habit into a new one. I cannot believe that it is enough to indicate some easy external method; the solution, as I say, is a question of change of mentality.

It is not difficult to issue from outside the mandates: *Let Hindu and Moslem unite*. At this the obedient Hindus may flock to join the *Khilafat* movement, for such conjunction is easy enough. They may even yield some of their worldly advantages in favour of the Moslems, for though that be more difficult, it is still of the outside. But the real difficulty is for Hindus and Moslems to give up their respective prejudices which keep them apart. That is where the problem now rests. To the Hindu, the Mussalman is impure: for the Mussalman, the Hindu is a *kafir*. In spite of their longing for *swaraj* neither can forget this inward obsession. I used to know an anglicised Hindu who had leanings towards Europe-an fare. Everything else he would heartily relish, but he drew the line at hotel cooked rice,— rice touched by Mussalman cooks, said he, refused to pass his lips. The same kind of prejudice which makes such rice *taboo*, stands in the way of cordial relationship. The habit of mind which religious injunctions have ingrained in us constitutes the age old fortress which holds our anti-Moslem feeling secure against penetration by outside *ententes*, whether on the basis of the *khilafat* movement or of pecuniary pacts.

Such like problems in our country become so difficult: be-cause they are of the inside; the obstructions are all within our own mind, which is at once in revolt if there be any proposal for getting rid of them. That is why we feel so strongly attracted if some external *solution* be suggested. It is when his own character stands in the way of making a living along the beaten track, that a person becomes ready to court disaster in a desperate gamble for becoming suddenly rich. If our countrymen accept the proposition that the *charkha* is the principal means of attaining *swaraj* then it has to be admitted that in their opinion *swaraj* is an external achievement. And therein lies the reason why, when the defects of character and the perversions of social custom which obstruct its realisation are kept out of sight, and the whole attention is concentrated on home spun thread, no surprise is felt but rather relief.

In these circumstances, if we take the view that the external poverty of our country claims our foremost attention—that one of the chief obstacles to *swaraj* will be removed if our cultivators employ their leisure in productive occupations, then it is for our leaders to think out the ways and means whereby such spare time may be utilised to the best advantage. And does it not then become obvious that such advantage is best to be secured in the line of cultivation itself?

Suppose that poverty should overtake me, then it would surely behove any adviser of mine, first of all to consider that literary work is the only one in which I can claim any length of practice. However great may be my mentor's contempt for this profession, he cannot well ignore it in advising me on how to earn a living. He may be able to show by statistical calculations that a tea shop in the students quarters would yield 75% profit for accounts which neglect the human element easily run into large figures. And if such tea shop enterprise should but assist in completing my ruin, that is not because my intellect is of a lower order than that of the successful tea vendor, but because my mind is differently constituted.

It is not feasible to make the cultivator either happier or richer by thrusting aside, all of a sudden, the habits of body and mind which have grown upon him through his life. As I have indicated before, those who do not use their minds, get into fixed habits for which any the least novelty becomes an obstacle. If an undue love for a particular programme leads one to ignore this psychological truth, that makes no difference to psychology, it is the programme which suffers. In other agricultural countries the attempt is being successfully made to lead the cultivators towards a progressive improvement of production along the line of cultivation itself, and there agriculture has made long strides forward by an intelligent application of science, the yield per unit of land being many times larger than in our country. The path which is lit up by the intellect is not an *easy*, but a *true* path, the pursuit of which shows that manhood is at work. To tell the cultivator turn the *charkha* instead of trying to get him to employ his whole energy in his own line of work is only a sign of weakness. We cast the blame for being lazy on the cultivator, but the advice we give him amounts rather to a confession of the laziness of our own mind.

The discussion, so far, has proceeded on the assumption that the large-scale production of homespun thread and cloth will result in the alleviation of the country's poverty. But after all that is a gratuitous assumption. Those who ought to know, have expressed grave doubts on the point. It is however better for an ignoramus like myself to refrain from entering into this controversy. My complaint is, that by the promulgation of this confusion between *swaraj* and *charkha*, the mind of the country is being distracted from *swaraj*.

We must have a clear idea of the vast thing that the welfare of our country means. To confine our idea of it to the outsides, or to make it too narrow, diminishes our own power of achievement. The lower the claim made on our mind, the greater the resulting depression of its vitality, the more languid does it become. To give the *charkha* the first place in our striving for the country's welfare is only a way to make our insulted intelligence recoil in despairing inaction. A great and vivid picture of the country's well-being in its universal aspect, held before our eyes, can alone enable our countrymen to apply the best of head and heart to carve out the way along which their varied activities may progress towards that end. If we make the picture petty, our striving becomes petty likewise. The great ones of the world who have made stupendous sacrifices for the land of their birth, or for their fellow-men in general, have all had a supreme vision of the welfare of country and humanity before their mind's eye. If we desire to evoke self-sacrifice, then we must assist the people to meditate thus on a grand vision. Heaps of thread and piles of cloth do not constitute the subject of a great picture of welfare. That is the vision of a calculating mind; it cannot arouse those incalculable forces which, in the joy of a supreme realisation, cannot only brave suffering and death, but reck nothing, either, of obloquy and failure.

The child joyfully learns to speak, because from the lips of father and mother it get glimpses of language as a whole. Even while it understands but little, it is thereby continually stimulated and its joy is constantly at work in order to gain fullness of utterance. If, instead of having before it the exuberance of expression, the child had been hemmed in with grammar texts, it would have to be forced to learn its mother tongue at the point of the cane, and even then could not have done it so soon. It is for this reason I think that if we want the country to take up the striving for *swaraj* in earnest, then we must make an effort to hold vividly before it the complete image of that *swaraj*. I do not say that the propositions of this image can become the immensely large in a short space of time; but we must claim that it be whole, that it be true. All living things are organic wholes at every stage of their growth. The infant does not begin life at the toe-end and get its human shape only after some years of growth. That is why we can rejoice in it from the very first, and in that joy bear all the pains and sacrifices of helping it to grow. If *swaraj* has to be viewed for any length of time, only as home-spun thread, that would be like having an infantile leg to nurse into maturity. A man like the Mahatma may succeed in getting some of our countrymen to take an interest in this kind of uninspiring nature for a time because of their faith in his personal greatness of soul. To obey him is for them an end in itself. To me it seems that such a state of mind is not helpful for the attainment of *swaraj*.

I think it to be primarily necessary that, in different places over the country small centers should be established in which expression is given to the responsibility of the country for achieving its own *swaraj;*—that is to say, its own welfare as a whole and not only in regard to its supply of homespun thread. The welfare of the people is a synthesis comprised of many elements, all intimately interrelated. To take them in isolation can lead to no real result. Health and work, reason, wisdom and joy, must all be thrown into the crucible in order that the result may be fullness of welfare. We want to see a picture of such welfare before our eyes, for that will teach us ever so much more than any amount of exhortation. We must have, before us, in various centres of population examples of different types of revived life abounding in health and wisdom and prosperity. Otherwise we shall never be able to bring about the realisation of what *swaraj* means simply by dint of spinning threads, weaving *khaddar*, or holding discourses. That which we would achieve for the whole of India must be actually made true even in some small corner of it,—then only will a worshipful striving for it be born in our hearts. Then only shall we know the real value of self–determination, *na medhaya na bahudha srutena*, not by reasoning nor by listening to lectures, but by direct experience. If even the people of one village of India, by the exercise of their own powers, make their village their very own, then and there will begin the work of realising our country as our own.

Fauna and flora take birth in their respective regions, but that does not make any such region belong to them. Man creates his own motherland. In the work of its creation as well as of its preservation, the people the country come into intimate relations with one another, and a country so created by them, they can love better than life itself. In our country its people are only born therein: they are taking no hand in its creation; therefore between them there are no deep-seated ties of connexion, nor is any loss sustained by the whole country felt as a personal loss by the individual. We must re-awaken the faculty of gaining the motherland by creating it. The various processes of creation need all the varied powers of man. In the exercise of these multifarious powers, along many and diverse roads, in order to reach one and the same goal, we may realise ourselves in our country. To be fruitful, such exercise of our powers must begin near home and gradually spread further and further outwards. If we are tempted to look down upon the initial stage of such activity as too small, let us remember the teaching of *Gita: Swalpamasaya dharmosya travate mahato bhayat*, by the least bit of *dharma* (truth) are we saved from immense fear. Truth is powerful, not in its dimensions, but in itself.

When acquaintance with, practice of, and pride in co-operative self-determination shall have spread in our land, then on such broad abiding foundation alone may *swaraj* become true. So long as we are wanting therein, both within and without and while such want is proving the root of all our other wants... want of food, of health, of wisdom,—it is past all belief that any programme of outward activity can rise superior to the poverty of spirit which has overcome our people. Success begets success; likewise *swaraj* alone can beget *swaraj*.

The right of God over the universe is His *swaraj*... the right to create it. In that same privilege, I say consists our *swaraj*, namely our right to create our own country. The proof of such right, as well as its cultivation, lies in the exercise of the creative process. Only by living do we show that we have life.

It may be argued that spinning is also a creative act. But that is not so: for, by turning its wheel man merely becomes an appendage of the *charkha*; that is to say, he but does himself what a machine might have done: he converts his living energy into a dead turning movement. The machine is solitary, because being devoid of mind it is sufficient unto itself and knows nothing outside itself. Likewise alone is the man who confines himself to spinning, for the thread produced by his *charkha* is not for him a thread of necessary relationship with others. He has no need to think of his neighbour,—like the silkworm his activity is centred round himself. He becomes a machine, isolated, companionless. Members of Congress who spin may, while so engaged, dream of some economic paradise for their country, but the origin of their dream is elsewhere; the *charkha* has no spell from which such dreams may spring. But the man who is busy trying to drive out some epidemic from his village, even should he be unfortunate enough to be all alone in such endeavour, needs must concern himself with the interests of the whole village in the beginning, middle and end of his work, so that because of this very effort he cannot help realising within himself the village as a whole, and at every moment consciously rejoicing in its creation. In his work, therefore, does the striving for *swaraj* make a true beginning. When the others also come and join him, then alone can we say that the whole village is making progress towards the gain of itself which is the outcome of the creation of itself. Such gain may be called the gain of *swaraj*. However small the size of it may be, it is immense in its truth.

The village of which the people come together to earn for themselves their food, their health, their education, to gain for themselves the joy of so doing, shall have lighted a lamp on the way to *swaraj*. It will not be difficult therefrom to light others, one after another, and thus illuminate more and more of the path along which *swaraj* will advance, not propelled by the mechanical revolution of the *charkha*, but taken by the organic processes of its own living growth.

Rabindranath Tagore

8. The Poet and the *charkha*

(It was after a couple of months that Gandhi wrote a rejoinder to Tagore's 'The Cult of the Charkha' in his journal, Young India *of 5 November 1925)*

When (Sir) Rabindranath's criticism of the *charkha* was published some time ago, several friends asked me to reply to it. Being heavily engaged I was unable then to study it in full. But I had read enough of it to know its trend. I was in no hurry to reply. Those who had read it were too much agitated or influenced to be able to appreciate what I might have then written even if I had the time. Now therefore is really the time for me to write on it and to ensure a dispassionate view being taken of the Poet's criticism or my reply if such it may be called.

The criticism is a sharp rebuke to Acharya Ray for his impatience of the Poet's and Acharya Seal's position regarding the *charkha*, and a gentle rebuke to me for my exclusive love of it. Let the public understand that the Poet does not deny its great economic value. Let them know that he signed the appeal for the All India Deshabandhu Memorial after he had written his criticism. He signed the appeal after studying its contents carefully and even as he signed it he sent me the message that he had written something on the *charkha*, which might not quite please me. I knew therefore what was coming. But it has not displeased me. Why should mere disagreement with my views displease? If every disagreement were to displease, since no two men agree exactly on all points, life would be a bundle of unpleasant sensations and therefore a perfect nuisance. On the contrary, the frank criticism pleases me. For our friendship becomes all the richer for our disagreements. Friends to be friends are not called upon to agree even on most points. Only disagreement must have no sharpness, much less bitterness, about them. And I gratefully admit that there is none about the Poet's criticism.

I am obliged to make these prefatory remarks as Dame Rumour has whispered that jealousy is the root of all that criticism. Such baseless suspicion betrays an atmosphere of weakness and intolerance. A little reflection must remove all ground for such a cruel charge. Of what should the Poet be jealous in me? Jealousy presupposes the possibility of rivalry. Well, I have never succeeded in writing a single rhyme in my life. There is nothing of the Poet about me. I cannot aspire after his greatness. He is the undisputed master of it. The world today does not possess his equal as a poet. My 'Mahatmaship' has no relation to the poet's undisputed position. It is time to realise that our fields are absolutely different and at no point overlapping. The Poet lives in a magnificent world of his own creation—his world of ideas. I am a slave of somebody else's creation—the spinning wheel. The Poet makes his *gopis* dance to the tune of his flute. I wander after my beloved Sita, the *charkha* and seek to deliver her from the ten-headed monster from Japan, Manchester, Paris etc. The Poet is an inventor—he creates, destroys and recreates. I am an explorer and having discovered a thing I must cling to it. The Poet presents the world with new and attractive things from day to day. I can merely show the hidden possibilities of old and even worn-out things. The world easily finds an honourable place for the magician who produces new and dazzling things. I have to struggle laboriously to find a corner for my worn-out things. Thus, there is no competition between us. But I may say in all humility that we complement each the other's activity.

The fact is that the Poet's criticism is a poetic licence and he who takes it literally is in danger of finding himself in an awkward corner. An ancient poet has said that Solomon arrayed in all his glory was not like one of the lilies of the field. He clearly referred to the natural beauty and innocence of the lily contrasted with the artificiality of Solomon's glory and his sinfulness in spite of his many good deeds. Or take the poetical licence in 'It is easier for a camel to pass through the eye of a needle than for a rich man to enter the Kingdom of Heaven'. We know that no camel has ever passed through the eye of a needle and we know too that rich men like Janaka have entered the Kingdom of Heaven. Or take the beautiful simile of human teeth being likened to the pomegranate seed. Foolish women who have taken the poetical exaggeration literally have been found to disfigure and even harm their teeth. Painters and poets are obliged to exaggerate the proportions of their figures in order to give true perspective. Those therefore who take the Poet's denunciation of the *charkha* literally will be doing an injustice to the Poet and an injury to themselves.

The Poet does not, he is not expected, he has no need, to read *Young India*. All he knows about the movement is what he has picked up from table talk. He has therefore denounced what he has imagined to be the excesses of the *charkha* cult.

He thinks for instance that I want everybody to spin the whole of his or her time to the exclusion of all other activity; that is to say that I want the Poet to forsake his muse, the farmer his plough, the lawyer his brief and the doctor his lancet. So far is this from truth that I have asked no one to abandon his calling, but on the contrary to adorn it by giving every day only thirty minutes to spinning as sacrifice for the whole nation. I have indeed asked the famishing to spin for a living and the half-starved farmer to spin during his leisure hours to supplement his slender resources. If the Poet spun half an hour daily his poetry would gain in richness. For it would then represent the poor man's wants and woes in a more forcible manner than now.

The Poet thinks that the *charkha* is calculated to bring about a deathlike sameness in the nation and thus imagining he would shun it if he could. The truth is that the *charkha* is intended to realise the essential and living oneness of interest among India's myriads. Behind the magnificent and kaleidoscopic variety, one discovers in nature a unity of purpose, design and form which is equally unmistakable. No two men are absolutely alike, not even twins, and yet there is much that is indispensably common to all mankind. And behind the commonness of form there is the same life pervading all. The idea of sameness or oneness was carried by Shankara to its utmost logical and natural limit and he exclaimed that there was only one Truth, one God Brahman, and all form, *nam rupa* was illusion or illusory, evanescent. We need not debate whether what we see is unreal; and whether the real behind the unreality is what we do not see. Let both be equally real if you will. All I say is that there is a sameness, identity or oneness behind the multiplicity and variety. And so do I hold that behind a variety of occupations there is an indispensable sameness also of occupation. Is not agriculture common to the vast majority of mankind? Even so was spinning common not long ago to a vast majority of mankind. Just as both prince and peasant must eat and clothe themselves, so must both labour for supplying their primary wants. Prince may do so if only by way of symbol and sacrifice but that much is indispensable for him if he will be true to himself and his people. Europe may not realise this vital necessity at the present moment, because it has made of exploitation of non-European races a religion. But it is a false religion bound to perish in the near future. The non-European races will not for ever allow themselves to be exploited. I have endeavoured to show a way out that is peaceful human and therefore noble. It may be rejected. If it is, the alternative is a tug of war, in which each will try to pull down the other. Then, when non-Europeans will seek to exploit the Europeans, the truth of the *charkha* will have to be realised. Just as, if we are to live, we must breathe not air imported from England nor eat food so imported, so may we not import cloth made in England. I do not hesitate to carry the doctrine to its logical limit and say that Bengal dare not import her cloth even from Bombay or from Banga Lakshmi. If Bengal will live her natural and free life without exploiting the rest of India or the world outside, she must manufacture her cloth in her own villages as she grows her corn there. Machinery has its place; it has come to stay. But it must not be allowed to displace the necessary human labour. An improved plough is a good thing. But if by some chance one man could plough up by some mechanical invention of his the whole of the land of India and control all the agricultural produce and if the millions had no other occupation, they would starve, and being idle, they would become dunces, as many have already become. There is hourly danger of many more being reduced to that unenviable state. I would welcome every improvement in the cottage machine but I know that it is criminal to displace the hand labour by the introduction of power-driven spindles unless one is at the same time ready to give millions of farmers some other occupation in their homes.

The Irish analogy does not take us very far. It is perfect in so far as it enables us to realise the necessity of economic co-operation. But Indian circumstances being different, the method of working out cooperation is necessarily different. For Indian distress every effort at cooperation has to centre round the *charkha* if it is to apply to the majority of the inhabitants of this vast peninsula 1900 miles long and 1500 miles broad. A Sir Gangaram may give us a model farm which can be no model for the penniless Indian farmer who has hardly two to three acres of land which every day runs the risk of being still further cut up.

Round the *charkha*, that is, amidst the people who have shed
their idleness and who have understood the value of cooperation, a national servant would build up a programme of anti-
malaria campaign, improved sanitation, settlement of village
disputes, conservation and breeding of cattle and hundreds of
other beneficial activities. Wherever *charkha* work is fairly established, all such ameliorative activity is going on according to the
capacity of the villagers and the workers concerned.

It is not my purpose to traverse all the Poet's arguments in
detail. Where the differences between us are not fundamental–
and these I have endeavoured to state—there is nothing in the
Poet's argument which I cannot endorse and still maintain my
position regarding the *charkha*. The many things about the *charkha*
which he has ridiculed I have never said. The merits I have
claimed for the *charkha* remain undamaged by the Poet's battery.

One thing, and one thing only, has hurt me, the Poet's belief,
again picked up from table talk, that I look upon Ram Mohun Roy
as a 'pygmy'. Well, I have never anywhere described that great
reformer as a pygmy much less regarded him as such. He is to me
as much a giant as he is to the Poet. I do not remember any
occasion save one when I had to use Ram Mohun Roy's name.
That was in connection with Western education. This was on the
Cuttack's sands now four years ago. What I do remember having
said was that it was possible to attain highest culture without
Western education. And when some one mentioned Ram Mohun
Roy, I remember having said that he was a pygmy compared to
the unknown authors say of the *Upanishads*. This is altogether
different from looking upon Ram Mohun Roy as a pygmy. I do
not think meanly of Tennyson if I say that he was a pygmy before
Milton or Shakespeare. I claim that I enhance the greatness of
both. If I adore the Poet as he knows, I do in spite of differences
between us. I am not likely to disparage the greatness of the man
who made the great reform movement of Bengal possible and of
which the Poet is one of the finest of fruits.

M.K. Gandhi

9. The Poet and the wheel

(In Young India *of 11 March 1926, Gandhi wrote a postscript to the controversy between him and Tagore.)*

In spite of the weakness of body to which the Poet himself referred in his address at the Abhoy Ashram, it was a good thing for Dr. Suresh Banerji, the manager of the Abhoy Ashram, at Comila to have drawn Dr. Tagore there. The reader knows that the Abhoy Ashram was established for the purpose of *khaddar* development. The Poet's acceptance of the address and such association as it may imply on his part with the *khaddar* movement, dispels if any dispeller was necessary, the superstition that the Poet is against the spinning wheel and the *khaddar* movement in every shape or form. In the epitome of his address published in *The Servant*, I find the following reference to the movements:

"The country is not one's own by mere accident of birth but becomes so by one's life's contribution. An animal has got its fur but man has got to spin and weave because what the animal has got, it has got once for all and ready-made. It is for man to rearrange and reshuffle for his purposes materials he finds placed before him."

But there are other pregnant facts in the address which are helpful to workers for, this is what the Poet has to say:

"That we were so long kept from realising India in her true self is due to the fact that we have not by daily endeavour created her by movement making her healthful and fruitful."

Thus he adjures us each one individually to make daily endeavour if we are to gain. In the very next sentence he asks us "not to cherish the dream that can be ours by some extraneous happening." "It can be ours" the Poet adds "in so far as we succeed in permeating our conciousness throughout the country by service".

He tells us also how to attain unity. "We could attain unity *only through* work." That is what the inmates of the Abhoy Ashram are actually doing. For through their spinning they are helping Hindus, Mussalmans, in fact every body, who needs help through that source. They are teaching untouchable boys and girls through their school and through it teach them to spin also. Through their Dispensary they are giving relief to the ailing irrespective of race or religion. They need to preach no sermon on unity. They live it. This work inspires the Poet and he therefore proceeds to say:

"Life is an organic whole. It is the spirit that after all matters. It is not a fact that there is lack of strength in our arms. The fact is that our mind has not been awakened.

"Our greatest fight here therefore is that against mental lethargy. The village is a living entity. You cannot neglect any one department of its life without injuring the other. We are to realise today the soul of our country as a great indivisible whole and likewise all our disabilities and miseries as one inter-related whole."

Referring to our failure, the Poet truly says:

"Man's creation can be beautiful in so far as he has given himself to his work. The reason why our enterprises in this country fail so often is that we give only a portion of ourselves to the cause dear to our heart. We give with the right hand to steal back with the left."

M.K. Gandhi

PART III

1929–1933

1929–1933

Notes on Documents

Tagore was away from India a good deal of time in 1929 and 1930 —for almost fourteen months in those two years—lecturing in Japan, Indo-China, Canada, USA, USSR and about five West European countries. No letters were exchanged with Gandhi in this period. (Chronology of Tagore's foreign trips in *Rabindranath Tagore: A Centenary Volume*, Sahitya Akademi, New Delhi, 1961). However, on 18 January 1930 Tagore visited Gandhi at Sabarmati, while on tour to collect funds for his school in Santiniketan. (See Appendix: Mahadev Desai's report in *Harijan*, 23 January 1930). Later that year when Tagore was in England he was pressed by journalists to comment on Gandhi's politics in the context of the Round Table Conference; most notable was Tagore's statement, supportive of Gandhi, in November 1930 (see Appendix: Tagore's statement, *The Spectator*, London, 15 November 1930). Gandhi contributed a message to the felicitation volume for Tagore in July 1931. In October that year Tagore sent a cable to Gandhi, then in England for the second Round Table Conference, on his birthday (Document 1).

In January 1932 Gandhi wrote at 4 a.m., minutes before his arrest, very touchingly of the impending resumption of the Civil Disobedience movement (Document 2). Documents 3, 4, 5, 6 form a group of letters which were exchanged between them while Gandhi was on fast at Yeravada Jail in September 1932. Tagore was so moved by the fast that he himself went to Pune and Gandhi, having gained success, broke his fast in Tagore's presence.

Another bunch of letters (Documents 7, 8, 9) pertain to the fast undertaken by Gandhi on the issue of caste restrictions on admission to the Guruvayyur temple; Tagore tried to dissuade Gandhi from fasting too frequently, lest "anything happens to you." Kalappan, mentioned in these letters (Document 8), started fasting on 20 September 1932 on the issue that Gandhi took up.

A third group of letters concern Gandhi's resolve to fast in May 1933 (Document 11, 12, 13, 14). Tagore publicly expressed his admiration for such an act of courage and moral strength (Document 14, published in *Harijan*). But his letters to Gandhi argued strongly against self-mortification and wilfully endangering a precious life. About this time Gandhi published in *Harijan* one of Tagore's letters on temples and mosques which "enclose" divinity (Document 10). Tucker mentioned in this letter was Boyed Tucker, an American missionary of the Methodist Church, who visited Tagore at Santiniketan in 1927 and again in 1932 when he was sent by Tagore to see Gandhi at Yeravada jail.

The last spate of letters of this period (Documents 15, 16, 17, 18) is a part of the fall-out of the Poona Pact mentioned earlier. Tagore began to have misgivings. We have to take note of a press-statement issued by Tagore on 24 July 1933 (see Appendix) to understand the background to these letters. Tagore had endorsed and celebrated the Poona Pact but on second thoughts he found it open to grave objections. The situation was "very painful" at that moment due to Gandhi's fast and "upon the settlement of this [pact] Mr. Gandhi's life depended, and the intolerable anxiety caused by such a crisis drove me precipitately to a commitment". Tagore added that he himself had no "experience in political dealings" and the conference which had previously arrived at the formula for the pact had "no responsible representatives of Bengal." Upon reconsideration, Tagore announced to the Press, some aspects of the pact appeared to him as unjust; in Bengal it would contribute to "keeping alive the spirit of communal conflict in our province in an intense form and making peaceful government of the country perpetually difficult."

Reacting to this Gandhi said that he was "not at all convinced that there was any error" or injustice in the pact; rather curiously, he invited the Poet "to convene a meeting of the principal parties and convince them that a grave injustice has been done to Bengal". (Document 15). At this, Tagore gave up, but not without a renewed protest against a violation of justice "for the sake of immediate peace"; he terminated further correspondence on the subject, saying that he "did not desire any answer". (Document 18).

EDITOR

1. Birthday Greeting telegram from Tagore

Santiniketan
2.10.1931

To: Mahatma Gandhi Care Horace Alexander Sellyoak (UK)

Our combined homage of reverent love to You on the happy occasion of your Birthday

Rabindranath Tagore

2. Gandhi to Tagore on the resumption of Civil Disobedience

Laburnum Road,
Bombay,
3 January 1932

Dear Gurudev,

I am just stretching my tired limbs on the mattress and as I try to steal a wink of sleep, I think of you. I want you to give your best to the sacrificial fire that is being lighted.

With love

M.K.Gandhi

3. Tagore's thoughts of Gandhi in jail on the eve of a fast

(Telegram sent by Tagore to Gandhi, a copy of which is kept in Rabindra Bhavan.)

19.9.1932

To: Mahatma Gandhi Yeravada Jail Poona

It is worth sacrificing precious life for the sake of India's unity and her social integrity stop Though we cannot anticipate what effect it may have upon our rulers, who may not understand its immense importance for our people, we feel certain that the supreme appeal of such self offering to the conscience of our own countrymen will not be in vain stop I fervently hope that we will not callously allow such national tragedy to reach its extreme length stop Our sorrowing hearts will follow your sublime penance with reverence and love.

Rabindranath Tagore

4. Gandhi seeks Tagore's blessing before starting a fast

(In Gandhi's own hand)

(Censored) Sd/- Illegible Major, I. M. S., Superintendent, Yeravada Central Prison.

Dear Gurudev,

This is early morning 3 o'clock of Tuesday. I enter the fiery gate at noon. If you can bless the effort, I want it. You have been to me a true friend because you have been a candid friend often speaking your thoughts aloud. I had looked forward to a firm opinion from you, one way or the other. But you have refused to criticise. Though it can now only be during my fast, I will yet prize your criticism, if your heart condemns my action. I am not too proud to make an open confession of my blunder, whatever the cost of the confession, if I find myself in error. If your heart approves of the action I want your blessing. It will sustain me. I hope I have made myself clear.

My love,

M.K. Gandhi

20.9.32.
10.30 a.m.

(Just as I was handing this to the Superintendent, I got your loving and magnificent wire. It will sustain me in the midst of the storm I am about to enter. I am sending you a wire. Thank you.)

M. K. G.

5. Tagore's relief at abandonment of the fast

Santiniketan,
Calcutta,
30 September 1932

Mahatmaji,

Our people are wonderstruck at the impossible being made possible in these few days and there is a universal feeling of immense relief at your being saved for us. Now is the opportune moment when a definite command from you will rouse the Hindu community to make a desperate effort to win over the Mahomedans to our common cause. It is more difficult of success than your fight against untouchability, for there is a deep-rooted antipathy against the Muslims in most of our people and they also have not much love for ourselves. But you know how to move the hearts of those that are obdurate, and only, I am sure, have the patient love that can conquer the hatred that has accumulated for ages. I do not know how to calculate political consequences, but I believe that nothing can be too costly which would enable us to win their confidence and convince them that we understand their difficulties and their own point of view. However, it is not for me to advise you and I shall fully rely upon your own judgement as to the course that should be taken. Only one suggestion I must venture to make to you that you might ask the Hindu Mahasabha to make a conciliatory gesture towards the other party.

I have no doubt that you are gaining strength and inspiring every moment strength and hope around you.

With reverent love,

I am ever yours,
Rabindranath Tagore

6. Gandhi's letter of thanks

9 October 1932

Dear Gurudev,

I have your beautiful letter. I am daily seeking light. This unity between Hindus and Muslims is also life's mission. The restrictions too hamper me. But I know that when I have the light, it will pierce through the restrictions, meanwhile I pray, though I do not yet fast.

I hope you were none the worse for the strenuous work in Poona and equally fatiguing long journey.

Mahadev translated for us your beautiful sermon to the villagers on 20th ultimo.

With love,

Yours
M.K.Gandhi

7. Gandhi on the fast

(The letter is in late Mahadev Desai's handwriting, signed by Gandhi. "With deep love" & "Yours"—only these two lines are in Gandhi's own hand.)

Yeravada Central Prison,
10 November 1932

Superintendent,
Yeravada Central Prison,
(Poona)

Dear Gurudev,

You must have seen the statement I have circulated to the Press. I want your blessings if I can have them for this further effort. I do not know whether you feel that this effort is, if possible, purer than before. The last fast had a political tinge about it and superficial critics were able to say that it was aimed at the British Government. This time if the ordeal has to come, it will not be possible to give any political colour to it. You will of course recall that the last fast was broken on the clearest possible notice that I might have to resume if there was any breach of faith by the so called caste Hindus. The prospective fast about Guruvayyur Temple is absolutely a point of honour. It is being made by the orthodox section of the centre of attack and is being given an allIndia significance. I rather like it. But it makes it all the more necessary for the liberalising influences to be collected together and set in motion in order to overthrow the monster of untouchability. I want your wholehearted cooperation if you feel as I do.

I hope you are keeping well.

With deep love,

Yours
M.K. Gandhi

8. Tagore on the impact of the fast

Visva-Bharati,
Santiniketan, Bengal,
15 November 1932

Dear Mahatmaji,

I can realise the sanctity of the promise given by you to Kelappan, and certainly nobody from outside can presume to criticise any actions that you may decide upon guided by your own direct revelation of truth. What I fear is that following so close upon the tremendous impact made on our consciousness by the recent fast, a repetition of it may psychologically be too much for us properly to evaluate and effectively to utilise for the uplift of humanity. The mighty liberating forces set in motion by your fast still continue to operate and spread from village to village, removing age-long iniquities, transforming the harshness of callously superstitious to a new feeling of sympathy for the distressed. Were I convinced that the movement has suffered any abatement or in any way shows signs of lacunae, I would welcome even the highest sacrifice, which humanity today is capable of making, the sacrifice of your life in penance for our sins. But all my experiences of the activities of the villages around us here, as well as of other localities, convince me that the movement generated by your fast continue to gain in strength and conquer formidable obstacles. The testimony of my friends from all parts of India confirm this truth. It may be that there are reactionary elements, but it seems to me that we should allow them time—the pressure of a growing public opinion is sure to win them over. Even as to the Guruvayyur temple, if my information is correct, excepting a few misguided individuals, the majority of men is overwhelmingly on the side of the reform. I pray and hope that the former will yet yield to sanity and constitutionally remove the legal barriers which seem to stand in the way of reform. Should we take too seriously the activities of some isolated groups of individuals and subject millions of our countrymen to the extremest form of suffering while they themselves are unquestionably on the side of truth ? The influence which is at work may have a check if anything happens to you. Should we risk that possibility now that we have won ? These are the thoughts which naturally rise in my mind and I was thinking of putting them before Mahadev when your letter arrived. I shall continue to follow events with my thoughts and prayers and fervently hope that those who now stand in the way of truth will be converted to it.

With reverent love,

Yours,
Rabindranath Tagore

9. Gandhi on Tagore's comforting letter

(Censored)

24 November 1932

Dear Gurudev,

Your precious letter comforts me. It is enough for me that you are watching and praying.

With deep love,

Yours,
M.K. Gandhi

10. Tagore on Hindu sects and the prayer hall at Santiniketan

March 1933

Dear Mahatmaji,

It is needless to say that I do not at all relish the idea of divinity being enclosed in a brick and mortar temple for the special purpose of exploitation by a particular group of people. I strongly believe that it is possible for the simple hearted people to realise the presence of God in the open air, in a surrounding free from all artificial obstruction. We know a sect in Bengal, illiterate and not dominated by Brahminical tradition, who enjoy a perfect freedom of worship profoundly universal in character. It was the prohibition for them to enter temples that has helped them in their purity of realisation.

The traditional idea of Godhead and conventional forms of worship hardly lay emphasis upon the moral worth of religious practices. Their essential value lies in the conformity to custom which creates in the minds of the worshippers an abstract sense of sanctity and sanction. When we argue with them in the name of justice and humanity it is contemptuously ignored for as I have said the moral appeal of the cause has no meaning for them and you know that there are practices and legends connected with a number of our sectarian creeds and practices which are ignoble and irrational.

There is a tradition of religion connected with temple worship, and though such traditions can be morally wrong and harmful, yet they cannot merely be ignored. There the question comes of changing them, of widening their range and character. There can be differences of opinion with regard to the methods to be adopted. From the point of view of the trustees of traditions they are acting according to an inherent sense of property in preserving them as they are, in keeping the enjoyment of idol worship in temples for exclusive groups of people. They not only deny the right of such worship to Christians and Mahomedans but to sections of their own community. Particular temples and deities are their own property and they keep them locked up in an iron chest. In this they are acting according to traditional religion which allows them such freedom, rather enjoins them to act in this manner. A reformer in dealing with such morally wrong traditions cannot adopt coercion and yet as in fighting with other wrong and harmful customs he must exert moral force and constantly seek to rectify them. This fight is necessary. I do not think Tucker makes this point clear.

As to the Santiniketan prayer hall it is open to all peoples of every faith. Just as its doors do not shut out anybody so there is nothing in the simple form of worship which excludes peoples of different religions. Our religious service could as well take place under the trees; its truth and sacredness would not at all be affected but perhaps enhanced by such natural environment. Difficulties of climate and season intervene, otherwise I do not think separate buildings are really necessary for prayer and communion with the Divine.

I have sent a poem for the 'Harijan'—translating it from one of my recent Bengali writings. I do hope it is one in spirit with the ideal of the Harijan which I read with much pleasure and interest. There can be no more hopeful sign for India than the fact that her repressed humanity is waking up as a result of the great fast.

With loving regards,

Yours sincerely,
Rabindranath Tagore

11. Gandhi's thoughts contemplating yet another fast

Yeravada Central Prison,
Poona,
2 May 1933

Dear Gurudev,

It is just now 1.45 a.m. and I think of you and some other friends. If your heart endorses contemplated fast, I want your blessings again.

My love and respects,

Yours,
M.K Gandhi

12. Tagore on Gandhi's fast

Glen Eden,
Darjeeling,
9 May 1933

Dear Mahatmaji,

Evidentally the telegram which I sent to you some days ago has failed to reach its destination though it has appeared in some of the papers.

You must not blame me if I cannot feel a complete agreement with you at the immense responsibility you incur by the step you have taken. I have not before me the entire background of thoughts and facts against which should be placed your own judgement in order to understand its significance. From the beginning of creation there continue things that are ugly and wrong—the negative factors of existence—and the ideals which are positive and eternal ever wait to be represented by messengers of truth who never have the right to leave the field of their work in despair or disgust because of the impurities and imperfections in their surroundings. It is a presumption in my part to remind you that when Lord Buddha woke up to the multitude of miseries from which the world suffers, he strenuously went on preaching the path of liberation till the last day of his earthly career. Death when it is physically or morally inevitable has to be bravely endured, but we have not the liberty to court it unless there is absolutely no other alternative for the expression of the ultimate purpose of life itself. It is not unlikely that you are mistaken about the imperative necessity of your present vow, and when we realise that there is a grave risk of its fatal termination we shudder at the possibility of the tremendous mistake never having the opportunity of being rectified. I cannot help beseeching you not to offer such an ultimatum of mortification to God for his scheme of things and almost refuse the great gift of life with all its opportunities to hold up till its last moment the ideal of perfection which justifies humanity.

However I must confess that I have not the vision which you have before your mind, nor can I fully realise the call which has come only to yourself, and therefore whatever may happen I shall try to believe that you are right in your resolve and that

my misgivings may be the outcome of a timidity of ignorance.
    With love and reverence,

                                                    Yours
                                        Rabindranath Tagore

13. Tagore on moral aspects of the fast

                                                    Darjeeling,
                                                    11 May 1933
Dear Mahatmaji,
    I am trying clearly to find out the meaning of this last
message of yours which is before the world today. In every
important act of his life Buddha preached limitless love for all
creatures. Christ said, "Love thine enemies" and that teaching of
his found its final expression in the words of forgiveness he
uttered for those who killed him. As far as I can understand, the
fast that you have started carries in it the idea of expiation for the
sins of your countrymen. But I ask to be excused when I say that
the expiation can truly and heroically be done only by daily
endeavours for the sake of these unfortunate beings who do not
know what they do. The fasting which has no direct action upon
the conduct of misdoers and which may abruptly terminate one's
power further to serve those who need help, cannot be universal-
ly accepted and therefore it is all the more unacceptable for any
individual who has the responsibility to represent humanity.
    The logical consequence of your example, if followed, will
be an elimination of all noble souls from the world, leaving the
morally feeble and down-trodden multitude to sink into the
fathomless depth of ignorance and inequity. You have no right to
say that this process of penance can only be efficacious through
your own individual endeavour and for others it has no meaning.
If that were true, you ought to have performed it in absolute
secrecy as a special mystic rite which only claims its one sacrifice
beginning and ending in yourself. You ask others actively to
devote their energy to extirpate the evil which smothers our
national life and enjoin only upon yourself an extreme form of
sacrifice which is of passive character. For lesser men than
yourself it opens up an easy and futile path of duty by urging

them to take a plunge into a dark abyss of self-mortification. You cannot blame them if they follow you in this special method of purification of their country, for all messages must be universal in their application, and if not, they should never be expressed at all.

The suffering that has been caused to me by the vow you have taken has compelled me to write to you thus—for I cannot bear the sight of a sublimely noble career journeying towards a finality which, to my mind, lacks a perfectly satisfying justification. And once again, I appeal to you for the sake of the dignity of our nation, which is truly impersonated in you, and for the sake of the millions of my countrymen who need your living touch and help to desist from any act that you think is good only for you and not for the rest of humanity.

With deepest pain and love,

Rabindranath Tagore

14. The message of the fast

(Harijan of 10, June 1933 carried this editorial note on the significance of Gandhi's fast quoting Tagore's statement.)

We pointed out in these columns how Gandhiji's penance had a message for everyone of us and how we should all try to understand and act on it. We adverted also to the danger of our failing to take advantage of the present feeling in the country and ensure enduring results in the cause of Harijan Service. Speaking of the fast last September, Dr. Rabindranath Tagore voiced this apprehension and made a stirring appeal to the whole country to unite in a campaign of purification and to bear ourselves in a way that will show to the world that we deserve to have amidst us a great personage like Gandhiji and that his sufferings and sacrifices on our behalf have not gone in vain. The appeal applies with greater force, if possible, to the recent fast and will bear repetition.

He said:

"Nothing can be more disastrous for us than the utter

lessening of the value of a heroic expression of truth by paying it the homage of a mere ceremonial expression of feeling by a people emotionally inclined. The penance which Mahatmaji has taken upon himself is not a ritual but a message to all India and to the world. If we must make that message our own, we should accept it in the right spirit. The truth of sacrifice could only be grasped by our genuine sacrifice. Let us try to understand the meaning of his message. From the dawn of human history, there has continued the assertion of superiority of one section of mankind at the expense of another, building the stronghold of pride and superiority upon the slavish humiliation of others. Though Man has practised this for ages, yet we must assert that it is inhuman. Human prosperity can never be stable on the foundation of slavery, which not only harms the slaves but ruins their masters. Their heavy burden drags us inevitably down and obstructs us at every step of our forward march. Those whom we humiliate gradually push us down the precipice of degradation."

Man-eating civilisation will decompose by disease and death, such is the law of the Lord of Man. The brand of ignominy by which we have deprived from elemental human pride a section of our fellow-countrymen has brought dishonour to the whole of India.

Mahatmaji has repeatedly pointed out the danger of those divisions in our country that are permanent insults to humanity but our attention has not yet been drawn to the urgency of social reformation with the same force as it has been to the importance of *khaddar* and economic recovery. The social inequities from which all our time-honoured loyalty, making it difficult for us to uproot them. Against that deep-seated moral weakness in our society, Mahatmaji has pronounced his ultimatum, and though it may be our misfortune to lose him in this battle, the proud privilege of the fight will be passed on to every one of us to be carried to the finish. It is the supreme charge of this fight which he is offering to us; if we can accept that wholeheartedly, then this day would be glorified. If we do not know how to accept this great challenge, if we cheaply dismiss it with ceremonial fasting for a day followed by indifference tomorrow and allow the noble life to be wasted and its great meaning lost, then our people will roll down the slope of degradation from sorrows and starvation to utter futility.

Great persons appeared from age to age all of a sudden. We do not find them whenever we want and it is a great good fortune to find them in our midst. Today there is no end to our suffering, degradation and persecution, disease and sorrow are being piled up from day to day; yet, transcending all, there is this sublime joy that an incomparable being is born in this land of ours and that we are breathing, within the same atmosphere. In Mahatmaji's life there is no distinction between the high and the low, the learned and the unlettered, the rich and the poor, amongst whom equally he has lavished his love and has proclaimed: "May happiness and well-being come to one and all". That proclamation was not a mere word, it came out of the depth of his suffering, and how much he has suffered, what torture, what humiliation! His external life is a history of uninterrupted suffering not only in India but outside. How many a time he had to face death itself. That suffering, however, was not for the fulfilment of his self-interest but for the good of all. After so much of insult and injury, he never retreated in anger but took all the suffering on his own head. His penance, his greatness, has staggered even his opponents. He achieves his purpose but never through violence. He triumphs through sacrifice, through suffering, through supreme penance.

What an intolerable agony there must be behind his decision to fast himself to death! If we do not understand him and recognise the sanctity of that penance, would we not be responsible for his martyrdom? He has courted death with the determination of equalising the high and the low. May that strength and that divine audacity inspire our spirit and our action.... Where man insults man, God himself turns his face. The poison of human degradation have been injected into the veins of Mother India through centuries. The crushing humiliation have we set upon the heads of countless millions and the whole country today is weak and staggering under that dead weight. It was impossible for the *Mahatma* to tolerate this sin. That is why the great *Tapasvi* is starving from day to day. A great curse was weighing on the nation for a long while and he came forward to expiate for our sins. Let us all unite with him in that supreme purification. He has triumphed over our fear, even over the fear of death. The world is looking on us, and the unsympathetic are even scoffing. If we fail to respond, then even this great event

would look like a cruel joke. If on the contrary the fire of his
spiritual strength kindled our soul, the whole world gaze with
wonder. May we all cry with one voice: "Victory to thee Oh
Tapasvi, May thy penance be fulfilled!" May that hymn of Victory
resound from shore to to shore. May the whole world realise the
inevitability of the triumph of truth. May Mother India be
glorified!"

15. Gandhi to Tagore on the Yeravada Pact

*(See Documents 16-18 in this part of the book and
Document 9 in Appendix)*

Ahmedabad,
27 July 1933

Dear Gurudev,
    I have read your Press message regarding the Yeravada
Pact, in so far as it applies to Bengal. It caused me deep grief to
find that you were misled by very deep affection for me and by
your confidence in my judgement into approving of a Pact which
was discovered to have done a grave injustice to Bengal. It is now
no use my saying that affection for me should not have affected
your judgement, or that confidence in my judgement ought not
to have made you accept a Pact about which you had ample
means for coming to an independent judgement. Knowing as I do
your very generous nature, you could not have acted otherwise
than you did and in spite of the discovery made by you that you
have committed a grave error you would continue to repeat such
errors if the occasions too were repeated.
    But I am not at all convinced that there was any error made.
As soon as the agitation for an amendment of the Pact arose, I
applied my mind to it, discussed it with friends who ought to
know and I was satisfied that there was no injustice done to
Bengal. I corresponded with those who complained of injustice.
But they, too, including Ramanandbabu*, could not convince me
of any injustice. Of course, our points of view were different. In
my opinion, the approach to the question was also wrong.

---

* Ramananda Chatterji, Editor, *Modern Review*, Calcutta.

A Pact arrived at by mutual arrangement cannot possibly be altered by the British Government except through the consent of the parties to the Pact. But no serious attempt seems to have been made to secure any such agreement. Your appearance, therefore, on the same platform as the complainants, I for one, welcome, in the hope that it would lead to a mutual discussion, instead of a futile appeal to the British Government. If, therefore, you have, for your own part, studied the subject and have arrived at the opinion that you have now pronounced, I would like you to convene a meeting of the principal parties and convince them that a grave injustice has been done to Bengal. If it can be proved, I have no doubt that the Pact will be re-considered and amended so as to undo the wrong said to have been done to Bengal. If I felt convinced that there was an error of judgement, so far as Bengal was concerned, I would strain every nerve to see that the error was rectified. You may know that up to now I have studiously refrained from saying anything in public in defence of the Pact, save by way of reiterating my opinion accompanied by the statement that if injustice could be proved, redress would be given. I am, therefore, entirely at your service.

Just now, I am absorbed in disbanding the Ashram and devising means of saving as much as can be for public use. My service will, therefore, be available after I am imprisoned, which event may take place any day after the end of this month. I hope you are keeping good health.

Yours sincerely,
M.K. Gandhi

16. Tagore's misgivings about Poona Pact

(See Document 9 in Appendix. Reproduced from a copy kept in Rabindra Bhavan.)

Uttarayan,
Santiniketan, Bengal,
28 July 1933

Dear Mahatmaji,
This is the copy of the message which, with very great pain and reluctance, I cabled to Sir Nripen [Sarkar] and from which

you will know how I feel about the Poona Pact. I am fully
convinced that if it is accepted without modification, it will be a
source of perpetual communal jealousy leading to constant disturbance of peace and a fatal break in the spirit of mutual co-
operation in our province.

    With love and reverence,

                                                Rabindranath Tagore

17. Gandhi's acknowledgement of Tagore's letter

(Original letter in Mahadev Desai's hand signed by Gandhi)
[Censored by Superintendent, Yeravada Central Prison, Poona]

                                         Yeravada Central Prison,
                                              7th August 33

Dear Gurudev
    Your letter of the 28th July enclosing copy of your cable to
Sir Nripen Sarkar on the Yeravada Pact was handed to me here
on the 4th instant. Evidently your letter crossed mine which I
wrote whilst I was in Ahmedabad. For the time being I am unable
however to send you anything but the bare acknowledgement.

                                             Yours sincerely,
                                              M.K. Gandhi

18. Tagore on inclusion of Bengal in Poona Pact

(From a copy kept in Rabindra Bhavan.)

8 August 1933

Dear Mahatmaji,

At this unhappy moment I am sure you need complete rest after the strenuous days of mental and physical strain, I do not wish to trouble you with any detailed discussion of the Poona Pact. You are satisfied that there was no injustice done to Bengal. I wish I could accept your words and remain silently contented about it but it has become impossible for me knowing for certain that the communal award advocated by the Pact, if it remains unaltered will inflict a serious injury upon the social and political life in Bengal. Justice is an important aspect of truth and if it is allowed to be violated for the sake of immediate peace or speedy cutting of some political knots in the long run, it is sure to come back to those who are apparently benefited by it and will claim a very heavy price for the concession cheaply gained. You know that I am not a politician, and I look upon the whole thing from the point of view of humanity, which will cruelly suffer when its claim to justice is ignored. I give you in this letter only my own considered opinion and do not desire any answer for it.

With love and reverence,

Yours sincerely,
Rabindranath Tagore

PART IV

1934–1941

1934–1941

Notes on Documents

Documents in this period centre around four major issues. First, the controversial statement of Gandhi linking the earthquake of Bihar in 1934 with the sin of casteism, which has been extensively commented upon in the 'Introduction' to this volume. The relevant documents are 3, 4, 6 and 7. In the middle of this controversy Tagore issued a statement defending Gandhi against his detractors (Document 5).

The second issue was the posture of the Congress establishment, led by prominent Gandhians, towards Subhas Chandra Bose who was forced to resign presidentship of the Congress. Tagore was unwilling to intervene too much into such matters but he was deeply worried about the fate of the Congress (Documents 18, 19). Gandhi wrote to Andrews on 15 January 1940 to assuage Tagore's anxieties and to assure Tagore that Subhas was "as my son" but he behaved "like a spoilt child" (see 'Introduction').

A third group of letters between Gandhi and Tagore arise out of their mutual concern for the financial stability of Visva-Bharati (Documents 8, 9, 10). Gandhi secured funding from various sources among his wealthy admirers (Gandhi to Tagore, 6 and 7 November 1937; see 'Appendix'). Gandhi did not like Tagore's "begging expeditions" like the one Tagore undertook in 1936 (Document 10).

Finally, there is another bunch of letters which arise out of the above. Tagore continued, till a very late age, to lead performances by the students of his Sangeet Bhavana at Visva-Bharati to raise funds. This Gandhi objected to and he declined the position of a Trustee of Visva-Bharati for this reason. Tagore maintained that presenting to the world his musical creations was his vocation, and a "poet's religion" (Documents 11, 12, 13, 14).

Apart from this, some events of the day cast their shadows on these letters, e.g. the repression in Midnapore after the assasination of the Magistrate (Documents 1, 12), the condition of the Andaman prisoners (see 'Appendix', Gandhi's cable to Tagore, 16 August 1937), C.F. Andrews' illness and death (Documents 24, 25, 26) and the like. Some of these exchanges are incomplete and fragmentary and these have been placed in the 'Appendix'.

Gandhi visited Santiniketan to meet Tagore in February 1940. Tagore's speech of welcome and Pyarelal's account of the Santiniketan pilgrimage are included in the 'Appendix'. Some letters connected with this visit (Documents 20, 21, 22, 23) are important. This is the occasion when Tagore requested Gandhi to take care of Visva-Bharati, "a vessel which is carrying my life's best treasure", and Gandhi assured Tagore of his support to that "common endeavour" (Documents 22, 23).

Two important pronouncements by Gandhi are not reproduced here since they are already available in his Collected Works. One is the press statement he made on his way from Santiniketan to Calcutta on 19 February 1940 (CWMG, Vol.LXXI, pp. 226-27) on the 'Communal Decision' in respect of representation in Bengal Legislature. Gandhi said that the Congress Working Committee "has neither accepted nor rejected the decision." His own opinion was that the case of Bengal was "the most glaring instance of injustice" in respect of "the wedge of the tremendous European vote between the two major communities." The other matter on which both Tagore and Gandhi made important statements was Eleanor Rathbone's open letter to Indians. Tagore's statement, practically from his deathbed, on 4 June 1941 was a masterpiece of sarcasm. The British are "scandalised at our ingratitude—that having drunk deeply at the wells of English thought we should still have some thoughts left for our poor country's interests... The British hate the Nazis for merely challenging their world mastery and Miss Rathbone expects us to kiss the hands of her people... for having riveted chains on ours." These documents are available in CWMG, Vol. LXXIV.

Tagore was ailing very often in these last years of his life and many letters are about that as well as Tagore's concern for Gandhi when he undertook some fasts (Documents 11, 15, 16, 17, 28). The day before his own birthday Gandhi wrote a rather touching letter to Tagore—"stay yet a while"—in 1940, his last letter to Tagore (Document 27). On Tagore's birthday in April 1941 they exchanged pleasantries in telegrams (Document 29). That was the last communication between them.

EDITOR

1. Gandhi on repression in Bengal

(In Gandhi's own hand)

21 January 1934

Dear Gurudev,

The news about the Govt measures in Midnapur has dazed me. They appear to be worse than the Martial Law measures in the Punjab in 1919. I get here only the *Hindu*. Are you doing anything? Is Bengal doing anything? Our cowardice chokes me. Or do I see cowardice where there is none? Can you give me any solace? I hope you are keeping well.

With deep love,

Ever Yours,
M.K. Gandhi

I am in Coonoor between 29th January & 5th February

2. Tagore on the "lawlessness" of the Government

31 January 1934

Dear Mahatmaji,

I have received your letter in which you mention the government measures in Midnapore. Midnapore is by no means an isolated case, it seems the accepted policy of the government is to terrify the people into submission. Detailed news about the latest manifestations of government lawlessness are just reaching us, but I have experience enough not to feel surprised. As for protest against these, I am afraid old people like me are of very little practical value. The government as well as my countrymen know my views and there is no sense in my issuing a fresh statement. But I hope I shall be able to discuss the matter in an article I shall set myself to write soon and thus make my protest in a manner which best suits my temperament and capacity.

With deep love,

Yours ever,
Rabindranath Tagore

3. Tagore on "divine chastisement" of Bihar

28 January 1934

Dear Mahatmaji,

   The press reports that you in a recent speech referring to the recent earthquake in Bihar spoke as follows, 'I want you, to be superstitious enough (sic) to believe with me that the earthquake is a divine chastisement for the great sin we have committed against those whom we describe as Harijans'. I find it difficult to believe it. But if this be your real view on the matter, I do not think it should go unchallenged. Herewith you will find a rejoinder from me. If you are correctly reported in the press, would you kindly send it to the press? I have not sent it myself for publication, for I would be the last person to criticise you on unreal acts.

   I am looking forward to meeting you here.

   With deep love,

Yours as ever,
Rabindranath Tagore

4. Gandhi's telegram to Tagore

Coonoor,
2 February 1934

To: Gurudev, Santiniketan.

   Your letter have (sic) given considered opinion Harijan posting advance copy if after reading it you deem necessary publish your protest it can be published at your end or mine as you desire.

M.K. Gandhi

5. Tagore's statement in defence of Gandhi

Santiniketan,
6 February 1934

For some time past, I have been noticing a spirit of hostility amongst a certain section of my countrymen against the latest activities of Mahatma Gandhi. One can take no exception to genuine criticism but there is always a difference between criticism and vilification. To one really great, the ready adulation as well as cheap sneers of the mob mean very little and I know Mahatmaji carries that greatness with him. But nonetheless I would be failing in my duty were I not to raise my voice of protest against the slanderous campaign that is being carried out against him. For, Mahatmaji is the one person who has done most to raise the people up from the slough of despondency and self-abasement to which they had fallen through centuries of servitude. His message of hope and faith has changed the entire outlook of the people, as if overnight. He has inspired courage and self-respect into the hearts of those who for centuries had patiently borne the load of indignity upon their heads and believed it to be eternal, and we cannot but offer our homage of admiration to one who has worked this miracle.

To malign a life so truly dedicated as his because of occasional differences of opinion seems to be carrying public ingratitude to the point of meanness. I have often disagreed with him in public and even quite recently have criticised his belief that the recent earthquake devastation in Bihar is a divine chastisement, for the sin of untouchability but I have enough regard for the sincerity of his religious convictions and his abiding love for the poor as to hold his differences of opinion with me with respect.

I offer him hearty welcome to Bengal and appeal to the people of my province to join with me in appreciating the great value of his life to our motherland.

Rabindranath Tagore

6. The Bihar earthquake

(The following is the statement issued by Tagore of protest against Gandhi's remark of "divine chastisement" of Bihar which appeared in Harijan, *16 February 1934.)*

It has caused me painful surprise to find Mahatma Gandhi accusing those who blindly follow their own social custom of untouchability of having brought down God's vengeance upon certain parts of Bihar, evidently specially selected for His desolating displeasure. It is all the more unfortunate, because this kind of unscientific view of things is too readily accepted by a large section of our countrymen. I keenly feel the iniquity of it when I am compelled to utter a truism in asserting that physical catastrophies have their inevitable and exclusive origin in certain combination of physical facts. Unless we believe in the inexorableness of the universal law in the working of which God himself never interferes, we find it impossible to justify his ways on occasions like the one which has sorely stricken us in an overwhelming manner and scale.

If we associate ethical principles with cosmic phenomena, we shall have to admit that human nature is morally superior to Providence that preaches its lessons in good behaviour in orgies of the worst behaviour possible. For, we can never imagine any civilised ruler of men making indiscriminate examples of casual victims, including children and members of the untouchable community, in order to impress others dwelling at a safe distance who possibly deserve severer condemnation. Though we cannot point out any period of human history that is free from iniquities of the darkest kind, we still find citadels of malevolence yet remain unshaken, that the factories, that cruelly thrive upon abject poverty and the ignorance of the famished cultivators, or prison-houses in all parts of the world where a penal system is pursued, which, most often, is a special form of licensed criminality, still stand firm. It only shows that the law of gravitation does not in the least respond to the stupendous load of callousness that accumulates till the moral foundation of our society begins to show dangerous cracks and civilisations are undermined. What is truly tragic about it is the fact that the kind of argument, that Mahatmaji uses by exploiting an event of cosmic disturbance far better suits the psychology of his opponents than his own, and it would not have surprised me at all if they had taken this opportunity of holding him and his followers responsible for the visitation of Divine anger. As for us, we feel perfectly secure in the faith that our own sins and errors, however enormous, have not enough force to drag down the structure of creation to ruins. We can depend upon it, sinners and saints, bigots and breakers of convention. We, who are immensely grateful to Mahatmaji for inducing, by his wonder working inspiration, freedom from fear and feebleness in the minds of his countrymen, feel profoundly hurt when any words from his mouth may emphasise the elements of unreason in those very minds—unreason, which is a fundamental source of all the blind powers that drive us against freedom and self-respect.

Rabindranath Tagore

7. Superstition vs. Faith

(Gandhi's spirited rejoinder to Tagore which was published in Harijan February 1934.)

The Bard of Santiniketan is Gurudev for me as he is for the inmates of that great institution. But Gurudev and I early discovered certain differences, and it cannot suffer by Gurudev's latest utterance on my linking the Bihar calamity with the sin of untouchability. He had a perfect right to utter his protest when he believed that I was in error. My profound regard for him would make me listen to him more readily than to any other critic. But in spite of my having read the statement three times, I adhere to what I have written in these columns.

When at Tinnevelly I first linked the event with untouchability, I spoke with the greatest deliberation and out of the fullness of my heart, I spoke as I believed. I have long believed that physical phenomena produce results both physical and spiritual. The converse I hold to be equally true.

To me the earthquake was no caprice of God nor a result of a meeting of mere blind forces. We do not know all the laws of God nor their working. Knowledge of the tallest scientist or the greatest spiritualist is like a particle of dust. If God is not a personal being for me like my earthly father, He is infinitely more. He rules me in the tiniest detail of my life. I believe literally that not a leaf moves but by His will. Every breath I take depends upon His suffrance.

He and His law are one. The Law is God. Anything attributed to Him is not a mere attribute. He is the Attribute. He is Truth, Love, Law and a million things that human ingenuity can name. I do believe with Gurudev "in the inexorableness of the universal law in the working of which God Himself never interferes." For God is the Law. But I submit that we do not know the Law or the laws fully, and what appears to us as catastrophes are so only because we do not know the universal laws sufficiently.

Visitations like droughts, floods, earthquakes and the like, though they seem to have only physical origins, are, for me, somehow connected with man's morals. Therefore, I instinctively felt that the earthquake was a visitation for the sin of untouchability. Of course, Sanatanists have a perfect right to say that it was due to my crime of preaching against untouchability. My belief is a call to repentance and self-purification. I admit my utter ignorance of the working of the laws of Nature. But even as I cannot help believing in God though I am unable to prove His existence to the sceptics, in like manner, I cannot prove the connection of the sin of untouchability with the Bihar visitation even though the connection is instinctively felt by me. If my belief turns out ill-founded, it will still have done good to me and those who believe with me. For we shall have been spurred to more vigorous efforts towards self-purification, assuming of-course, that untouchability is a deadly sin. I know fully well the danger of such speculation. But I would be untruthful and cowardly if, for fear of ridicule, when those that are nearest and dearest to me are suffering, I did not proclaim my belief from the house-top. The physical effect of the earthquake will be soon forgotten and even partially repaired. But it would be terrible, if it is an expression of the divine wrath for the sin of untouchability and we did not learn the moral lesson from the event and repent for that sin. I have not the faith which Gurudev has that "our own sins and errors, however enormous, have not got enough force to drag down the structure of creation to ruins." On the contrary I have the faith that our own sins have more force to ruin that structure than any mere physical phenomenon. There is an indissoluble marriage between matter and spirit. Our ignorance of the results of the union makes it a profound mystery and inspires awe in us, but it cannot undo them. But a living recognition of the union has enabled many to use every physical catastrophe for their own moral uplifting.

With me the connection between cosmic phenomena and human behaviour is a living faith that draws me nearer to my God, humbles me and makes me readier for facing him. Such a belief would be a degrading superstition, if out of the depth of my ignorance I used it for castigating my opponents.

M.K. Gandhi

8. Tagore's appeal to Gandhi about Santiniketan

Santiniketan, (Birbhum)
12th September 1935

My dear Mahatmaji,

I am glad Suren had an opportunity to discuss with you in detail the financial situation of the *asrama* during his recent visit to Wardha. I know how busy you are with your various activities and though I have often thought of telling you of my difficulties I have never done so before. But Charlie insisted that you must be informed about the situation and then only I gave permission to discuss it with you. Over thirty years I have practically given my all to this mission of my life and so long as I was comparatively young and active I faced all my difficulties unaided and through my struggles the institution grew up in its manifold aspects. And now, however, when I am 75 I feel the burden of my responsibility growing too heavy for me, that owing to some deficiency in me that my appeals fail to find adequate response in the heart of my people though the cause that I have done my utmost to serve is certainly valuable. Constant begging excursions with absurdly meagre results added to the strain of my daily anxieties and have brought my physical constitution nearly to an extreme verge of exhaustion. Now I know of none else but

yourself whose words may help my countrymen to realise that it
is worth their while to maintain this institution in fullness of its
functions and to relieve me of perpetual worry at this last period
of my waning life and health.

   With deepest love,

                                                    Rabindranath Tagore

9. Gandhi undertakes to help Tagore

                                                                Wardha,
                                                    13 October 1935

Dear Gurudev,
   Your touching letter was received only on 11th inst. when
I was in the midst of meetings. In the hope of delivering it to me
personally Anil needlessly detained it. I hope he is now quite
restored to health. Yes, I have the financial position before me
now. You may depend upon my straining every nerve to find the
required money. I am groping. I am trying to find the way out.
It will take sometime before I can report the result of my search
to you.
   It is unthinkable that you should have to undertake another
begging mission at your age. The necessary funds must come to
you without your having to stir out of Santiniketan.
   I hope you are keeping well. Padmaja who was with you a
few days ago, is here for the day and has been telling me how you
have aged.
   With reverential love,

                                                                Yours
                                                         M.K. Gandhi

10. Gandhi arranges required funds for Santiniketan

(Letter in Gandhi's own hand.)

Delhi,
27 March 1936

Dear Gurudev,

God has blessed my poor effort. And here is the money. Now you will relieve the public mind by announcing cancellation of the rest of the programme.

May God keep you for many a year to come.

Yours with love,
M.K. Gandhi

Delhi,
27 March 1936

Respected Sir,

Please find the enclosed draft for Rs.60,000 which we believe is the deficit on the expenses on Shantiniketan to cover for which you have been exhibiting your art from place to place. When we heard this we felt humiliated. We believe that at your advanced age and in your weak state of health you ought not to have to undertake these arduous tours. We must confess that we know very little of the institution except the name. But we have not been unaware of your great fame as the Poet of the age. You are not only the greatest Poet of India, you are the Poet of Humanity. Your poems remind one of the hymns of the ancient *Rishis*. You have by your unrivalled gifts raised the status of our country. And we feel that those whom God has blessed with means should relieve you of the burden of finding the funds required for the conduct of the institution. Our contribution is a humble effort in that direction. For reasons which need not be stated we prefer to remain anonymous. We hope that you will now cancel all the engagements taken for raising the sum above mentioned.

Praying for your long life to continue the service you are

rendering to our country.

> We remain
> Your Humble Countrymen

11. Tagore nominates Gandhi as a Life Trustee

10 February 1937

My dear Mahatmaji,

    I have taken the liberty of nominating you as a Life Trustee of our Visva-Bharati. In these last frail years of my life it will give me great consolation to know that the Institution to which I have given the best part and energy of my life will have you as one of its guardians. You will see from the Bulletin of Statutes and Regulations that is being sent under a separate cover that no strain of actual work will be put upon you, save what is entailed in occasional advice and decision in regard to matters that touch the financial security of the Institution. I feel justified in sharing my responsibilities with you for I know that no difference in our spheres of activity can loosen the bond of mutual love and common aspiration. I hope you will allow me that privilege.

> Yours affectionately,
> Rabindranath Tagore

Mahatma M.K.Gandhi,
Wardha, C.P.

12. Gandhi asks Tagore to recall Life-Trusteeship

(CWMG, *Vol.LXIV*)

Segaon, Wardha,
19 February 1937

Dear Gurudev,

    I got your letter of the 10th instant five days ago. Your trust in me and affection for me are there to be seen in every line but what about my amazing limitations? My shoulders are too weak to bear the burden you wish to impose upon me. My regard to you pulls me in one direction, my reason in the opposite, and it would be folly on my part to surrender reason to emotion in a question like the one that faces me. I know that if I undertake the trust I would not need to go into details of administration but it does imply capacity for financing the Institution and what I heard two days ago has deepened my reluctance for, I understand that in spite of your promise to me in Delhi you are about to go to Ahmedabad on a begging expedition. I was grieved and I would ask you on bended knees to forgo the expedition if it is really decided upon. And in any case I would beg of you to recall my appointment as one of the Trustees.

With love and reverence,

M.K. Gandhi

13. Tagore's reply

(This letter was sent on 26-2-37.)

Dear Mahatmaji,

You have grievously misjudged me on mere suspicion which is so unlike your great and gracious ways that it has started me into a painful amazement. I feel ashamed to have to assert that it was never my intention financially to exploit you or your name when I asked you to accept the trusteeship of Visva-Bharati. However, if it has been a mistake on my part, be the reason what it may, I readily withdraw my request and ask to be forgiven.

In your letter you have strangely accused me of contemplating to break my promise and go to Ahmedabad for the purpose of raising funds. You were not certain of the facts, and had no justification for hinting such a charge against me. Allow me to be frank in return and to tell you that possibly your own temperament prevents you to understand the dignity of the mission which I am glad to call my own,—a mission that is not merely concerned with the economic problem of India or her sectarian religions, but which comprehends the culture of the human mind in its broadest sense. And when I feel the urge to send abroad some poetical creation of mine, which according to me carries within it a permanent standard of beauty, I expect, not alms or favour, but grateful homage to my art from those who, have the sensitiveness of soul to respond to it. And if I have to receive contribution in the shape of admission fees from the audience, I claim it as very much less than what is due to me in return for the rare benefit conferred upon them. Therefore, I must refuse to accept the term "begging expedition" as an accurate or worthy expression coming from your pen.

It is a part of a poet's religion to entertain in his life a solemn faith in his own function, to realise that he is specially called to collaborate with his Creator in adding to the joy of existence. Let me confess that I should like nothing better than proudly to sit by the side of the artists trained by me when they try to give perfect expression to my dreams of beauty in their rhythmic movements and voice, and so be able to tell them that they have done well.

Yours sincerely,
Rabindranath Tagore

14. Gandhi on Tagore's "begging expedition"

(CWMG, *Vol.LXIV*)

Seagaon, Wardha,
2 March 1937

Dear Gurudev,
Your letter has caused me much distress. That a letter which was written out of love and reverence should have been so misunderstood is a revelation. There was no question of suspicion and, therefore, no question of misjudging you. I simply put before you my meaning of trusteeship. I have been trustee before now of several institutions and I have worn myself out to see that they were properly financed. Acceptance of the burden by me of Visvabharati could mean nothing to me unless it at least meant that I would be able to discharge the financial burden. As to the breach of promise, I thought myself to be so near you that I could dare playfully to accuse you of a contemplated breach of promise. My motive was absolutely plain. I wanted, somehow or other, to wean you from any further begging expedition—a phrase which you and I used often enough in Delhi. Of course I know your

religion and all India is proud of it. Let us have as much of it as you can give but never with the burden hanging over your head of collecting money for Visva-Bharati against the expression of yourself before the public.

I hope this letter will undo the grief that has been caused to you by my previous letter.

With love and reverence,

Yours,
M.K. Gandhi

15. Tagore thanks Gandhi for his message of "affectionate anxiety"

(Written by Tagore in his own hand.)

Santiniketan,
19 September 1937

Dear Mahatmaji,
The first thing which welcomed me into the world of life after the period of stupor I passed through was your message of affectionate anxiety and it was fully worth the cost of sufferings which were unremitting in their long persistence.

With grateful love,

Rabindranath Tagore

Mahatma Gandhi,
Wardha

16. Gandhi writes a letter with his left hand

(CWMG, *Vol.LXVI*)

Seagaon, Wardha,
23 September 1937

Dear Gurudev,

Your precious letter is before me. You have anticipated me. I wanted to write as soon as Sir Nilratan sent me his last reassuring wire. But my right hand needs rest. I did not want to dictate. The left hand works slow. This is merely to show you what love some of us bear towards you. I verily believe that the silent prayers from the hearts of your admirers have been heard and you are still with us. You are not a mere singer of the world. Your living word is a guide and an inspiration to thousands. May you be spared for many a long year yet to come.

With deep love,

Yours sincerely,
M.K. Gandhi

17. Tagore's birthday greetings to Gandhi

Santiniketan, 2-10-37

To: Mahatma Gandhi Wardha

We are all grateful for the great gift of your life

Rabindranath Tagore

18. Tagore's letter requesting "balm to the wound" inflicted on Bengal

"Uttarayan",
Santiniketan, Bengal,
29 March 1939

Dear Mahatmaji,

At the last Congress session some rude hands have deeply

hurt Bengal with an ungracious persistence. Please apply without delay balm to the wound with your own kind hands and prevent it from festering.

    With love,

Ever yours,
Rabindranath Tagore

Mahatma Gandhi,
Birla House,
Albuquerque Road,
New Delhi.

19. The Congress

(This article by Tagore published in July 1939 in Modern Review *is a critique of the developments that had overtaken the Congress; the original Bengali version, in the form of a letter to the poet Amiya Chakraborty was published in* Pravasee)

I sit down to write to you in a perturbed state of mind.

There was a time, not so very long ago, when the mind of the great mass of our countrymen was desert-like, its unfertile expanse divided into isolated sections between which all commerce was obstructed, resulting for India, in a succession of poverty-sticken epochs. All of a sudden came the rise into power of the new Congress organisation, a wide-branching tree that held out large promise of future fruit. Surprising was the change it wrought in the mass mind, as it learnt to hope, forgot to fear, and ceased to shrink from the very idea of casting off its bonds. What had seemed a while ago to be beyond the bounds of the possible was no longer felt to be unattainable. The feebleness of spirit that dreaded to desire was at length cured. And this stupendous change was due to the unbounded faith in India's destiny of one single man—a fact which already shows signs, here and there, of fading from public recollection.

Of course I know that, however dependent the new Congress regime may be on the personality of its founder, and great though that personality undoubtedly is, it will nevertheless

be necessary from time to time to enlarge its scope and improve
its working. But too much of a hurry to disturb the adaptation to
its present circumstances which has grown with the growth of the
Congress, may break up its very foundation. For it has to be
admitted that no other genius seems to have arisen amongst us
who is competent to bring about a radical change in it without
damage to its organic cohesion. That is why I think that this vast
field of endeavour, where the different forces of the country may
meet and join hands, needs must continue to be developed, for
the present, under the guidance of the Mahatma who gave it
birth.

As you know, I have never been a blind follower of
tradition,—that is to say, I have not believed that our national
welfare could be made secure by fixing once for all some principle
or method that was once found to be good, nor do I now feel it
to be true that however great the Congress organisation may have
grown, its aims and objects should be stereotyped for all time,—
rather do I devoutly wish that such a calamity may not befall it.
At the same time, whenever I realise the immense value of this
organisation as created by a great-souled Master, I cannot but be
perturbed at the possible consequences of piecemeal attacks on it
from the outside. Such reforms as are found to be necessary must
come from within itself.

Many of us still remember the original National Congress
that started political agitation in India. It made no attempt to look
into, to awaken, the mind of the people, its appealing glances
were all directed to the authorities above. What it called freedom
lay in the lap of dependence on others—this was the obsession it
could not get rid of. I need hardly remind you that I have
hesitated to cry shame on the poverty of spirit of the begging and
praying Salvation Army into which that Congress had resolved
itself.

We all know whose was the magic wand that touched into
life the deadly torpor into which the country had fallen, making
it conscious of its own powers, proclaiming non-violence to be
the true creed of the brave. Of this new life which Mahatmaji gave
to India, the stage of initiation is not yet passed, and further
advance along its way should still be under the guidance of the
Master. Like Nandi who stood guard at the entrance to Shiva's
hermitage I must raise my warning finger for all that the Mahat-

ma has to teach may not yet have reached us. When the rigour of Shiva's meditation was untimely broken, a raging conflagration was the only result.

So far, for one side of the question. The other side also deserves anxious consideration. When the powers of the Congress had but begun to unfold, it had little to fear from within. Now it is at the height of its prestige; it has gained world-wide recognition; the doors of Government at which its predecessors of old had vainly knocked, are now hospitably open to it, even ready to show it honour. But Manu, the ancient law-giver has warned us to beware of honour. For where power rises into eminence, toxins are created that eventually destroy it,—be it Imperialism or Fascism, have they not been generating the seeds of their own downfall? It may likewise be that the heat created by· the growing power of the Congress is rising to an unhealthy temperature. The higher command who are at its helm are apt in moments of crisis, to lose their head, and cannot hold to a straight course. Have we not seen lapses in regard to the vital matters of mutual courtesy and forbearance of constitutional procedure which had hitherto been sources of its strength,—lapses at the bottom of which lies pride of power?

The Christian scriptures have warned us how difficult it is for bloated prosperity to pass through the narrow gate of the Kingdom of Heaven. Freedom can be won only by putting forth the best in man, that is what I understand the teaching of the Mahatma to be. But those who have come together to control the field of our high endeavour—are their minds broadly tolerant, unswayed by personal bias? When they create ruptures by wounding one another is that for the sake of pure principle—is there no trace in it of the heat that is born of love power, pride of power? The cult of *shakti* that is gradually growing up within the Congress fold shows itself in its true colours when Mahatmaji's followers find it in their hearts to proclaim him as the equal of Hitler and Mussolini. Can it be at all possible for those whose reverence goes out to these gatherers of victims for human sacrifice, properly to maintain the purity of the citadel of Truth build by the selfless ascetic whom they would follow? I have the highest respect for Jawaharlal, who is always ready to lead an assault against abuse of power by wealth or blind faith, or imperialistic politics. Of him I ask whether the keepers of the

Congress stronghold have not on occasions shown dangerous signs of the intoxication of personal power? I have my own doubts, but at the same time I do not hide from myself the fact that my knowledge of political happenings is very insufficient.

On this point it is necessary to say something further. Bengal seems to have made up its mind at the last sitting of the Congress Committee, the Bengali people were treated with contumely. To be too ready to believe such a charge is nothing but a sign of weakness. It is hardly a proof of political sanity to allow ourselves to be continually afflicted with the suspicion that every one around us is conspiring against us. But the fact remains that in spite of the uniting centre which the Congress represents, the provinces are showing lamentable signs of separatist tendencies.

The Hindu-Moslem disunity is both lamentable and alarming, because nothing is more difficult to bridge than the gulf created by religious differences. On the other hand, the disunity between the provinces is owing to a lack of proper mutual understanding, due to differences of habits and customs. Thus Religion and Custom have between them usurped the throne of Reason, thereby destroying all clarity of mind. In countries where customs are not blindly sacrosanct, where religious beliefs have not cut up society into warring sections, political unity has come as a matter of course. Our Congress has not had the advantage of being able to grow up in an atmosphere of social tolerance, rather it has had to function in spite of social antagonisms which have set up impassable barriers every few miles—barriers which are guarded night and day by forces wearing the badge of religion.

Whatever the reasons may be, the fact remains that our provinces have not been welded together. I remember to have said somewhere that a coach of which the wheels are wobbly, the box shaky, and the whole body creaky; is all very well so long as it remains propped up in its stable,—there it may even be admired as a whole; but if it be dragged by horses through the street, it loudly complains of the lack of inward unity. That is what the Congress has done. It has dragged the provinces of India out on the highway of a common political freedom, and its internal discords are thereupon becoming apparent at every step. This being our plight, it behoves the authorities of the Congress to be very circumspect in their movements, for mutual suspiciousness is lying in wait to exaggerate the implications of every lapse, or inconsiderate gesture. That is what seems to have happened in the case of Bengal, and the relations between it and the Congress high command have been strained to breaking point. Personally I am not aware that anything has happened which made this inevitable. And yet, while the popular mind is thus exercised, it will be difficult for the leaders of Bengal to steer a correct course.

To me it is evident that Mahatmaji, having mapped out a particular line along which he advises the country to travel on its way to freedom, is naturally on the alert to see that no disturbing factor be allowed to bring about a deviation from it. Having successfully steered the ship of Congress so far, his reluctance to let it be taken out of its appointed course cannot reasonably be construed as a desire to wield dictatorial power. Men of genius would be unable to fulfil their destiny unless they had unbounded confidence in themselves, a confidence which they are wont to fortify by their faith in divine inspiration. In spite of occasional serious mistakes, Mahatmaji may claim to have had sufficient proof in his successes of his being on the right track and he is moreover, entitled to believe that none but himself can worthily complete the picture of national welfare which he has conceived and outlined. It may well be that he has many a further touch in mind with which it is to be perfected in due course. If these finishing touches are not given under his direction, with the patient attention and reverence due to the master from his followers, the picture as a whole may suffer. In these circumstances, say I, we need must rely for its completion on its creator, especially as it is still in the stage of unfinished growth.

Here I should confess that I do not always see eye to eye with Mahatmaji, by which I mean that had I been endowed with his force of character, my scheme of work would have been different. What that scheme is, I have indicated in some of my previous writings. But though I may have the imagination to conceive, I have not the power to carry out. Only a few men in the world have this power. And since our country has had the good fortune of giving birth to such a man, the way should be kept clear for his progress—I certainly would never think of impeding it. The time will doubtless come when Mahatmaji's errors and omissions will have to be made good; then will each one of us, according to his zeal and capacity have the opportunity of making his contribution. For the present, let the Congress proceed to the destination towards which it is heading. I will not say, like a blind follower, that there can be no other bourne beyond. Others there may be and are; but the time to take on other pilots will come when the first part of the journey is over.

I have referred to my own scheme. That was the outcome of my conviction that politics is but a part of the social system,— as is borne out by the history of every country. To be enamoured of some political system apart from its social foundation, will not do. Triumphal structures of different shapes and sizes raise their heads on the other side of the seas. We may be sure that none of them are built on foundations of sand. And when we set to work to imitate any super-structure that has caught our fancy, we should not forget the necessity of fitting it to some adequate foundation in the depths of our own social mentality.

I have recently taken refuge on a secluded hill-top, far from the scene of the recent political excitement, and after a long time I am getting the opportunity to survey both India and my own attitude with dispassion. I can see clearly that politics has to do with two different sets of forces,—one may be called mechanical, the other spiritual. In these days of crisis Europe is pacing backwards and forwards between the two. Neither is easy to secure, or work with; both have their price, the proper application of both require long preparatory training. We who have been so long in subjection know what the impact of mechanised force is like, but we cannot even dream of bringing it under our own control. The utmost we can think of is to purchase the alliance of some other power by getting into its debt. But history has shown us that to cultivate this kind of unequal friendship is like digging a channel to give entry to the crocodile—resulting in a feast for the latter at the expense of the digger.

There was a time when the issue of battle depended on personal bravery and physical strength. Now has come the day of weapons wrought by science which require a high degree of intellectual skill for their proper use. Any fight with those is unthinkable for us, with our untrained body and mind. This was realised from the very beginning of our political life, wherefore our former leaders were content with launching their fleet of petition, carrying paper-boats. But this reduced our politics to a mere game. Then arrived Mahatmaji with a solution for our utter lack of material equipment. Unflinching he came, with head held high, to prove that battle could be effectively waged against wrong without mechanical resources. He started experimental campaigns along different lines—and though in none of them can it be asserted that he has won through—he has extracted from his very defeats, lessons showing the way to ultimate victory. He has been busy ever since inculcating in the country the need of training in restraint and spiritual faith necessary to wield the weapons of non-violence.

It is comparatively easy to raise an army for violent warfare. A year's drilling is sufficient to fit men to be sent to the seat of war, but to train the spirit in the methods of non-violence takes more time. We have had enough of attempts to get together a table of untrained enthusiasts. Such crowds may be used to break down the work of rivals, but they cannot build up anything of value. They go to pieces when met by determined counter-attack. Those nations of the world who are now in fighting trim, rely for their strength of the education of masses of their people. The present age is the age of the trained mind not of blustering muscle. And everywhere in the East to say nothing of Japan, educational institutions have been made for the people at large. So long as our masses remain bound to blind tradition it is hopeless for us to expect to make any move forward. And so, after his discovery that an undisciplined mob is not a fit instrument for non-violent work—Mahatmaji has cried a halt in his campaign of civil disobedience, and turned his attention to mass education. So far, all is fairly clear.

But when I come to the contending political groups of the day with their rival methods of political advancement, round which endless controversies are ragings, I am beset with doubts and cannot see the issue clearly. My main difficulty in arriving at any definite conclusion may be due to my very meagre knowledge of what is actually happening in the different political circles. I know that those who have the power can make possible the seemingly impossible. Mahatmaji is one of those who have this power; but it would be going too far to say that he is the only one, or that all he undertakes must be successful. And if any other

—powerful personality inspired with a different ideal should arise—the latter—in turn, will not stay his hands because of the doubts or protests of others. It may even be that he will have to cut adrift from the main body and work alone to form another organisation, of which it will take us time to appraise the proper value. Should such a personality come forth from within the Congress, I would watch his progress—and wish him success—but from a distance. It would be beyond my capacity, altogether out of my sphere of work to join hands with him in any way.

The responsibility would be so great, the effects so far-reaching, the consequences so incalculable, that their burden could only be shouldered by one who has the necessary degree of self-confidence.

Our scriptures tell us that the worship of *Ganesha*—the Lord of the Masses must come before all other worship. In the service of our country our first duty must be to work for the welfare of the mass of its people,—to make them healthy in body and mind, happy in spirit; to foster their self-respect, to bring beauty into their daily work—their daily life; to show them the way to strive together in mutual respect, for mutual welfare. So far as my limitations have permitted, I have been doing this for the last forty years or so. And when Mahatmaji's call awakened the country, it was my fervent hope that he would rouse the powers of all sections of our people, in all their variety, to work in the different departments of national endeavour. For it is my belief that a realisation of the country's welfare means to believe in it, to know it in its fullness. Its true freedom would consist in gaining the fullest scope for its own obstructed powers.

Rabindranath Tagore

20. A telegraphic invitation from Tagore

Santiniketan, 20-1-40

To: Mahatma Gandhi Segaon Wardha

Just learnt from papers your visit to Bengal. Hope you will spend a few days with me at Santiniketan.

Rabindranath Tagore

21. Prompt acceptance by telegram

Wardhaganj
Date 23, H.8, M.20

To: Gurudev Santiniketan

Arranging reach Santiniketan fifteenth or sixteenth staying there least two days love.

Gandhi

22. "My life's best treasure": Tagore on Visva-Bharati

(Letter handed over by Tagore to Gandhi at the time of his departure from Santiniketan on 2 February 1940)

Dear Mahatmaji,

You have just had a bird's-eye view this morning of our Visva-Bharati centre of activities. I do not know what estimate you have formed of its merit. You know that though this institution is national in its immediate aspect, it is international in its spirit offering according to the best of its means India's hospitality of culture to the rest of the world.

At one of its critical moments you have saved it from an utter breakdown and helped it to its legs. We are ever thankful to you for this act of friendliness.

And, now, before you take your leave from Santiniketan, I make my fervent appeal to you, accept this institution under your protection giving it an assurance of permanence if you consider it to be a national asset. Visva-Bharati is like a vessel which is carrying the cargo of my life's best treasure and I hope it may claim special care from my countrymen for its perservation.

Rabindranath Tagore

23. Their "common endeavour": Gandhi on Visva-Bharati

On the way to Calcutta,
19 February 1940

Dear Gurudev,

The touching note that you put into my hands as we parted has gone straight into my heart. Of course Visva-Bharati is a national institution. It is undoubtedly also international. You may depend upon my doing all I can in the common endeavour to assure its permanence.

I look to you to keep your promise to sleep religiously for about an hour daily during the day.

Though I have always regarded Santiniketan as my second home, this visit has brought me nearer to it than ever before.

With reverence and love

Yours,
M.K. Gandhi

24. Gandhi's telegram about the health of Andrews

(Rabindra Bhavan Archives)

CA2
Calcutta 26 Feb 40
13H.40 M. Recd at 14H.10M.

To: Gurudev Santiniketan

Charlie better Hope you are not thinking of coming see him He seems disturbed over prospect I want assure him you will not exert yourself Am here till tomorrow

Love

(Sender's name missing)

25. Tagore to Gandhi

Santiniketan, 27-2-40

To: Mahatma Gandhi Birla Park Calcutta Ballygunge

Your telegram feel happy with Charlies improvement On your advice shall not go to see him.

Rabindranath

26. Proposal for a joint appeal

(CWMG, *Vol.LXXII*)

Seagaon, Wardha,
5 May 1940

Dear Gurudev,

Ten Thousand apologies for the delay in replying to Rathin's letter. Pressure on my limited time is unbearable. The result is an accumulation of arrears. But I have not been idle about your proposal. I discussed it fully with Roger Hicks. I have been thinking over the thing independently. The conclusion is set forth in the enclosed amended draft. You will revise it as you like. You will give it the polish which you alone can give.

Somehow or other I could not reconcile myself to an appeal for the hall and the hospital. Santiniketan was his as much as it is yours. What can be better than that the thing to which he had given himself and from which he had derived inspiration would be put on a permanent basis? The sum asked may be too little. It should then be increased. I have stated that originally Santiniketan was founded by the Maharishi. There is an apparent contradiction in the statement. You will please deal with it.

The idea that the appeal should be signed by us three is, I think, quite good.

I have not sent a copy to the Bishop.

If you do not like my proposal and if you will retain the original, please do not hesitate to do so.

I hope you are keeping well.

With love,

Yours sincerely,
M.K. Gandhi

27. Gandhi's last letter to Tagore

(Written during Tagore's serious illness in 1940)

Delhi,
1 October 1940

Dear Gurudev,

You must stay yet awhile. Humanity needs you. I was pleased beyond measure to find that you were better.

With love,

Yours,
M.K. Gandhi

28. Tagore's last letter to Gandhi

(During Tagore's illness, Sept-Oct 1940)

6 Dwarakanath Tagore Lane,
Calcutta

To: Mahatma Gandhi Wardha

Your constant good wishes have brought me back from the land of darkness into the land of light and life and my first offering of thanks goes out to you.

Rabindranath

29. Gandhi and Tagore exchange telegraphic greetings

(Gandhi's greetings on Tagore's 81st birthday—13 April 1941)

To: Gurudev Shantiniketan

Four score not enough may you finish five
Love

Gandhi

(The Poet's reply)

To: Mahatma Wardha

Thanks message but four score is impertinence, five score intolerable

Rabindranath

APPENDIX

NOTES ON DOCUMENTS IN
THE APPENDIX

I have placed in the Appendix a few letters and writings which
have a bearing on those included in the main body of the text in
the preceding pages. Some of these documents in the Appendix
are trivia—fragments of letters, telegrams, press statements and
the like. Some of these are significant, but could not be included
in the preceding text since these did not form a part of the
exchanges between Gandhi and Tagore.

Among the important documents are: the letter Tagore
wrote to Viceroy Chelmsford in May 1930 renouncing his knighthood as an act of protest (Document 1); Gandhi's essay entitled
'Condition of the Swaraj' (Document 2) to which Tagore adverts
in his essays on the *charkha* and Non-cooperation; Tagore's
statement—a subtle political argument—to *The Spectator* of London in defence of Gandhi's decision not to attend the Round
Table Conference in 1930 (Document 4); and Tagore's press
statement in September 1934 on the "higher ideals in politics"
represented in Gandhi's *dharma yuddha* (Document 14).

Document no.10 below is to be read together with Tagore's
letter to Gandhi of 28 July 1933 (Document 16 in Part III). This is
the press statement, simultaneously issued by Tagore, expressing
his reservations concerning the "Poona Pact" and the consequent
"communal award" in respect of the province of Bengal. In this
statement Tagore is critical of his own role in legitimising, so to
speak, the Poona Pact and he regrets that he was unable to foresee
how grave a damage was being done to the prospects of communal harmony in Bengal. Gandhi, initially unresponsive to these
second thoughts offered by Tagore, conceded that some injustice
was involved in the communal award in respect of Bengal (see
Notes on Documents in Part IV of this book).

An important statement from Tagore was elicited by Shri
Mahadev Desai. The latter asked Tagore (Document 15) for his
opinion on the question of conversion of Harijans to Sikhism, a

question of importance because (a) "you cannot separate culture from religion" and renuniciation of Hinduism was tantamount to renunciation of a culture; (b) moreover," the converts will vote not as Hindus, but as Sikhs". Tagore's reply was very forthright: (a) it is unfortunate and indefensible that the "spirit of division, keeping down a large section of our (i.e. Hindu) community, is in the permanent structure of our religion", however much we might try to give the ancient texts "a civilised gloss". (b) Second-ly, Tagore is unconcerned "whether they vote as Hindus or Sikhs" because that is "of much lesser importance than what affects our humanity and forms our mental attitude to our fellow-beings" (Document 16). The entire letter is of great significance.

I have included two eye-witness accounts of encounters between Gandhi and Tagore. The first describes Tagore's visit to Gandhi's *ashram* in 1933, and the second Gandhi's "pilgrimage" to Santiniketan in 1940 (Documents 3 and 22).

A large number of telegrams which passed between Tagore and Gandhi have been preserved in the Visva-Bharati Archives at Rabindra Bhavan. A spate of cables was usually set off by the fasts undertaken by Gandhi (Documents 5, 6, 7, 8, 11) and, on the other hand, by the signs of declining health of Tagore (Documents 25, 26, 27). Apart from these the Appendix includes some brief letters concerning their mutual friend C.F. Andrews who died on 5 April 1940 (Documents 12, 13, 23, 24); collection of funds for Visva-Bharati (Documents 18, 19); and, finally, Tagore's Welcome Address to Gandhi on the last occasion they met, at Santiniketan in February 1940 (Document 21). From September 1940 Tagore was almost continuously ill and Gandhi's anxiety is evident in the letter he wrote on the eve of his own birthday in October 1940: "you *must* stay yet a while" (Document 27, Part IV). In April 1940 when Tagore completed 80 years, they exchanged greetings by telegrams. Tagore's physical condition steadily de-teriorated and he was removed from Santiniketan to Calcutta on 25 July 1941 to undergo surgery. Gandhi kept in touch through cables to the poet's son, Rathindranath (Documents 26, 27). Tagore died in Calcutta, in the house in which he was born, on 7 August 1941. The obituary written by Mahatma Gandhi ap-peared in most newspapers the next day (Document 28).

EDITOR

1. Tagore's letter to the Viceroy renouncing his knighthood

(Tagore wrote the following letter to His Excellency Lord Chelmsford, the Viceroy, giving voice to what Indians felt about the atrocities in Jallianwala Bagh and renouncing his knighthood.)

30 May 1919

Your Excellency,

The enormity of the measures taken by the Government in the Punjab for quelling some local disturbances has, with a rude shock, revealed to our minds the helplessness of our position as British subjects in India. The disproportionate severity of the punishments inflicted upon the unfortunate people and the methods of carrying them out, we are convinced, are without parallel in the history of civilised governments, barring some conspicuous exceptions, recent and remote. Considering that such treatment has been meted out to a population, disarmed and resourceless, by a power which has the most terribly efficient organisation for destruction of human lives, we must strongly assert that it can claim no political expediency, far less moral justification. The accounts of the insults and sufferings undergone by our brothers in the Punjab have trickled through the gagged silence, reaching every corner of India, and the universal agony of indignation roused in the hearts of our people has been ignored by our rulers—possibly congratulating themselves for imparting what they imagine as salutary lessons. This callousness has been praised by most of the Anglo-Indian papers, which have in some cases gone to the brutal length of making fun of our sufferings, without receiving the least check from the same authority, relentlessly careful in smothering every cry of pain and expression of judgement from the organs representing the sufferers.

Knowing that our appeals have been in vain and that the passion of vengeance is blinding the noble vision of statesmanship in our Government which could so easily afford to be magnanimous as befitting its physical strength and moral tradition, the very least that I can do for my country is to take all consequences upon myself in giving voice to the protest of the millions of my countrymen, surprised into a dumb anguish of terror. The time has come when badges of honour make our

shame glaring in their incongruous context of humiliation, and I
for my part wish to stand, shorn of all special distinctions, by the
side of my countrymen who, for their so-called insignificance, are
liable to suffer a degradation not fit for human beings. And these
are the reasons which have painfully compelled me to ask Your
Excellency with due deference and regret to relieve me of my title
of knighthood which I had the honour to accept from His Majesty
the King at the hands of your predecessor, for whose nobleness
of heart I still entertain great admiration.

Yours faithfully
Rabindranath Tagore

2. The Conditions of *swaraj*

(In the issue of Young India *of 23 February 1921, Gandhi clearly
enunciated the pre-conditions on the part of Indians for the
attainment of "swaraj")*

Swaraj is easy of attainment before October next, if certain
simple conditions can be fulfilled. I ventured to mention one year
in September last, because I knew that conditions were incredibly
simple and I felt that the atmosphere in the country was responsive. Past five months' experience has confirmed me in the
opinion. I am convinced that the country has never been so ready
for establishing *Swaraj* as now.

But it is necessary for us as accurately as possible to know
the conditions. One supreme indispensable condition is the con-
tinuance of non-violence. Rowdyism, hooliganism, looting that
we have recently witnessed are disturbing elements. They are
danger-signals. We must be able to arrest their progress. The
spirit of democracy cannot be established in a year in the midst
of terrorism whether governmental or popular. In some respects,
popular terrorism is more antagonistic to the growth of the
democratic spirit than the governmental. For the latter strength-
ens the spirit of democracy, whereas the former kills it. Dyerism
has evoked a yearning after freedom as nothing else has. But
internal Dyerism, representing as it will terrorism by a majority,

will establish an oligarchy such as stifle the spirit of all free discussion and conduct. Non-violence, therefore, as against the Government and as between ourselves, is absolutely essential to speedy success. And we must be able to devise means of observing it on our part in spite of the gravest provocations.

The next condition is our ability to bring into being the Congress organisation in terms of new Constitution, which aims at establishing a Congress agency in every village with a proper electorate. It means both money and ability to give effect to Congress policies. What is really needed is not a large measure of sacrifice but ability to organise and to take simple concerted action. At the present moment, we have not even succeeded in carrying the Congress message to every home in the 77 lacs of villages of India. To do this work means at least 250 honest workers for as many districts, who have influence in their respective districts and who believe in the Congress programme. No village, no circle need wait for instructions from headquarters for founding their respective organisations.

There are certain things that are applicable to all. The most potent thing is *swadeshi*. Every home must have the spinning wheel and every village can organise itself in less than a month and become self supporting for its cloth. Just imagine what these silent revolution means and there would be no difficulty in sharing my belief that *swadeshi* means *swaraj* and *swadharma*.

Every man and woman can give some money—be it, even a pice—to the Tilak Swaraj Fund. And we need have no anxiety about financing the movement. Every man and woman can deny himself or herself all luxury, all ornamentation, all intoxicants at least for one year. And we shall have not only money but we shall have boycotted many foreign articles. Our civilization, our culture, our *swaraj* depend not upon multiplying our wants—self-indulgence, but upon restricting our wants—self-denial.

We can do nothing without Hindu-Muslim unity and without killing the snake of untouchability. Untouchability is a corroding poison that is eating into the vitals of Hindu society—*Varnashrama* is not a religion of superiority and inferiority. No man or God can consider another man as inferior to himself. He must consider every man as his blood-brother. It is the cardinal principle of every religion.

If this is a religious battle, no argument is necessary to

convince the reader that self-denial must be its supreme test. *khilafat* cannot be saved, the Punjab humanity cannot be redressed, without godliness. Godliness means change of heart—in political language, changing the angle of vision. And such a change can come in a moment. My belief is that India is ripe for that change.

Let us then rivet our attention on:

(1) Cultivating the spirit of non-violence.

(2) Setting up Congress organisations in every village.

(3) Introducing the spinning wheel in every home and manufacturing all the cloth, required for our wants, through the village weaver.

(4) Collecting as much money as possible.

(5) Promoting Hindu-Muslim unity and

(6) Ridding Hinduism of the curse of untouchability and otherwise purifying ourselves by avoiding intoxicating drinks and drugs.

Have we honest, earnest, industrious, patriotic workers for this very simple programme? If we have, *swaraj* will be established in India before next October.

M..K. Gandhi

3. The Poet's visit

(The issue of Young India, *dated 23 January 1930 carried a report of Tagore's visit to Gandhi's Satyagraha Ashram in Ahmedabad, written by Mahadev Desai.)*

The Poet, who is touring this part of the country on begging mission for the Vishva-Bharati, honoured our *ashram* with a visit on the 18th instant. He had a cold, and the signs of strain, exhaustion and, if he will pardon me, of old age, were quite visible on his noble countenance. But he stayed with us longer than we had expected with the result that we had one of the pleasantest evenings we had for many a day.

"I am seventy now, Mahatmaji," he said. "and so am considerably older than you."

"But", said Gandhiji with a hearty smile, "when an old man of 60 cannot dance, a young poet of 70 can dance."

"That is true", said the Poet appreciating the compliment. But he seemed to envy Gandhiji's ready-made prescriptions for a happy old age when he said, "You are getting ready for another arrest cure. I wish they gave me one."

"But," said Gandhiji, "You do not behave yourself," and there was a peal of laughter in the little room where the Poet and the man at the wheel were sitting.

The Poet talked in his usual manner on all varieties of subjects, all of us listening with rapt attention. He had vivid in his memory the picture of a Korean who had visited him. The man was dreaming dreams of a new Korea.

"How will you fight exploiting Japan?" the Poet had asked him, and he had said:

"The world may be divided into two classes—exploiters and exploited, and it is only by means of the combination of the exploited that we can fight Japan.

"That combination is coming, and one day we will find all the exploited people together, and we will find even the Japanese exploited fighting by the side of us."

"Won't it be true, Mahatmaji? Prosperous people can never combine, it is only the oppressed and the downtrodden who can combine. That was his idea."

"Very true, very true," said Gandhiji. "And he said," added the Poet, "that we cannot fight the exploiters with their weapons. That is modern weapons; but the day is coming when the whole world will fight on our side. He perhaps got the idea from the Russians who have made the world nervous today. However much we might try to barricade ourselves against Russia, the invasion of an idea can never be stopped. We had *brahman* supremacy, then *kshatriya* supremacy, now we have a *vaishya* supremacy, and we are going to have a *shudra* supremacy for numerically they are in a majority."

He talked with intimate knowledge of the affairs in China and elsewhere, and said, "no Government could endure that was not truly representative of the masses. They must be educated and they must know how to express their wants, and the Government must be responsive to those wants."

The Poet's apology, for having taken up much of Gandhiji's time gave Gandhiji an opportunity to harp on his favourite subject.

"No," he said, "you have not wasted my time. I have been spinning away without allowing a break in the conversation. For every minute that I spin there is in me consciousness that I am adding to the nation's wealth. My calculation is that if one crore of us spun for an hour every day, and so turned an idle hour to account we could add Rs.50,000 every day to the national wealth. Our income is only 7 pice per day, and even a single pie added to it is quite considerable. But even the 7 pice is not the average income of the poorest of us, for it includes the income of our millionaires also. That means that there are millions who do not earn even 7 pice per day and millions must be starving. Sjt. Birla tells me that we are paying 80 crores of rupees as interest but that we have not got the wherewithal to pay it and that inspite of the so-called favourable trade balances we are getting more and more impoverished. That is to say, our debts are not remunerative.

In such a poor and vast country even a pie per day for 300 millions of people means much. The spinning wheel is not meant to oust a single man or woman from his or her occupation. It seeks only to harness every single idle minute of our millions for common productive works. Unintelligent, resourceless and hopeless as they are, they have nothing better, more handy, and more paying to look to. They cannot think of adding to their agricultural produce. Our average holding is something less than 2 acres, and even that average, like our average income, includes the hundreds of acres of the Zamindars. The bulky recommendations of the Agricultural Commission contain nothing of value for the poor agriculturist and what they have proposed will never take effect."

"Oh, these Commissions are no use," said the Poet, "They will end in adding a few more departments, that is all. I have no faith in them."

The Poet was keen on knowing what exactly Gandhiji wanted to place before the country during the present year.

"I am furiously thinking night and day," said Gandhiji, "and I do not see any light coming out of the surrounding darkness. But even if we could not think of a programme of effective resistance, we could not possibly refrain from declaring the country's objective to mean Independence especially as Dominion Status is said to mean what we have never understood it to mean."

As they were thus talking away the crowd in the room was getting bigger and bigger like a snowball, and the Poet felt inclined to go.

"But you are coming to Ahmedabad on your way back," said Gandhi. "And if you get out at Ahmedabad you cannot escape me. So we look forward to your coming again, and we hope you will give us the benefit of your stay for at least twenty-four hours, as you did long ago."

As the Poet prepared to go, the boys and girls of the *ashram* waylaid him at the prayer ground where they had gathered to pay their respects to him. A warm garland, the *kumkuma* marks on the Poet's broad-head, and a song was all that they could offer. The Poet in return gave them his blessings which they will treasure for many a long day.

"Talking," he said, is a wasteful effort and involves unnecessary exercise of the lungs. "Rather than talk, as I usually have to do, I shall leave you a message in just a single sentence. It is this that the sacrifice needed for serving our country must not consist in merely emotional enthusiasm which is indulged in as a sort of luxury, but it should be a real discipline of truth and a severe discipline of truth. I know that you boys and girls are going through it and will go through it as long as you have your great teacher with you. I know you will fulfil the great promise I claim from you. Let us not think of making a political picnic of speeches and other demonstrations, but willingly accept the drudgery and trouble of quiet silent work. It is not here even necessary for me to say so. It is there in the atmosphere. I feel deeply the influence of it all around you and I envy you. I have no faith in noisy demonstrations. Let us not talk, but have faith in silent work, faith in humble beginnings, and I know Truth will take wing of itself and like fire will spread through the country, though its origin may be small and insignificant. Let us no longer blow the siren and allow the steam to be wasted away."

4. Tagore on Gandhi's absence at the Round Table Conference

(The following is Tagore's 'Letter to the Editor' published in The Spectator *of London, dated 15 November 1930. It seeks to explain Gandhi's absence at the first Round Table Conference. The editor of the* The Spectator *added his own comments, which are appended here.)*

Sir,

I have often been asked to give my opinion about Mahatma Gandhi's rejection of the invitation to the Round Table Conference because his terms were found impossible to be at once accepted by the British Government. I am not competent to discuss this question from a narrowly political point of view, though I am sure it has another perspective of meaning, which needs serious consideration.

Through the blinding mist of the past, the time is struggling to appear when people's destinies are no longer to be moulded and modelled by the politicians, who are the modern medicine men of diplomacy. The collaboration of the world mind is daily acquiring a supreme value for all important national problems, and the centre of gravity is shifting from the exclusive conference of national interest to the conference of moral judgement of all nations. Every day the idea is growing clearer in our minds that the affairs which once were jealously considered as special to one's own country do concern all humanity when they comprehend moral issues. The potent force of public opinion has already extended its field of activity across all political barbed wire fences of individual countries, and the human world is rapidly developing its universal organ of voice and sense of hearing to a very high degree of sensitiveness.

This has generated a power which national organisations of all free countries are busily exploiting for their own interest with the help of a large expenditure and often of unscrupulous means and messengers. We have seen how in the late war, while the manufacture of the poison gas which has its range of mischief only within the battlefield was not neglected, dissemination of poisonous slanders was also carried on far and wide with lavish extravagance. The instruments of propaganda have become to-day a permanent political necessity, not only for informing the world of facts, but also deluding it; and insinuations against their rivals and victims are sown broadcast by Governments through the agencies that seem inoffensive and camouflage that has the appearance of moderation and fairness.

But all this has a great meaning proving that our history has come to a stage when moral force has to be acknowledged even by politics and be captured at any cost, even at the cost of truth. This fact is all the more remarkable because the efficiency of the physical and material power has in this present scientific age, attained a degree of virulent perfection never before achieved. And yet this power hesitates today to assert its unashamed supremacy except in rare cases of short sighted stupidity and fanatical barbarism. The necessity to give a dog a bad name and then to hang it certainly proves a higher moral spirit than the defiant spirit that allows a dog to be hanged without the accompaniment of a libellous justification.

The invitation to a Round Table Conference accorded to the representatives of a people who can with perfect impunity be throttled into silence or trampled into a pulp, is in itself a sign of the time undreamt of even half a century ago. Mahatma Gandhi may not believe in the success of its obvious purpose, but he must acknowledge that it represents the same moral principle which he himself invokes on behalf of his countrymen in their endeavour after self-government. The real importance of this Conference is not in the opportunity it may offer of a cooperation with the British politicians, but with the soul force of the whole world. We must know that this Conference is going to hold its sittings before the world-tribunal whose approbation it is eager to win.

When the continents began to be formed on the geography of the earth, the amount of the land was insignificant, as it were, comtemptuously tolerated by the all-pervading reign of the sea, which kicked it and lashed it and nearly smothered it under an engulfing protection. But those very uncertain points of concession, scarcely solid, were significant of a fruitful future. We human beings have the cause to be thankful for that precarious geological, small favour, surrounded by unfathomable restrictions. And today, when on the one hand the police batons are bloodily busy cracking our unresisting heads and admiringly defended by authorities, majestically aloof from the tragic scene, a beckoning gesture from the other shore has reached the disarmed multitude of India, denuded of educational facilities, in the shape of an invitation to a Conference. I do not know if it is too small or ineffectual, but there is no doubt that it is a moral gesture, the gesture inspired not merely by the political necessity but the necessity of a world sanction. And I believe that it would have been worthy of Mahatma Gandhi if he could have accepted unhesitatingly the seat offered to him, even though the conditions were not fully acceptable to himself. To come there without any absolute assurance of ρolitical success would all the more enhance the significance of his moral mission. God's great boons come humbly through small openings, and we on our part should be humble when we hail them, trust them, and by our own merit make them bear the best fruits. The gifts that have any real value claim for their perfecticn our own faith and sacrifice.

This present age waits for a new and noble technique for all reparations of national maladjustment. Mahatma Gandhi is the one man in the present age who has preached it and shaped it through his movement of non-violent resistance in South Africa and India. And now he has had the opportunity to introduce the moral spirit of that movement into a Conference, which only he has made compellingly possible, and which only he could have used as a platform wherefrom to send his voice to all those all over the world, who truly represent the future history of man, a history that has to be built upon the foundation of numerous immediate failures and futile sufferings. Any such Conference can never be from the beginning a ready-made apparatus into whose rigid narrowness one must squeeze and torture oneself for accomadation. It waits for a man of genius, as he surely is, to turn it into an instrument for giving expression to the spirit of the age in the field of political intercommunication. I feel sad that such an opportunity has been lost for the moment, for India and for all the world. For, today is the age of co-operation in all departments of life including politics, the age of the creation of the continent in which all the human islands are to merge their isolation for a grand festival of civilization.

But here my pen stops, for I have suffered, and my suffering has been too cruel and too recent for me to leave it aside and think of a millennium that is still remote. I have known what has been done in Dacca, and from the light of that I can read the story of the Peshawar tragedy.

These people, the rulers of the world, are afraid of the judgement of their own peers, but are not afraid of the suffering caused by themselves. The time made safe for the weak will be slow in its journey through a long moral path which is still in the making. In the meanwhile, the mother's tears are flowing in our neighbourhood, and the wretched dumbness of the desolated homes is a burden we find difficult to remove from our hearts. There are wounds that cry for their immediate healing of their pain, and I am silenced by my own shame as I try to talk of an age when the tedious ceremony of exorcism is completed by which the devil is made to slink away for his own safety and self-interest. Those of our brothers who have suffered, till their hearts are ready to break, cry to me angrily: "Stop that discussion about the future; it is natural and therefore healthy for us to struggle through the process of the suffering which we have undertaken on our own soil, and instead of appealing to the world to take our side, let us, unarmed and resourceless, stand up and defy the mighty power and say : We fear thee not. We do need redress of our wrongs, but we need even more our self-respect, which nobody outside our own selves can restore to us."

I do not know how to answer them, and say to myself : "Possibly they are wiser with the natural wisdom of the sufferer."

It was the great personality of Mahatma Gandhi which inspired this courage, under persecutions frankly brutal or cowardly insidious, into the heart of the dumb multitudes of India, suffering for ages from the diffidence of their own human power. I myself have too often doubted the possibility of such a sudden quickening of life in a country whose mind has remained parched under a long drought of education. But a miracle has happened through the magical touch of Mahatma's own indomitable spirit and his courageous faith in human nature. And after this experience of mine, I hesitate to doubt his wisdom when he holds himself aloof from the invitation that seems to offer the opportunity for at least the beginning of an endeavour which, through the usual path of diplomacy, with its tortuous bends and sudden pitfalls of reaction, may at last lead us to our goal. Let me believe in his firmness of attitude, and not in my doubts.—

I am, Sir,
Rabindranath Tagore

(The following note by the Editor of *The Spectator* was appended at the end of Tagore's letter. "Although we do not share all Rabindranath Tagore's views, we welcome his outspoken letter. We are sure that it correctly represents views widely held in India. At the moment it is of the utmost importance that we, in Great Britain, should recognize the need for making a supreme effort to win Indian belief in our faith. Editor, *The Spectator*.)

5. Tagore's telegram of good wishes for the "penance"

(Copy of a telegram sent by Tagore to Gandhi on 22 May 1933.)

May your penance bring you close to the bosom of the Eternal away from the too burdensome pressure of life's malignant facts thus freshening your spirit to fight them with vigorous detachment.

Rabindranath Tagore

6. Telegram about Gandhi's condition

(Original telegram kept in Rabindra Bhavan.)

O KC Poona D G 23 18
23 May 1933

To: Rabindranath Tagore Darjeeling
Mahatmaji deeply moved by prayer his condition unchanged letter follows *pranams*

Amiya*

---

* Amiya Chakraborty was one of Tagore's close associates.

7. "Your prayer great help in this ordeal": Gandhi

(Original telegram kept in Rabindra Bhavan.)

O SG Poona 23 32
23 Mar 33

To: Rabindranath Tagore Darjeeling

Mahatmajis message tell Gurudeva I treasure your gift I realise your presence with me Your prayer great help in this ordeal Gods will be done Mohandas

Pranams

AMIYA

8. Tagore's telegram on the conclusion of fast

Darjeeling
27-5-33

Relieved from poignant anxiety. With thankful heart we welcome this great day when from death's challenge you come out victorious to renew your fight against sacrilegious bigotry simulating piety and moral degeneracy of the powerful.

Rabindranath

9. Tagore's press statement on Bengal and the Poona Pact

(A Press statement by Tagore from Santiniketan on 24 July 1933. Text of cable to Sir Nripendranath Sircar.)

I remember to have sent a cable to the Prime Minister, not to delay in accepting the proposal about communal awards sent to him by Mr. Gandhi. At that moment a situation was created which was extremely painful, not affording us the least time or peace of mind to think quietly on the possible consequences of the Poona Pact, which had already been arrived at and in the conference, of which no responsible representatives of Bengal took part. Upon the settlement of this question Mr. Gandhi's life depended, and the intolerable anxiety caused by such a crisis drove precipitately to a commitment which I now realise as a mistake from the point of view of our country's permanent interest.

Never having any experience in political dealings, while entertaining a great love for Mr.Gandhi and a complete faith in his wisdom in Indian politics, I dared not wait for further consideration, which was unfortunate as justice has certainly been sacrificed in the case of Bengal. I have not the least doubt now that such an injustice will continue to cause mischief for all parties concerned, keeping alive the spirit of communal conflict in our province in an intense form and making peaceful government of the country perpetually difficult.

That the British Government refuses to reconsider this subject of vital importance to us, while all other proposals contained in the White paper are being freely rehandled does not surprise or hurt me too much, but that the Indian members of the Conference belonging to provinces different from ours should not only remain apathetic but actively take part in Bengal's misfortune is terribly ominous, presaging no good for our future history.

10. Gandhi on inability to visit Calcutta

(Original telegram kept in Rabindra Bhavan.)

O H K
Lahore 13 8 50 Recd at 12 H. 4 M
13 July' 34

To: Gurudev Santiniketan
       Your kind wire Calcutta visit Instant friends Anxious settlement Domestic quarrels all dates booked Pray forgive

Gandhi

11. Gandhi on breaking fast at Wardha

(Original telegram kept in Rabindra Bhavan.)

Wardha Date 14 Aug '34 10H 20M
Recd. at 12H. 8M.

To: Gurudev Santiniketan

By Gods blessing broke fast Am well Love

Gandhi

12. Gandhi seeks Tagore's consent to Andrews' visit to Poona

(Original telegram kept in Rabindra Bhavan.)

Wardhaganj 10 Sept., 34 10H.50M
Recd. 7 H. 34 M.

To: Gurudev Santiniketan

Andrews just got on way station your wire third which was redirected Simla he must keep official appointment Poona Wednesday where he is proceeding arrangement was for him pass day here and then proceed Shantiniketan both He and I very sorry over mishap wire please wire whether Andrews might break journey here one day or proceed Shantiniketan without break love

Gandhi

13. Tagore thanked for compliance with Gandhi's request

(Original telegram kept in Rabindra Bhavan.)

(Wardha 11 Sept. 34 14H. 45M.)
Recd. at 15H. 49M.

To: Gurudev Santiniketan
Deeply grateful wire Charlie today Bombay Care advocate
Bhulabhai Poona tomorrow Servindia Wardha Friday love

Gandhi

14. Moral warfare

(In this short piece in Modern Review *of September 1934,
Tagore explains the dimensions of moral warfare—dharma
yuddha of Gandhi.)*

By segregating ethics to the Kingdom of Heaven and
depriving the Kingdom of Earth from its use man has up to now
never seriously acknowledged the need of higher ideals in
politics or in practical affairs. That is why when disagreements
occur between individuals—violence is not encouraged but
punished, but when the combatants are nations, barbaric methods are not only not condemned but glorified. The greatest of
men like Buddha or Christ have from the dawn of human
history stood for the ideal of non-violence, they have dared to
love their enemies and defied tyrannism by peace, but we have
not yet claimed the responsibility they have offered us.

Fight is necessary in this world, combat we must and
relentlessly against the evils that threaten us, for by tolerating
untruth we admit their claim to exist. But war on the human
plain must be what in India we call *dharma yuddha*—moral
warfare. In it we must array our spiritual powers against the
cowardly violence of evils. This is the great ideal which Mahatma Gandhi represents, challenging his people to fearlessly apply
man's highest strength not only in our individual dealings but
in the clash of nation and nation.

In the barbaric age men's hunger did not impose any limits

on its range of food which included even human flesh but with the evolution of society this has been banished from extreme, possibilly in a like manner, we await the time when nothing may supposedly justify the use of violence whatever consequences we are led to face. Because, success in a conflict may be terrible defeat from the human point of view, and material gain is not worth the price we pay at spiritual cost. Much rather should we lose all than barter our soul for an evil victory. We honour Mahatma Gandhi because he has brought this ideal into the sphere of politics and under his lead India is proving everyday how aggressive power pitifully fails when human nature in its wakeful majesty bears insult and pain without retaliating. India today inspired by her great leader opens the new chapter of human history which has just begun.

15. Mahadev Desai seeks Tagore's views on conversion of Harijans to Sikhism

(Original handwritten letter.)

As at Wardha,
20 December 1936

Revered Gurudev,

A number of people have been quoting your opinion on the question of the conversion of Harijans to Sikhism in support of their own contention that to embrace Sikhism is the only way to retain Hindu Culture and yet renounce Hinduism. Bapu could not believe that you could ever have given your assent to a proposition like this. If Sikhism is a part of Hinduism there is no question of renouncing the latter. One may, though he may be a Hindu, hold Sikh beliefs or Buddhist beliefs, as he does Shaiva or Vaishnava beliefs. That however is no renunciation of Hinduism. If he renounces Hinduism, he renounces Hindu Culture and all that goes by that name, for you cannot separate culture from religion. Culture is a reflection of one's religion. And Sikhism at best is no religion or philosophy but an attempt to reform Hindu practices. There can, on this ground too, be no question of conversion to Sikhism!

I need not bother you with the political aspect of the question, for the very insistence on conversion to Sikhism must take a political colour, for the converts will vote not as Hindus but as Sikhs! This political motive vitiates the whole question.

Would you mind setting out your considered opinion on the matter?

With profound *pranams*

Yours sincerely,
Mahadevi

P.S. Although I am writing this from Faizpur, you may, if you reply to this after the 28th, address it to Wardha. Should you be free to reply to it earlier, you may address it to Tilaknagar, Faizpur. Nandababu's* influence is to be seen in every line and contour of this Congress and Exhibition.

16. Tagore's clarification

(In typescript with corrections in Tagore's own hand.)

Santiniketan, Bengal,
4 January 1936 [1937]

My dear Mahadeo,

I am not surprised that you should have requested me to explain fully my views with regard to the question of conversion of Harijans to Sikhism. At the very outset, let me tell you that I have not actually advised them to change their religious faith, but pleaded the case of Sikhism if, for reasons well known to all of us, they contemplated such a radical step. I hold the same view with regard to Buddhism as well.

In everyday use, Hinduism is just a way of life, and however great its philosophical and cultural basis may be, that alone will not atone for all the social injustices perpetrated throughout ages, in its name. Our religion divides the society into so many graded groups, and those at the bottom are not only denied bare social justice, but are constantly made to feel themselves as less than human. Santanists are not very far wrong when they claim that this spirit of division, keeping down a large section of our community, is in the permanent structure of our religion forming

---

* The reference is to Nandalal Bose's art panels and other decorations at the Faizpur Congress.

the basis of our society as can be proved by the injunctions of our ancient lawgivers such as Manu, Parasara and others.

Many of us try to give their texts a civilised gloss but such individual interpretations do not help the victims or touch the social autocrats in their behaviour. There are some modern incidents of their defeat such as had happened even so late as in the time of Chaitanya, which was quickly followed by reaction and we cannot be certain that the future of the social reform already achieved by our modern pioneers is permanently assured.

I am hardly concerned about the political aspect of the case.—Whether they vote as Hindus or Sikhs is, according to me, of much lesser importance than what affects our humanity and forms our mental attitude towards our fellow beings. Long ago, it is now nearly 25 years, in a poem [title not deciphered] I had uttered my denunciation of the society that has raised itself on the indignity imposed upon the majority of our population in India and made her ready for centuries of defeat and degradation. My cry has been a feeble cry in a wilderness that has obstructed along its history of dense growth the path of light and repeated efforts of those pathmakers, who were the predecessors of the present great guide of our nation. Mahatmaji with his phenomenal hold upon the masses has indeed stirred us up, but yet I do not know how long we must wait for his teaching to work effectively at the noxious roots in the dark depth of the soil. At the same time, we must know that disasters that dog the footsteps of evils do not wait to consult our own time for their mitigation, for the medicine which is sluggishly slow in its curative effect is too often overtaken by death.

I do hold the view that Buddhism or Sikhism were attempts from within at the eradication of one of the most intractable social deformities in Hinduism that turns into ridicule our aspiration for freedom. It was indeed a great day not only for the whole of Indian Sikhs but also for the whole of India when Guru Govind, defying the age long convention of the Hindu Society, made his followers one, by breaking down all barriers of caste and thereby made them free to inherit the true blessings of a self-respecting manhood. Sikhism has a brave message to the people and it has a noble record. How great would be its effect, if this religion can get out of its geographical provincialism, shed its exclusiveness inevitable in a small community and acquire a nationwide perspective one can only guess. I do not find anything in their religious practices and creeds which hurt my human dignity. My father often used to offer his worship in Amristar Gurudwara, where I daily accompanied him but I never could imagine him at the Kali's temple in Calcutta. Yet, in his culture and religion he was a Hindu and in his daily living maintained a purer standard of Hinduism than most of those who profess it by words of mouth and pollute it in their habits. I therefore do not fear that their conversion to Sikhism or Buddhism will mean also their neglecting or abandoning Hindu culture.

I felt very happy that Nandalal proved once again his great worth. But I never had any doubts about his making Faizpur arrangements an unqualified success.

With loving blessings,

Yours sincerely,

Rabindranath Tagore

17. Gandhiji's assurance to Tagore about Andaman prisoners

(From the original telegram: Pyarelal Papers, courtesy: Pyarelal. CWMG, Vol.LXVI)

[On or after 16 August 1937]

To: Gurudev Santiniketan

Pray depend upon my doing utmost end Andaman crisis. Love

Gandhi

18. About donations to Visva-Bharati

(From the manuscript of Mahadev Desai's diary, courtesy: Narayan Desai; CWMG, Vol. LXVI.)

6 November 1937

The (Birla) Brothers will, whether with or without the help of friends, provide Rs.1,000 per month, Rs.800 being for the school of Indology and Rs.200 per month for Nandababu's art school, as long as these departments continue satisfactorily.

Calcutta,
8 November 1937

Dear Gurudev,

Your messenger has brought your precious note with receipts. I have done nothing. It is God's prompting; your labours and prayers have borne fruit. May you have complete rest from worry and toil over the financial difficulties.

I am well, thanks.

Love,

M.K. Gandhi

19. Tagore thanks Gandhi for aid to Visva-Bharati

Santiniketan,
7 November 1937

Dear Mahatmaji

Your love for me has greatly exceeded my expectation and I assure you that the gift you have bestowed on me is a gift of profound peace and freedom from daily worries that had been sapping my strength. I have struggled almost single-handed for about forty years for a cause which has failed to find a helping hand in a neighbourhood jealously antagonistic and therefore when I am nearing the end of my journey suddenly to be blessed with an unquestioning sympathy lavish in generosity overwhelms my famished heart with joy. I have no other words to say. God bless you. With love,

Yours affectionately
Rabindranath Tagore

20. Tagore's message to the Press about Gandhi's health

21.1.38

I trust that everything will be done to help Mahatmaji to recover health at this critical juncture and that those in authority will also do all in their power to expedite the release of those political prisoners who have given their word of honour that they have altogether eschewed violence.

Rabindranath Tagore

21. Tagore's welcome address to Gandhi

(Tagore's address of welcome to Gandhi on the occasion of the latter's visit to Santiniketan in February 1940.)

17 February 1940

I hope we shall be able to keep close to a reticent expression of love and reverence in welcoming you into our ashram and never allow it to overflow into any extravagant display of phrases. Homage to the great naturally seeks its manifestation in the language of simplicity, and we offer you these few words to let you know that we accept you as our own and as one who belongs to all humanity.

Just at this moment there are problems that darken our destiny. These, we know, are crowding your path and none of us is free from their attack. Let us for a while pass beyond the bounds of this turmoil and make our meeting today a simple meeting of hearts whose memory will remain when all the moral confusions of our distracted politics will be allayed and the eternal value of our true endeavours will be revealed.

Rabindranath Tagore

22. The Santiniketan pilgrimage

(In March 1940, Gandhi with his entourage, revisited Santiniketan for the last time. Mahadev Desai's report of the "pilgrimage" was published in Harijan *of 9 March 1940.)*

In the course of a letter which he wrote on the eve of his visit to Santiniketan Gandhi described it as a 'pilgrimage.' As an institution that, pending his arrival, invited and gave shelter, under its hospitable roof, to members of his 'family' on their return to India from South Africa, it has always claimed a soft corner in his heart. And the sweet associations of Gurudev and Borodada, the late Mr. Pearson and Deenbandhu, Andrews have only heightened that feeling. To attune himself to that feeling, or perhaps under the stress of that feeling, Gandhiji before starting made a drastic reduction in his entourage, cutting down to the barest minimum irrespective of every other consideration, and though many at that time failed to catch its import, it gave Gandhiji in the retrospect, a supreme satisfaction to have taken that unbending moral stand as the only course befitting the solemnity of the occasion.

This was to be his third visit to Santiniketan, the last one being fourteen years ago—in 1925. He knew it was overdue. Every report about Gurudev's failing health accompanied by a 'love message' from the Poet that Deenbandhu sent to Gandhiji from time to time, reminded him of it. It was Deenbandhu who had acted as the 'go-between' on the present occasion, when he conveyed to Gandhiji the Poet's pressing invitation to visit Santiniketan. But by a cruel irony when that long looked for visit actually came he was not there to witness it. He had been suddenly taken ill a few days before and removed to the Presidency Hospital, Calcutta, in a precarious condition. He was more than a member of the 'joint family' of Gurudev and Gandhiji and the shadow of this domestic illness overhung and tinged the whole of Gandhiji's Santiniketan visit.

A small reception had been arranged for Gandhiji on the afternoon of the day of his arrival. It was held in *Amrakunja*, a spot rendered sacred by its associations with the late Maharishi Debendranath Tagore, Gurudev's father. It was here, tradition says, that he used to sit and sometimes remain absorbed in

meditation from eventide till daybreak. By his will he converted
it into a place of universal worship of one Brahma, the Formless
and Invisible, and a sanctuary for all wild animal life.

The function commenced with a chanting of the Poet's
favourite Upanishadic text, with the haunting refrain

"Those who come to know Him,
       They attain to immortality."

The address of welcome was read by Gurudev himself. It
was short and impressive. But Gandhiji's thoughts were far away
with Charlie Andrews in Calcutta. On a previous occasion
Deenbandhu had sung.

"And I have seen His face—
       have seen and known
This sacrament was given

                        *   *   *   *

And I can wait the dawning of the day,
       The day-star on my night already shining.
The shadow and the veil shall pass away,
       Death shall make true my dreaming."

And now as he lay hovering between life and death. Gandhiji
made a feeling reference to him in his reply.

"My uppermost feelings on arriving here are about
Deenbandhu," he began. "Perhaps you do not know that the first
thing I did yesterday morning on alighting from the train at
Calcutta was to pay him a visit in the hospital. Gurudev is a
world poet, but Deenabandhu too has the spirit and temperament
of a poet in him. He had long yearned to be present on the present
occasion, to drink in and store up the memory of every word,
movement and gesture relating to the meeting with Gurudev. But
God had willed it otherwise and he now lies in Calcutta, stricken
down and unable even to make full use of his speech. I would like
you all to join me in the prayer that God may restore him to us
soon and, in any case, may grant his spirit peace.

"I have not come here as a stranger or a guest. Santiniketan
has been more than a home to me. It was here that the members
of my South African family found warm hospitability in 1914,
pending my arrival from England, and I too found shelter here
for nearly a month. The memories of those days crowd in upon
me as I see you all, here assembled before me. It grieves me that

I cannot prolong my stay here as I would have loved to. It is a question of duty. In a letter to a friend, the other day, I described my present trip to Santiniketan and Malikanda as a pilgrimage. Santiniketan has truly, this time, proved for me a 'niketan' of 'Santi' — an abode of peace. I have come here leaving behind me all the cares and burdens of politics, simply to have Gurudev's *darshan* and blessings. I have often claimed myself to be an accomplished beggar. But a more precious gift has never dropped into my beggar's bowl than Gurudev's blessings to-day. I know his blessings are with me always. But it has been my privilege today to receive the same from him in person, and that fills me with joy."

The next day the whole morning was devoted to making a round of all the various departments of Santiniketan, followed by a visit to Sriniketan. Kshitishbabu, "the sole survivor" of the older group of teachers whom Gandhiji had contacted during his last visit to and stay at Santiniketan, acted as the guide. It was a privilege in the Vidyabhawan to meet Haribabu, the compiler of the Bengali dictionary, who has, single-handed, after twenty eight years of continuous labour completed a work which entitles him to be ranked with literary giants like Shri Nagendranath Bose, the author of Bengali *Viswakosha*, and Prof. Murray of the Oxford Dictionary fame. Sixty-four volumes of his monumental work, we were told, have already been published, and the complete set, when it is ready in another three years' time, will run into eighty and cost from 40 to 50 rupees each.

In the China Bhawan or the Department of Chinese Culture, Prof. Tan-Yuan Sen was not there, being away with the China's goodwill deputation that is touring India, but his good wife was there to meet Gandhiji. Gandhiji was here shown the library of Chinese books that the Chinese nation has presented to the Visva-Bharati. The Chinese children, Gandhiji was told, were not one whit behind any other in establishing a freemasonry with their Santiniketan chums, and felt quite at home with them undeterred by the "language difficulty".

In the section of Islamic culture, Gandhiji was delighted to see an original manuscript transcribed in his own beautiful caligraphic hand by that Philosopher Prince—Dara Shikoh, who through his mysticism arrived at a catholicity and breadth of religious outlook that was unheard of in those days and is rare even in our own. In a monograph published by the Department we are told how he patronised men of all denominations, saints, theologians, philosophers and poets of every creed and community, studied Sanskrit, became deeply interested in the Vedanta and Yoga Philosophy, and from the learned pandits of Benares and contacts with yogis, initiated himself into the practices of Yoga. Denounced by the fanatical set as a heretic he was nevertheless a true Mussalman. In a lengthy introduction to the *Upanishads* which he himself translated into Persian, he has explained how he was led to their study through his search after Reality. "Subtle doubts came into my mind for which I had no possibility of solution and, whereas the Holy Koran is almost totally enigmatical and at the present day the understanders thereof are very rare, I became desirous to collect into one view all the revealed books, as the very word of God itself might be its own commentary, and if in one book it be compendious in another book it might be found diffusive." Proceeding he adds that as a "mystic enthusiast and ardent advocate of the unity of God", he searched for Reality no matter in what language, and that in quest for Truth, in the higher stages of its realisation, religion is of no matter." And so he came to `Upanishads' "which are a treasury of monotheism." And yet it was not that he wanted to raise a hybrid growth by grafting Hindusim on Islam or *vice versa.* As Dr. Yusuf Hussan has pointed out " he was actuated by a desire to prove that both Islam and Hinduism in appearance so fundamentally dissimilar, are essentially the same. Both represent spiritual efforts of man to realize Truth and God."

The last to be visited was the Kala Bhawan, Shri Nandababu's *sanctum sanctorum* of art. "Like Krishna, he hides himself behind his work," was the epigrammatic description given of him by a friend to Gandhiji. Retiring, shy, reserved, he is the pattern of humility and unassuming un-ostentatiousness. He lives only in and for his art which he has taken as his spiritual *sadhana.* "You cannot become an artist," he is fond of telling his pupils, "unless you identify yourself with the humblest and the meanest of God's creation". A gentler soul has hardly ever breathed. All the children are his chums, and it is a common sight to see Nandababu make a detour to avoid a bunch of youngsters engaged in a 'lark' lest he should intrude upon their 'freedom'!! "Art is a jealous and exacting mistress" is another favourite saying of his. But though fastidious and meticulous to a degree in his devotion to his ideal, he has never been known to send away an aspiring artist without an encouraging word.

His genius is only matched by his industry. There is hardly a nook or a corner in Santiniketan but bears the impress of his art and industry. A wall to him is only a bed for the execution of a fresco or a bas-relief panel, a ceiling simply a surface for bearing his cartoons, a lump of clay plastic material to be turned into a beautiful model. As a friend remarked half seriously, half in banter, if Nadababu had his way, he would use our great globe itself as material for turning out some cosmic piece of art! It gave Gandhiji particular satisfaction and joy to know that next to Bengal, Gujarat had provided Nandababu the largest number of pupils.

Gandhiji had several intimate talks with Gurudev. But they are of too sacred and personal a character for recapitulation here. At seventy-nine the Poet's countenance shows no diminution in its lustre, the eyes burn brighter than ever, the step is firm although he needs support and moves about only with difficulty. The voice has lost none of its vigour or its sonorous musical quality, and the spirit retains all the freshness and irrepressible exuberance of youth. He insisted upon Gandhiji witnessing the performance of his favourite musical pantomime, *Chandalika*, in which his grand-daughter played the principal part. He personally supervised the rehearsal and even delayed the programme by a quarter of an hour till he was satisfied that everything was tip-top. It was a sight to be remembered when at one stage he almost jumped to the edge of his seat and broke out into a musical interpolation to provide the cue when the performers had or seemed to have lost it. His enthusiasm must have got an infectious quality in it, for I have never seen Gandhiji follow with such sustained and rapt interest any entertainment as he did this one during the full one hour that it lasted.

From a bare spot that Santiniketan is originally said to have been and notorious for being the haunt of dacoits, it has under the magic of Gurudev's personality grown to its present size, and yet, as Kshitishbabu remarked to Gandhiji with a sigh, "the scholars who are engaged in research work are cramped for space, and when enough accommodation is forthcoming, who knows, the present race of scholars at any rate may have run its course!".

23. Rathindranath Tagore's letter to Gandhi about a memorial for Andrews

April 1940

Dear Mahatmaji,

All these days, ever since the sad news of Mr. Andrews' death reached him, father has been thinking of what could be done to perpetuate the memory of that great life in some suitable form which while it may be a fitting tribute of a grateful people should at the same time provide opportunities for carrying on the noble work which his life embodied. As it is a matter which is sure to occupy your thoughts as well, father would be greatly helped in arriving at a decision by your advice and suggestion. We have placed some tentative proposals before him which he approves and which he would like you to consider. Your judgement in this matter will be surer and truer than any one else's and father hopes you will exercise it freely in amending or altering these proposals. If any public appeal is to be issued, it may best be done jointly in the name of yourself, the Lord Bishop of Calcutta and father, who were perhaps Mr. Andrews' three closest friends and associates. I shall be grateful if you let us have your advice in this matter. I am also writing to the Lord Bishop of Calcutta about it.

Father sends you his love.

Yours respectfully,
Rathindranath Tagore

24. Tagore on a suitable memorial to Andrews

13 May 1940

My dear Mahatmaji

I entirely agree with you with regard to the suggestions about Charlie's memorial but I am not sure if it would be proper for me to sign the appeal. It might be misconstrued as Santiniketan is involved. An appeal by you and the Bishop would perhaps carry a greater weight; or you may get a few other common friends of your own choice to sign it along with you, perhaps including the Head of the Cambridge Mission. I shall however leave the decision entirely with you.

Herewith you will find a somewhat altered and elaborated draft for the appeal together with the one sent by you. I felt, a little elaboration was needed also a little change, specially with regard to the Hall of Christian Culture in view of some suggestions offered to my son by the Bishop. The project of such a Hall was much in Charlie's mind lately, and we feel we are carrying out his own wish in including it. But here also I leave the last word with you. You will kindly proceed without any further reference to me. But after the final form has been decided upon and signed by you, you may send it to my office for the printing and despatch of it to probable donors. A mere appeal in the press would not do; we have to follow it up by personal correspondence.

I have come up to Kalimpong for the summer months and any further correspondence may be sent here direct. Knowing the value of your time, I would request you not to bother to write yourself; Mahadeo can very well inform me of your wishes.

Yours sincerely,
Rabindranath Tagore

25. Gandhi's telegram thanks Tagore for a song

Wardhaganj
Date 31 Hours 18.
Recd. here at 8H. 35M.

To: Gurudev Santiniketan

Received your song only last night when Navin Dhiru came Thank God though frail in body your mind vigorous enough for new songs.

Gandhi

26. Gandhi's enquiry about Tagore's health

(Original telegram kept in Rabindra Bhavan.)

Post mark: Santiniketan,
17 July 1941

O QL
Wardha 16 Jul 41 16H. 55M Recd at 7H.50M.

To: Gurudev Santiniketan
Press reports disturbing wire exact condition

Gandhi

27. Gandhi's telegram to Rathindranath Tagore

1 August 41
Wardhaganj Date 1 H.12

To: Rathindranath Tagore Calcutta
Thank God hope speedy complete recovery

Gandhi

28. Obituary of Tagore by Mahatma Gandhi

(From a copy: Pyarelal Papers, Courtesy: Pyarelal. Also The
Bombay Chronicle, *8 August 1741* and *CWMG, Vol. LXXIV.)*

7 August 1941

In the death of Rabindranath Tagore, we have not only lost
the greatest poet of the age, but an ardent nationalist who was
also a humanitarian. There was hardly any public activity on
which he has not left the impress of his powerful personality. In
Santiniketan and Sriniketan, he has left a legacy to the whole
nation, indeed, to the world. May the noble soul rest in peace and
may those in charge at Santiniketan prove worthy of the responsibility resting on their shoulders.

Laser typesetting at Sriram Graphics, C4A/5A Janakpuri, New Delhi 110058
and printed at Jay Kay Offset Printers, Rohtak Road, Nangloi, Delhi - 110041